Essentials of Medicolegal Death Investigation

Essentials of Medicolegal Death Investigation

Matthew M. Lunn

ELSEVIER

AMSTERDAM • BOSTON • HEIDELBERG • LONDON
NEW YORK • OXFORD • PARIS • SAN DIEGO
SAN FRANCISCO • SINGAPORE • SYDNEY • TOKYO
Academic Press is an imprint of Elsevier

Academic Press is an imprint of Elsevier
125 London Wall, London EC2Y 5AS, United Kingdom
525 B Street, Suite 1800, San Diego, CA 92101-4495, United States
50 Hampshire Street, 5th Floor, Cambridge, MA 02139, United States
The Boulevard, Langford Lane, Kidlington, Oxford OX5 1GB, United Kingdom

Library of Congress Cataloging-in-Publication Data
A catalog record for this book is available from the Library of Congress

British Library Cataloguing-in-Publication Data
A catalogue record for this book is available from the British Library

ISBN: 978-0-12-803641-9

For information on all Academic Press publications visit our website at https://www.elsevier.com/

Publisher: Sara Tenney
Acquisition Editor: Elizabeth Brown
Editorial Project Manager: Joslyn Chaiprasert-Paguio
Production Project Manager: Lisa Jones
Designer: Miles Hitchen

Typeset by TNQ Books and Journals

Dedication

This book is dedicated to my wife, Rachel, and my amazing family who have always loved, encouraged, and supported me.

Contents

4. Common Natural Diseases and Disorders

5. Asphyxiation

6. Blunt-Force Injuries

Preface

This book is designed to be an introduction to the medicolegal death investigation field for students as well as a reference for practicing professionals. The reason I wanted to write this book was to fill a gap. Previous books have focused on the forensic pathologist or on the crime scene investigator while discussing the concepts of medicolegal death investigation. The field has grown significantly since its early inception, and I felt it was time for a experienced, board-certified medicolegal death investigator to write a book.

I have had the privilege to learn from some of the best in the business. From my mentor, John Kraemer, to the dedicated professionals who volunteer significant time to the American Board of Medicolegal Death Investigators (ABMDI), I have learned so much from so many. I have had numerous opportunities to discuss the importance of quality medicolegal death investigations with law enforcement, medical, and homeland security professionals from all across the country, but the most important aspect of the position for me was always working one-on-one with families who are thrust unexpectedly into a situation where their loved one has died and they now must figure out what comes next. Continuing to improve the science behind what medicolegal death investigators do and why as well as improving certification of medicolegal professionals, especially in rural parts of the country, are essential areas of growth for the profession, but it will never be more important than properly notifying someone of the death of their loved one.

It is my desire that you the reader find this to be a helpful resource in your professional pursuits, and I hope you always put the decedents and their loved ones at the forefront of anything you do.

Chapter 1

Introduction to Death Investigation

Chapter Outline

The study of medicolegal death investigation is one that encompasses a number of other disciplines. A medicolegal death investigator uses principles from medicine, criminal justice, and social sciences to dutifully fulfill his/her role in the death investigation system. Like a health-care provider, the medicolegal death investigator must be well versed in understanding medical conditions, common treatments, and medications for various health conditions and, above all else, be exceptional at obtaining a complete medical, social, and family history. Criminal justice principles are an area that the medicolegal death investigator must familiarize himself/herself with, as well.

While a majority of the investigator's role is to understand how someone's chronic medical conditions or acute life events may have contributed to their death, it is also important for the medicolegal death investigator to understand many common criminal justice principles. These could include securing the scene, properly documenting findings with photographs and writing, and properly identifying and securing items of evidentiary value. Understanding basic legal issues is also important for the medicolegal death investigator to stay abreast on. The principles of social science should also be discussed in the training of any professional in this field.

One of the major roles not often thought of when discussing proper investigation of someone's death is the role the medicolegal death investigator plays in working with family and other covictims. Communicating knowledge about what happened to a decedent as well as showing empathy for someone who has just experienced a loss is crucial to properly service the community. Additionally, being able to understand and discuss a family's religious and cultural beliefs allows the medicolegal death investigator to fully investigate

Essentials of Medicolegal Death Investigation. http://dx.doi.org/10.1016/B978-0-12-803641-9.00001-X

what happened to someone while still honoring the beliefs of a diverse community.

Oftentimes, the success of a medicolegal professional is dependent on their ability to integrate the medical, legal, and social science knowledge. However, when dealing with the family and friends of someone who has died, the treatment and care shown will determine how the general public views on not only that particular professional, but the death investigation system as a whole. This will be discussed further in later chapters, but one must always be mindful that the members of the general public who the medicolegal death investigator has come in contact with likely has very little-to-no knowledge of how the system works, and it is incumbent on the medicolegal office to have policies that realize the importance of taking care of families and covictims.

Before someone can begin to study the science, medicine, and investigative technique of being a medicolegal death investigator, it is important to understand the confines of the system in which one works. While no system is perfect, many changes have been occurring recently with the idea of improving and standardizing death investigations in the United States. However well-intentioned these efforts may be, the reality of the current state of systems in the country makes it difficult to find a simple solution to a very complex issue.

The ultimate goal of any transition in forensics, whether it be in medicolegal death investigation or in another discipline, should be consistency. The idea that a person's death in a resource-rich area is treated differently than an individual who dies in a limited funding or resource-deprived area should be unacceptable to not only professionals but the general public. Unfortunately, the reality is that the general public does not view the death investigation system in this country as a priority until they are unexpectedly thrust into this world through unexpected circumstances in their own personal life.

DEATH INVESTIGATION SYSTEMS IN THE UNITED STATES

The various death investigation systems in the United States can only be described as a potpourri of various levels of funding and requirements for who can carry out this important public health and safety function. Over the last couple of decades, the medicolegal community has seen a push to improve the minimum standards for the individuals who work in and oversee these offices, but to understand where we are going we must first discuss the origins of death investigation.

The first death investigation systems were quite primitive and were designed to ensure the best interest of the Crown in England dating back to the 9th century. As part of this function, the original coroners would collect a form of taxes from the decedent's estate. In the United States, a similar system originated here, but over time it has slowly began to evolve into a more medically focused function of public health and safety. This started with the state of Massachusetts requiring physicians to respond to deaths in 1877 and in 1918 New York City developing what could be described as the first medical examiner system in the country (Hanzlick & Combs, 1998; Spitz & Fisher, 1982). Over time, depending on the current politics and economic strength of the country, there have been shifts toward more of a medical examiner system than that of a coroner system, but that trend has started to cool off in the last decade or so. That being said, there is a renewed interest in this topic at the federal level.

The two basic systems just mentioned that are currently in use in the United States are offices that are either run by a coroner or run by a medical examiner. Death investigation systems run by a coroner are usually county-based offices that are headed by an elected, although in some instances appointed, official. This official could have a multitude of experiences and educational background prior to being the coroner. In Colorado, to be the county coroner, one must simply be a registered voter in that county, have a high school diploma or GED, and have no felonies on their criminal record. As one can imagine, this creates a situation where someone with little-to-no medical or investigative experience could be tasked with overseeing this important public health and safety function. The argument could also be made that there is no need for a medical examiner or similar professional to oversee this function. The government is best served by someone with budget and management experience who is directly responsible to the constituents in which the office serves. In a period in this country's history where public funds are ever so scarce and meeting the community's needs with less is a way of life, having someone with the necessary background in fiscal matters could be of great benefit. The other system in use in the United States is that of a medical examiner run office.

A medical examiner office is run by a physician, whose training will be discussed a little later in the chapter, but they have completed a medical education, oftentimes with specialized training in forensic pathology. The physicians who oversee these offices are traditionally appointed based on their education and experience. In large offices, these individuals are usually board-certified forensic pathologists (Hanzlick, 2007). In fact, offices that seek national accreditation from the National Association of Medical Examiners (NAME) must have a board-certified forensic pathologist as the chief medical examiner, otherwise they are not eligible for accreditation (NAME, 2013). The benefit of this system is that someone who is specifically educated and trained in both medicine and forensic science is overseeing the system designed to handle the said function. When a decision is made about whether a decedent needs an autopsy or can have their regular primary care provider sign their death certificate, these physicians have the proper background to give the definitive answer. Conversely, these physicians rarely have much, if any, background and education in fiscal matters or management. This could lead to an office that has the necessary qualifications to perform the duties, but a lack of understanding on how to effectively implement policies and directives. The federal government, through various task groups and committees, has recommended the implementation of medical examiner offices over an elected coroner system to insure the best possible outcome in every death investigation.

The National Academy of Science Report (2009) Strengthening Forensic Science in the United States: A Path Forward, provides a number of recommendations in a multitude of forensic disciplines. As it relates to medicolegal death investigation, their first recommendation was to make funding available for jurisdictions to replace their current coroner system(s) with medical examiner offices. The ultimate goal being that all coroner offices should be eliminated. This, however, is a more difficult task than simply putting money toward an issue. There are legislative issues that would require a change to various state constitutions, and this could be difficult given political connections that coroners, as elected officials, have (Hanzlick, 2007). Fig. 1.1 provides a breakdown of the states that have a particular type of death investigation system, and Fig. 1.2 is a picture of the autopsy suite at the Iowa Office of the State Medical Examiner. The facilities in Iowa are not common for medical examiners or coroners across the country. Many jurisdictions lack basic storage, security, and proper facilities to perform the important work that needs to be done for the public's health and safety.

The idea that a major change to a medical examiner only system is coming in the near future is not realistic. Each office, whether medical examiner or

Death Investigation System by State			
State ME	County/Regional ME	Coroner	Mix
Iowa	Michigan	South Carolina	New York
Maine	Florida	Louisiana	Pennsylvania
New Hampshire	Arizona	Indiana	Ohio
Vermont	Tennessee	North Dakota	Kentucky
Massachusetts		South Dakota	Georgia
Connecticut		Nebraska	Alabama
Rhode Island		Kansas	Mississippi
West Virginia		Colorado	Arkansas
Maryland		Wyoming	Missouri
Virginia		Idaho	Illinois
North Carolina		Nevada	Wisconsin
Delaware			Minnesota
Oklahoma			Texas
Utah			Montana
New Mexico			California
Oregon			Washington
New Jersey			Hawaii
Alaska			

FIGURE 1.1 A breakdown of the states that have a particular type of death investigation system. *Reproduced from a survey of more than 60 of the nation's largest medical examiner and coroner offices conducted by ProPublica, FRONTLINE, and NPR.*

FIGURE 1.2 Autopsy suite at the Iowa Office of the State Medical Examiner.

coroner, has its strengths and weaknesses. J. Michael Murphy, former Coroner for Clark County (NV), believes "the truth always is found somewhere in the middle of each respective point of view. The quality of the work performed by any office lies squarely upon the shoulders of the chief executive officer no matter Coroner or Medical Examiner (2015)." The debate will continue, but the likely outcome may come in the form of standards for the individual practitioners as a way to increase reliability within the death investigation system as opposed to the individual running the office.

PROFESSIONALS INVOLVED IN DEATH INVESTIGATIONS

Many different professionals and agencies make up the response to a death investigation. We have already briefly discussed the medical examiner and coroner offices, but these are not the only agencies that have a statutory responsibility to look into the death of an individual. The easiest way to discuss all of those involved is to take a look at a "routine" death from discovery through to disposition at a mortuary.

When an individual is found deceased, the first step in the process is the individual that found the decedent, usually referred to as the "RP" or reporting party, will call 9-1-1 to notify emergency services. This generates an initial response from two to three different departments. The first arriving individual is almost always a patrol officer who responded after the emergency call was put out by the dispatcher. This individual has many initial responsibilities to ensure a proper investigation can follow. First, the officer will try to provide life-saving care if at all possible. If the officer believes he/she may have a person that can be resuscitated, they will likely start CPR and possibly hook up an automated external defibrillator (AED) to the individual before the next professionals in this process, the fire department and/or emergency medical services, arrive on scene. If the individual found unresponsive is a viable patient, the emergency medical providers will transport the individual to the hospital. However, if after an evaluation the emergency medical providers believe the individual is not a viable patient they, usually in consultation with online medical control via a telephone call to speak with a local emergency room physician, will pronounce death. While all of this is going on, that initial responding officer(s) must begin securing the scene to make sure that nothing is removed or unnecessarily introduced into the scene. For the sake of this discussion, we will assume that the individual was pronounced dead on scene.

Once death has been confirmed by the emergency medical providers, they should exit the scene without altering it any further. The one important caveat to this is that any medical interventions that were performed on the decedent cannot be removed at this time. This includes everything from attempts, successful or not, to start intravenous or intraosseous fluids, electrocardiogram or defibrillator patches, endotracheal or other airway devices, and any other interventions that may have been performed on the decedent in an attempt to evaluate and/or treat the individual.

At this time, other professionals are beginning to arrive on scene. This usually will include other patrol officers as well as a patrol supervisor (usually a sergeant). It is often the responsibility of the patrol supervisor to contact the medical examiner/coroner office, detectives from the law enforcement agency with jurisdiction, and the crime lab. It is largely dependent on the various law enforcement jurisdictions what type of response the medicolegal death investigator can expect, in addition to their response to a scene. Some jurisdictions will send at least one detective and one criminalist to respond and document every scene, others will only send these individuals if the death is suspicious or believed to be a homicide. Additionally, not every death scene will require a scene response from the medical examiner/coroner office's medicolegal death investigator.

This, like the response of the law enforcement agency, is largely based on office protocols and state statutes. Some offices will respond to any and all death scenes. This could include deaths in a home, business, nursing facility, hospice center, or hospital. Additionally, some offices may not respond to all home deaths, especially when the decedent is elderly, has a significant and documented medical history, and law enforcement on-scene does not believe there are any signs of foul play. It is important to note that while this may be a standard practice in all areas, it is the medicolegal professional who is best qualified to examine a decedent and review their medical, family, and social history to determine if an individual died of natural causes and can have their death certificate signed by their primary care provider or if further investigation is required. There is some cursory research that shows if a decedent lived in a small to midsize jurisdiction they are more likely to have a scene response to their death. In very large jurisdictions, there may be less of a likelihood that a medicolegal death investigator will response, even if the case is a homicide (Clark, 2015). This illustrates the need for national standardization of policies and acceptable medicolegal office staffing levels.

Resources and the size of the population served play a significant role on the response of the medical examiner/coroner office to death scenes. Ideally, every death would generate a scene response, but that is not a feasible model. As an example, Los Angeles County's Medical Examiner-Coroner Office only responded to around 20% of the scenes out of the total number of deaths reported to their office (Los Angeles County, 2013), whereas Larimer County's (CO) Medical Examiner Office responded to almost 35% of the scenes out of the total number of deaths reported to their office (Larimer County, 2014). There is, however, an obvious difference in population and deaths investigated between the two departments. Los Angeles County has a very densely populated urban jurisdiction of around 10 million people, and Larimer County has a population of around 300,000 that is very rural. This comparison is not to draw a conclusion that one way of handling deaths is preferred over the other, but each office has to make the determination for how best to respond to the deaths within their jurisdiction to ensure that proper certification of death is being performed. Population, funding, and personnel provide significant limitations to an office and what they can do. That being said, the more an office is able to respond to death scenes, the less likely is that possible other causes of death, besides natural disease processes, are falling through the cracks.

Medicolegal death investigators are professionals who are trained and credentialed to conduct scene investigations, collect evidence, and work with the general public for a death to be accurately certified. The need for such a professional credential came out of the National Institute of Justice's (NIJ) National Guidelines for Death Investigation (1997). Out of this document and the subsequent *Death Investigation: A Guide for the Scene Investigator* (Clark, 1999) primary tasks were identified for what makes a proper and competent medicolegal death investigator. These tasks include everything from responding to scenes, communicating with other agencies as well as families, body examination, and identifying and collecting evidence.

In some jurisdictions law enforcement officers still perform tasks which are now routinely done by medicolegal death investigators in the majority of the country. The problem with law enforcement handling these functions is that it does not recognize the importance of a separate, yet parallel investigation. Law enforcement officials are trying to determine what, if any, crime occurred. The medicolegal death investigator is trying to determine the circumstances surrounding the death so that the proper certification can be made on a death certificate. If a crime has been committed, law enforcement cares who is responsible while medicolegal death investigators care about the disease process or injury that leads to the decedent's death; but for this happening, the decedent would still be alive. Once the medicolegal death investigator has completed his/her scene investigation a determination is made whether the individual can be released to a mortuary or if he/she needs to be brought into the medical examiner/coroner office for further examination, which may include an autopsy.

Now, consider our example of an individual who has died in the field (outside of a care facility or hospital). If the individual's death requires an autopsy, the decedent will be brought into the medical examiner/coroner office to be evaluated by the next professional in the death investigation system, the forensic pathologist. The autopsy is the quintessential medical procedure for documenting natural disease processes and evidence of injury. The types of deaths, which require an autopsy will be discussed later in this book, but in general, deaths that are sudden, unexpected, or violent require an autopsy to be performed.

The autopsy will be performed by a forensic pathologist; a medical professional who has completed an undergraduate education, medical school, a pathology residency, and a forensic pathology fellowship. This author recognizes that all pathologists who perform medicolegal autopsies have not completed a fellowship in forensic pathology or become board certified as a forensic pathologist, but for this text this will be assumed. Forensic pathologists are often assisted by forensic autopsy technicians in the morgue.

Forensic autopsy technicians are individuals who assist the forensic pathologist in the performance of the autopsy. Their role depends on the needs of the physician they are working with. Many forensic autopsy technicians play an important role by taking photographs, collecting data such as height and weight, taking fingerprints, and eviscerating the organs for the pathologist to examine. Fig. 1.3 depicts autopsy technicians assisting by taking photographs of the decedent prior to autopsy. The training and education for these individuals is quite variable depending on what office you are working with.

Many forensic autopsy technicians have some level of education in health care or core sciences, particularly with classes in anatomy. Some offices around the country hire and start the majority of their staff out as forensic autopsy technicians, and then promote from this pool of employees for their medicolegal death investigators openings. In some offices, particularly in academic settings, it is not uncommon to have a certified pathologists' assistant working with the forensic pathologist. Pathologists' assistants usually hold a graduate-level degree and are certified nationally through the American Society for Clinical Pathology. In addition to their roles in the autopsy suite, they often take on additional roles in the pathology department as well as provide teaching function within their academic setting.

Some offices will incorporate radiologic technologists and photographers into their staff to assist with the routine activities of the office. The radiologic

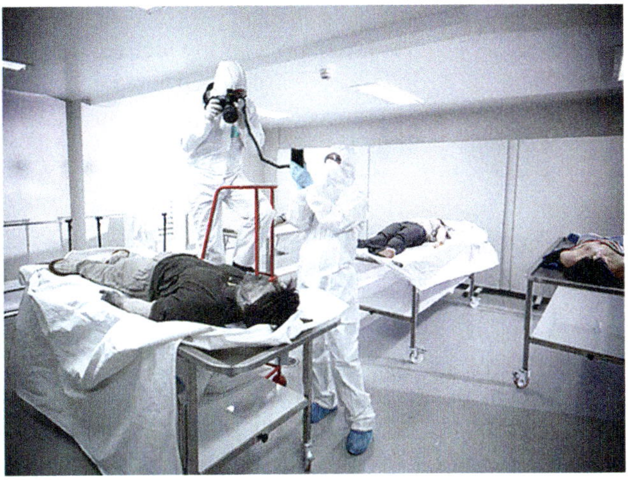

FIGURE 1.3 Autopsy technicians taking photographs of the decedent prior to autopsy.

technologists provide assistance with radiographs or other medical imagine to assist the forensic pathologist in determining cause and manner or death. Oftentimes, particularly in smaller offices, there is a finite amount of training for the medicolegal death investigators and autopsy technicians to perform this function. This is acceptable due to requirements that maintaining the licensing of individuals who perform radiographs is limited only to living individuals. The use of a dedicated photographer is also a luxury not afforded by many offices. The work of the individual tasked with this function, whether full-time or as part of their regular work activities, plays an important role in documenting not only signs of trauma or disease processes, but also taking negative photographs to show nothing is improper with the area being shown. Additionally, larger offices may have their own histology technicians and toxicology staff. The majority of offices, however, will outsource them.

Another important professional that should be involved immediately in the death investigation process is the victim advocate. These individuals usually work with the law enforcement agency or district attorney's office, and their function is to be there for covictims from the initial stages to guide them through the process that they have just been thrust into. A covictim is a family member, friend, or close acquaintance of the decedent. According to DeHart (2003), victim advocates intervene to reduce the risk to affected parties and provide prevention services to both direct and indirect victims of crime. These professionals often have a background in counseling, social work, or spiritual care. The victim advocate could be a full-time member of a department or the department could rely heavily on as-needed volunteers who often receive a lot of in-house training to function in the role. This role is crucial in the response to an unexpected death.

Best practice should dictate that a victim advocate is called for covictims as soon as an individual is pronounced deceased. This will accomplish two important tasks. First, the covictims will have someone present very quickly to provide comfort and information on the process. Second, the victim advocate frees up the law enforcement and medical examiner/coroner professionals from having to work with the covictims while trying to focus on the initial aspects of their investigation. Additionally, if a decedent will not require an autopsy these professionals can start the conversation with the next of kin about selecting a mortuary they would like to use for final arrangements. This will allow the decedent to be transported directly to a mortuary and not to the morgue to be held until arrangements can be made.

If an individual were to die in a nursing home or hospital, the nurses and physicians in these settings play an important role in the death investigation system. Many offices, particularly in large metropolitan areas depend heavily on these medical professionals for their opinion on what caused a decedent's death, and if any trauma or drugs of abuse could have played a role. In a smaller jurisdiction a full-time staff might have the ability to go to the hospital or nursing home to review each case. In major metropolitan areas, it is not uncommon for natural deaths that occur in these facilities to be either called in to be discussed with a medicolegal investigator, or for the facilities to fax in a report that will then be reviewed. If a medical examiner/coroner office relies on health-care workers to help monitor and assess deaths within their jurisdiction, it is common to have someone from the office routinely provide training so that gaps in the system can be minimized.

JURISDICTIONAL ISSUES

The agency that has jurisdiction over a decedent or a particular scene is usually laid out by the various state statutes. These statutes and how they affect a medical examiner/coroner office are constantly evolving. For this reason, it is important that at least one person within the office stays up to date so that there are not unintended legal issues. Additionally, many agencies or associations are involved in the legislative process to avoid any negative or unintended consequences for the medicolegal community through legislation. In many instances, legislative intent is not always obvious, so having a review with an attorney to provide guidance is often required. At a minimum, legislation that affects the medical examiner/coroner should outline which deaths fall under their jurisdiction.

The wording varies from state to state, but legislation generally outlines that the medical examiner/coroner has the responsibility to investigate sudden, unexpected, and traumatic deaths. This involves deaths not under the care of a physician; as a result of an injury, drug abuse, or mismanagement; in-custody; complications associated with anesthesia or a medical procedure; and cases of neglect/abuse.

Each jurisdiction defines under the care of a physician differently. For some jurisdictions it could mean only deaths where they were currently under the care and for some it might mean having been treated by a physician within the last hours to days. This is for jurisdictional issues only. Just because an individual died at home and hasn't seen their primary care provider or a treating physician within the last few months does not mean that this individual is required to be taken to the medical examiner/coroner office for an autopsy. It might be the case that the decedent was older and had a number of chronic health conditions. So, it is likely that this type of a case, while reportable and a scene investigation may be done, may be signed out by the decedent's primary care provider after the medicolegal death investigator contacts that provider to discuss the case with them.

While natural deaths usually account for the majority of deaths investigated by a medical examiner/coroner office (this will be discussed later in the book), deaths involving trauma make up another significant portion of the cases investigated. When most people think of traumatic deaths, they envision motor vehicle crashes and gunshot wounds. However, other types of trauma leading to death must also be investigated.

Any trauma sustained by an individual can adversely affect their overall health, especially those with chronic health conditions. The classic case is an elderly individual with chronic health conditions who falls and fractures his/her hip. There could be a multitude of issues associated with this. Two common issues are associated with death in these individuals. The first is a pulmonary thromboembolism. The results of venous stasis in a mobility limited individual could result in a venous thrombosis that could travel to the lungs. The second issue that could arise would be heart failure in a person with a cardiac history. The trauma is such that it overwhelms the decedent's body, which is already weakened due to chronic health conditions (DeMaria, Kenney, Merriam, Casanova, & Gann, 1987). Later in the book we will discuss a multitude of common traumatic injuries observed by a medicolegal death investigator.

Cases involving drug abuse or mismanagement are important to fully investigate. This is a broad category that encompasses improper taking of medications, whether prescribed to the decedent or not, as well as drugs of abuse. While drug abuse continues to be a problem some data show that, as a whole, there are some improvements. The National Survey on Drug Use and Health (NSDUH) (2014) revealed that the percentage of minors who self-reported having used illicit drugs in the last month prior to the survey has gone down from 10.1% in 2009 to 8.8% in 2013 (Center for Behavioral Health Statistics and Quality, 2015). However, total drug abuse for all individuals of age 12 years or older has stayed around 2.6% in the same period. There have also been some alarming statistics related to prescription opioid and heroin deaths which will be discussed later in the book.

In-custody deaths present unique challenges and must be fully investigated to ensure that nothing improper occurred while an individual was in the custody of a government entity. These deaths have come under increased scrutiny as of late with concerns that law enforcement officials are using unnecessary force which has resulted in fatalities. These instances range from the fatal shooting of a suspect to cases of excited delirium. Additionally, deaths that occur in a jail or prison should be properly investigated to ensure there are no signs of trauma or foul play not just from jailers but from the other inmates as well.

Instances of medical misadventures as well as complications associated with anesthesia should also be carefully reviewed by the medicolegal death investigator. These types of deaths are important to investigate because, like all deaths, important information can be gathered, which may help improve the care of future patients.

DEATH CERTIFICATES

One of the major functions of a death investigation system is to certify the cause and manner of death for cases that fall within their jurisdiction. This is done simply by signing the death certificate. The function of signing the death certificate is important because this public health record serves as a permanent record that an individual has in fact died. This document is almost always required to settle estates and for the purposes of filing a life insurance claim. It also serves as a means of statistical data to help guide public policy on addressing issues related to mortality (CDC, 2003). This very fact plays out everyday at the national, state, and local level.

The settling of financial affairs is often what family members of a decedent will think of when they are thrust into the criminal justice and medical examiner/coroner world due to a sudden death, second only to it stating to them what in fact killed their loved one. It is not uncommon to need the death certificate before family members can have access to bank accounts to pay expenses, and it would almost always be needed to sell off and settle an estate such as the closing of bank accounts or selling real estate. Additionally, there may be a financial stake in how the death certificate is signed.

A decedent may have had a life insurance policy that stated if he/she committed suicide, the policy would not pay out to the surviving beneficiary. Conversely, if an individual died from a violent act, as an example, there may be a clause that causes the policy to pay out at a higher rate. Additionally, if the death is suspicious and the beneficiary cannot be cleared by law enforcement of having anything to do with the death, the claim may not be paid out at all until that suspicion can be lifted. This is important for the medicolegal death investigators to understand so as to ensure the death certificate, if they are charged to sign it, is done in a correct fashion with all the available information at their disposal to make the most educated opinion as to the cause and manner of death that they can.

In a medical examiner system, it would be highly unlikely that the medicolegal death investigator would sign a death certificate. Exceptions to this might be if the investigator is a physician himself/herself or is another health-care provider, such as a physician assistant or nurse practitioner, who is allowed by state law to sign to the cause and manner of death. In a coroner system, however, it is not uncommon to have a nonphysician signing the death certificate.

The importance of the statistical significance the death certificate plays cannot be understated. The information placed on a death certificate, even though each state's death certificate is slightly different, is how the CDC collects and disseminates information to improve the health of everyone. These data can help show whether factors such as medical treatment and lifestyle factors are improving the overall health of a given population or the situation is getting worse. Additionally, the data could tell us about health disparities within a population.

As an example, if it appeared in the data that a certain percentage of the population in a geographical area was having a higher prevalence of fatal motor vehicle accidents, public health and safety officials have to examine the reasons why this may be occurring at a greater rate than the general population. From a medical standpoint, if an ethnic minority was suffering from a particular condition at a higher rate than the general population, we would want to know that to help understand the causes behind that difference. This is an important way in which the care physicians provide to their patients can be affected, and a way to help set national priorities as they relate to improving the lives of everyday Americans (Warner & Chen, 2012). It may not seem like it in the everyday, hectic life of a clinical provider but the availability of resources made available to combat various conditions and diseases is related to the data that is collected on the death certificate.

The data collected from death certificates around the country helps to guide public policy and funding to address the issues that are identified. If there appear to be a great number of automobile fatalities, then funding will likely be made available to study the safety of vehicles and what interventions can be done to increase the likelihood that an individual survives an accident. If there are a high number of deaths related to a specific form of cancer, funding priorities could be shifted to affect the greatest change based on this information. However, the findings that are presented from the data are only as good as the information that is collected in the field by health-care providers and professionals from the medical examiner and coroner offices.

Reliability of the available data is a major concern, and the medicolegal death investigator can play a pivotal role in this. The process that is gone through to collect all of the necessary information must be done consistently across not just one investigator's caseload, but across the office, the system, and even across the country. If everyone collects different kinds of information instead of an agreed upon list of basic findings that must be noted, then the data will not mean anything. To aid this, many offices and even some national organizations will put out standard forms that can be utilized by medical examiner and coroner personnel to ensure the necessary information is collected at every scene, every single time they are dispatched out to investigate a death. Improving the reliability of the information captured during a death investigation is only one major trend nationally.

NATIONAL EFFORTS

There are various national groups that utilize the death certificate data to help guide national priorities when addressing deficiencies in the current death investigation system. The NIJ had the Scientific Working Group on Medicolegal Death Investigation (SWGMDI) and now the focus is associated with a larger, more directed, and organized effort with the entire forensic community with the National Institute of Standards and Technology's (NIST) Organization of Scientific Area Committees (OSAC). The purpose of both the NIJ and NIST efforts are to improve death investigation through standardizing the investigative process from planning through the signing of death certificates.

This is accomplished through developing best practices, policies, and professional requirements for practice developed by subject matter experts (SME). The use of SMEs is one of the many ways in which standards can be developed. However, even with using professionals to develop best practices there is always the need for public comments from others that have a stake in the standards being developed.

The stakeholders that could have an interest in standards related to medicolegal death investigation include prosecutors, defense attorneys, law enforcement professionals, and crime scene investigators. This is not an all-inclusive list, but it does illustrate a diverse group that provides an important perspective that may not be realized by SMEs. This is true for all professions. Sometimes when a professional is so close to the process they might not understand how their practice affects those down the line. In addition to these national efforts, there are certifying bodies and membership organizations that have been championing this effort since the beginning of the profession.

The American Board of Medicolegal Death Investigators (ABMDI) is a national, nonprofit that was incorporated in 1999 to serve as the independent organization to certify death investigators across the country. There are two certification levels, registry diplomat and fellow (board certified), which both rely on experience in an office, the mastery of skills, and the ability to pass a national examination which covers the 29 tasks that were developed by the NIJ in their publication, National Guidelines for Death Investigation (ABMDI, n.d.). Certifying medicolegal death investigators and ensuring that offices are hiring and retaining these professionals is one way in which there can be an elevated standard to which a profession is held to. This is not to say that every certified death investigator is going to be the best possible professional every time, just like you couldn't say that every physician is the same simply because they met the same standard to practice. However, by creating a bar to measure all medicolegal death investigators against, medicolegal offices can say to the members of the community that they are striving for excellence by promoting the best possible practices in death investigation. The same can be said about medicolegal offices that achieve accreditation.

The two prominent medical examiner and coroner membership organizations are the National Association of Medical Examiners (NAME) and the International Association of Coroners & Medical Examiners (IAC&ME). Both organizations lobby for their members, provide training, and offer an accreditation program for medicolegal offices. Again, just because an office is accredited does not mean that it is one of the best offices in the country without question. What it does mean is that it has the proper policies and procedures in place that a leader office must have to be successful.

Medicolegal death investigators, like any professional, must always strive to serve their population based on an unbiased eye for the truth based on the current literature in the field, with strict adherence to ethical standards, and with the decedent and their family members at the forefront of all decisions that are made. Without this, they are doing a disservice to the population they serve and could create significant negative consequences for the families and covictims who are left behind after a death occurs.

REFERENCES

American Board of Medicolegal Death Investigator, n.d. Welcome to ABMDI. Retrieved from: http://www.abmdi.org.

Center for Behavioral Health Statistics and Quality. (2015). *Behavioral health trends in the United States: Results from the 2014 National Survey on Drug Use and Health* (HHS Publication No. SMA 15-4927, NSDUH Series H-50). Retrieved from http://www.samhsa.gov/data/.

Centers for Disease Control and Prevention. (2003). *Medical Examiners' and Coroners' Handbook on Death Registration and Fetal Death Reporting*. DHHS Publication No. PHS 2003-1110. Hyattsville, MD.

Clark, S. (2015). Accreditation and certification. In *International Association of Coroners and Medical Examiners Conference: Las Vegas, NV.*

Clark, S. C. (1999). *Death investigation: A guide for the scene investigator.*

DeHart, D. D. (2003). *National Victim Assistance Standards Consortium: Standards for Victim Assistance Programs and Providers*. Columbia, SC: Center for Child and Family Studies, University of South Carolina.

DeMaria, E. J., Kenney, P. R., Merriam, M. A., Casanova, L. A., & Gann, D. S. (1987). Survival after trauma in geriatric patients. *Annals of Surgery, 206*(6), 738.

Hanzlick, R. (2007). The conversion of coroner systems to medical examiner systems in the United States: a lull in action. *The American Journal of Forensic Medicine and Pathology, 28*(4).

Hanzlick, R., & Combs, D. (1998). Medical examiner and coroner systems: history and trends. *Journal of the American Medical Association, 279*(11), 870–874.

Larimer County Medical Examiner. (2014). *Annual Report.*

Los Angeles County Medical Examiner. (2013). *Annual Report.*

National Academy of Science Report. (2009). *Strengthening Forensic Science in the United States: A Path Forward.*

National Association of Medical Examiners (NAME). (2013). *Inspection and accreditation policies and procedures manual.*

Spitz, W. U., & Fisher, R. S. (1982). *Medicolegal Investigation of Death* (second ed.). Springfield, IL: Charles C Thomas Publisher.

United States Department of Justice Office of Justice Programs. (1997). *National Guidelines for Death Investigation*. Washington, DC.

Warner, M., & Chen, L. H. (2012). Surveillance of injury mortality. In *Injury Research* (pp. 3–21). US: Springer.

Chapter 2

Death Scene Basics

Chapter Outline

The vast majority of medicolegal death investigators in this country work very heavily in the field doing death scene investigations as opposed to working at a physical location for the majority of their workday. Depending on the size of the office, the investigators for a medical examiner or coroner office could work on a per call basis if the jurisdiction is small and does not handle a lot of deaths each week, or they could work a set shift schedule in a large office that could see the investigator handling a number of death scenes within the course of a single shift. Regardless of the volume handled by the medicolegal death investigator, their skills, knowledge, and understanding of scene basics as well as legal principles such as chain of custody are paramount for them to be successful at evaluating and documenting a scene, performing a body examination, and working closely with the family and other covictims of the decedent whose death they are called upon to investigate.

SCENE EVALUATION

The scene evaluation starts with the first responding police and fire/EMS personnel. From a law enforcement perspective, the officers must be able to secure the scene and ensure the safety of those who are there and those who are responding. The scene is secured by removing individuals who are there and making sure nobody else enters the scene before there is a proper investigation. The scene is made safe by identifying and removing, if possible, the threats to life and property.

Determining how large the scope of a scene perimeter takes knowledge and experience. Sometimes this is a simple task. If the decedent is an elderly individual with significant medical history and had an active do not resuscitate order, the perimeter might just simply be asking family to leave the bedroom until the medicolegal death investigator arrives. If the scene is in a public place

Essentials of Medicolegal Death Investigation. http://dx.doi.org/10.1016/B978-0-12-803641-9.00002-1

and a criminal act has occurred, the scene could be quite large and include multiple locations. It is the responsibility of the law enforcement agency to establish the scene perimeter and then secure it throughout an investigation. Setting up an appropriate perimeter is also a key aspect to ensuring a scene is safe.

Scene safety is one of the first things that are ingrained into first responders as they go through their training programs prior to or at the beginning of employment. The idea being that if they are unable to be safe and free from harm, they will not be able to assist others. Essentially, without a safe scene, they could become additional victims themselves. In the field of medicolegal death investigation there are a number of issues that professionals should be aware of to ensure their own safety. They include the possibility of violence, environmental issues, and chemicals.

By the time the medicolegal death investigator responds to a scene, the threat of violence from family members and bystanders is usually minimized and eliminated. However, this is still something to be mindful of. Situations can quickly escalate, particularly in a scene where an individual or individuals have died as a result of violence. There have also been instances of secondary devices used in mass fatality incidents specifically designed to injury those responding to provide aid to victims. While secondary devices are not something someone outside of a military environment are likely to come upon, it is still something that should be considered if there is a large scale terrorist attack in a major city. Another example would be the recent incidents of attacks on law enforcement personnel. Crowds can form quickly, particularly in officer-involved shootings, and there should always be an increased sense of security during these investigations.

Environmental issues are also important to be mindful of. This category covers a lot of different factors. Weather certainly fits in this category. If weather has played a role the hazards can be quite evident. If there has been a major weather event such as a hurricane, tornado, or flood, the threat might still be present and it would be best to secure the area for a later time to perform your examination of the decedent. There may also be secondary dangers as a result of a storm. The structure in which a decedent is found could be unstable due to damage, or there could be live power lines down on the ground, as examples. The ambient temperature is also important to be mindful of. If the weather is extremely hot, having adequate hydration and being able to take breaks during an investigation in a shaded or air conditioned area are important. On the other end of the temperature extreme, if the weather is extremely cold the medicolegal death investigator must be properly clothed to be able to safely work in the cold weather for extended periods of time. Additionally, the structure, a decedent is found in, could present significant environmental issues.

In addition to weather, structural issues such as confined spaces present dangers to the medicolegal professional. Confined spaces can be the cause of death in an individual due to lack of oxygen in an environment, and without the proper training the medicolegal death investigator could become another victim. The same is true with a damaged environment like with a structure affected by fire. The decedent may be very difficult to reach, particularly in a structure that is a total loss, and could require special equipment to access. In both of these scenarios, and any other environment that requires an advanced level of training, it is best to rely on the assistance of other professionals. The fire department is often a great resource for this specialized training. Additionally, some areas have technical rescue groups that could be of great assistance. An example of this would be in the Mountain West where there are various groups that specialize in mountain rescue operations. If a large corporation has many confined spaces, they too might have their own technical rescue team that would be available to assist and knowledgeable about the specific dangers and areas of the commercial structure.

Chemical hazards are also a significant safety concern of the medicolegal death investigator. These types of situations are becoming more commonplace with the increased prevalence of certain types of chemical suicides (these will be discussed in greater detail in a later chapter). Chemical exposures to the medicolegal professional can also occur in an industrial facility or at the scene of a motor vehicle accident involving a commercial truck transporting chemicals. In any of these situations it is the best practice to allow a hazmat unit to mitigate any situation before anyone else enters the scene. Cross-agency training should be done with the medicolegal office and area hazardous materials teams so that both groups of professionals know the needs and procedures for various situations. This is an opportunity to train these types of teams to take proper photographs while they are working a scene and how the loss of evidence can be minimized.

Once the scene has been secured and is safe, the first thing the medicolegal death investigator should do once he/she arrives on scene is meet with the supervising law enforcement official. The initial conversation with law enforcement should be brief so that the medicolegal death investigator does not start to form an opinion about what happened based on another agency's interpretations. It is also prudent to introduce yourself to any family, friends or colleagues of the decedent that may be on scene. This is not the time to interview the witnesses, but merely to let them know you are on scene and will be speaking with them shortly. Now it is time to enter and start to document the scene.

Photographs are the first step to properly documenting a scene prior to doing any exam or evidence collection. It is important to photograph everything prior to introducing anything new, including yourself, into the scene or moving anything from its original location. If a crime lab representative is there too it is often best to handle this task in conjunction with their scene photographs and walk-through. Fig. 2.1 depicts firearm evidence at a scene with evidence makers laid by the crime lab. This is something that should only

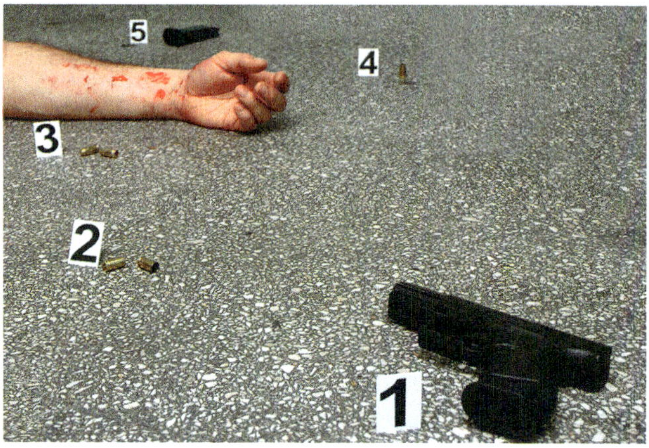

FIGURE 2.1 Firearm evidence at a scene with evidence makers laid by the crime lab technician.

be done after photographs without the markers have been taken, which will be discussed later in the text. Having a crime scene investigator and the medicolegal investigator doing them separately only delays the process and deprives both agencies of the open discussion that could occur in the initial finding of items of possible evidentiary value.

The general rule of thumb for photographs is that you start with the big picture and then focus in toward the details. Various scenes will require either more or less photographs be taken to accurately document the scene. As an example, a multiple stab wound homicide will inevitably require more photographs be taken than an elderly individual found unresponsive in bed with no suspicion of foul play. Regardless of the scene, a set of specific photographs should be captured on every scene response so that an accurate record of how the decedent was found can be established in case anyone needs to go back and review the case.

The first photograph should be a large picture of the entire area showing where the decedent was located within a given space. If the decedent was found in bed, this photograph could be obtained by standing in the doorway to the room. If the decedent was found in an outdoor location, this initial photograph should be wide enough so that there are multiple objects within the shot to allow others reviewing the photographs to easily be able to determine the location in the future. A good example for a motor vehicle accident would be the street signs on the corner. The next shot is a slightly closer photograph that simply shows the whole body. This is important because it will show the position in which the decedent was found. This can be used later with findings during your physical examination to see if what you are seeing on scene makes sense. From here, the next photographs will show specific sections of the decedent's body.

An identification photograph is next and is essential on every case. First, it can always be used to go back and confirm, at least visually, that the individual is who you believe them to be. Second, if a person is starting to decompose, this photograph might capture his/her appearance when he/she is still visually identifiable but may continue to decompose and have a distorted appearance by the time an autopsy is performed. The next six photographs are all of the body, both anterior and posterior. The decedent should be placed in a fully supine position and photographs taken of their body in sets of three; one of the head, neck, and chest (including the upper arms); one of the abdomen (including the distal aspects of the arms) and pelvis; and one of the lower extremities. There should be overlapping to these photographs to ensure that all areas of the body are represented in the photographs. The decedent should then be log-rolled into a prone position and the same set of three photographs obtained. These photographs should be taken at a 90-degree angle so that there is no distortion in the way parts of the body are represented visually in the photograph. More photographs may need to be taken during this step if the decedent was fully or partially clothed. There should be a photograph depicting the decedent with the clothing items, and then the items should be partially displaced to take another photograph showing the skin underneath. These photographs constitute the bare minimum for photography. Additional photographs may be taken at this point to show specific items close-up.

These close-up photographs could be used to document tattoos, injuries, identifying marks on the body, or important items around the scene. Whenever close-up photographs are taken, you will need to at least have one photograph that is at a slightly wider range and then the accompanying close-up photograph to be able to locate the finding easily at a later time. This is especially true if you are documenting injuries on a body.

If only close-up photographs are obtained, one could present the medicolegal death investigator the photographs at a later time, say in court, and without the medium-range picture locating the injury on the body, the investigator would not be able to differentiate where the injury was. The same could be said for items of value found around the scene. The common additional photographs taken on a death scene by the medicolegal death investigator could be of prescription medications, drugs of abuse, items that may have caused or contributed to a decedent's injuries, or items that could speak to the cause and manner of death such as a suicide note. All are important items that help tell the story about what happened to this individual. Negative photographs are also important in properly documenting a case.

Negative photographs are pictures that show something that illustrates nothing is wrong in this picture or, said another way, there was nothing that contributed to the decedent's death as it relates to this part of the body. This might not seem like an important step for the medicolegal death investigator, and one might ask, why take a picture of nothing? The reality is that these negative photographs are extremely helpful when reviewing the case to show definitively what the investigators saw on scene. They also are very helpful later on if there are claims that a decedent was potentially abused or mistreated by a caretaker prior to his/her death. A series of high-quality negative photographs of the decedent's body on scene can dispel these concerns.

The use of a ruler in the photographs should also be considered. The ruler allows for the item being shown to have a size indicator. If a ruler is used, there should be a photograph with and without the ruler. The second picture, without the ruler, is essentially a negative picture used to show that the ruler was not covering up anything else. In addition to photographs, some medicolegal death investigators utilize diagrams to document the scene further.

The use of diagrams is nowhere near as prevalent as photographs, which all medicolegal death investigators should utilize on all scenes, but can still be very useful in properly documenting a scene. Diagrams need not be elaborate or all-encompassing for each item in a room to be useful. The main items in the room and their relation to the body as well as other pieces of evidence can be extremely useful in showing how the scene presented itself. Additionally, these diagrams can be of benefit to individuals who review the case file at a later time. The forensic pathologist reviewing the case prior to an autopsy will have a better understanding about the details of the case, and if the case were to go to trial it could prove to be of benefit to a group of lay jurors who are trying to understand what the medicolegal death investigator saw on scene when he/she first arrived. Oftentimes, the crime lab personnel will document the scene with a diagram and they are often the more well equipped to perform this task. In addition to more practice at diagramming various scenes, criminalists will also tend to have more appropriate digital measurement equipment and software to recreate these documents.

PERFORMING AN EXAM

The decedent is the most important piece of evidence in any death investigation, whether criminal or not. In a criminal case, the decedent is the crucial piece of evidence that a crime has occurred, and the decedent might have evidence on or in them to connect an offender to the event. The decedent may have had a close, physical, interaction with the offender and his/her DNA could be left on the body. If a weapon was used, a recovered projectile from a gun could be recovered and used to link the crime to an offender's firearm. If it is a noncriminal matter, the body is certainly the most important piece of evidence. The decedent's body can reveal the trauma he/she may have sustained from a motor vehicle accident or show natural disease that has been affecting the decedent for a prolonged period of time.

Performing a proper body exam is an essential start to the death investigation process. The exam should be essentially the same whether the decedent's death was expected due to chronic health conditions, or whether it was a sudden, violent death. Making sure that you do your exam the same, regardless of the case type, will lessen the chances that you will miss something on any case you encounter. It will also ensure that you, as the medicolegal professional, will be accurately documenting all findings and not just signs of foul play. Properly documenting identifying marks and signs of natural disease are also important.

Performing a physical exam on a decedent is quite similar to an examination done by a primary care provider during a routine physical one. It is a head-to-toe look at a person's body to see if there are signs of normal development as well as signs of disease or trauma. Due to this, the physical exam is quite easy to teach if the medicolegal death investigator has a background in health care. Each section of the decedent's body should be visually examined as well as palpated to ensure accurate documentation of findings.

The visual examination, or inspection, allows for the medicolegal death investigator to obtain a great amount of information without having to actually do anything invasive. Fig. 2.2 depicts an initial visual examination by an investigator prior to moving the decedent. Some of the things the medicolegal death investigator should look for are as follows: Does the decedent's position they are found in suggest they were in bed, seated, or collapsed from a standing position? Is there any evidence that would suggest this was a traumatic event or their body was in a position that was detrimental to their ability to breathe normally? How about any changes to their skin color or signs of decomposition? All are important factors to consider when trying to determine what happened to this individual, and all can be obtained by simply looking at the individual and their surrounding environment. This is also where the medicolegal death investigator starts to document information that will be used later during interviews with family, friends, and bystanders to decide if the

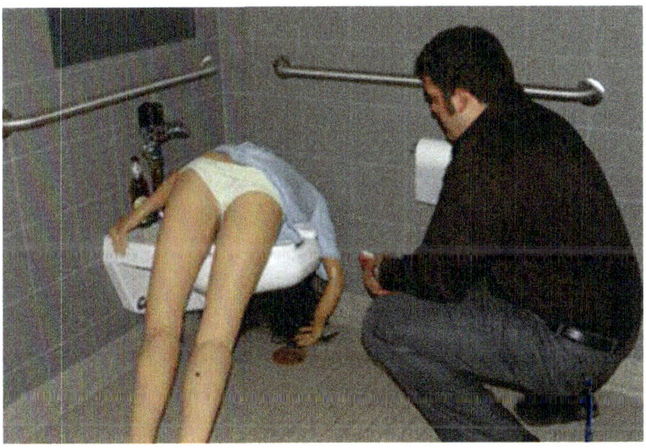

FIGURE 2.2 An initial visual examination by an investigator prior to moving the decedent.

story that is being told makes sense based on the information that you are being provided.

Palpation is an essential function to any physical examination of a decedent. There is a lot of information that can be obtained during this part of the physical examination. By palpating a decedent, you can determine his/her general body temperature, feel for any deformities or evidence of swelling, and can determine if the positioning of various body parts is consistent with normal anatomy. While palpating the decedent, the medicolegal death investigator can also determine if there is fluid collecting in the tissues or if crepitus is present. Palpation should be done with the pads of the fingers due to their increased sensitivity as opposed to other parts of the hand. For assessing algor mortis (body temperature) the back of the hand should be utilized to assess temperature since the skin is thinner (Bledsoe, Porter, & Cherry, 2006). This judgment of body temperature is simply if you believe the individual feels hot, warm, cool, or cold. Since there is not a scientific way to utilize a core body temperature as a means to determine time since death, very few medicolegal offices still perform a core body temperature on scene. There are certain exceptions to this, which will be discussed later on in the book.

Starting with the head and neck, the medicolegal death investigator should visually inspect the tissues to note any injuries or deformities. Any findings, as with anywhere on the body, should be documented on a body diagram that should ideally be integrated into an investigator's scene form. After the visual inspection is complete, one should palpate the cranium using both hands and moving from the back of the cranium all the way to the front. This can be followed by a complete palpation of the facial bones and the decedent's jaw. This is also a good time to assess whether rigor mortis, which will be discussed later in the chapter, is present or not. Rigor mortis is something that will need to be assessed throughout your examination with small and large muscles. At this point it is important to fully examine the oral airway.

The medicolegal death investigator should assess the decedent's teeth as to whether they are present, and if so, what condition they are in. The decent could be indentureless, have teeth that are in poor repair, or being in good repair. Any evidence of trauma should be documented. The lips' undersurfaces, buccal mucosa, frenulum, and tongue should also be examined for signs of trauma. Once the mouth has been examined, the eyes should be checked. With the eyes the medicolegal death investigator should be looking for the color of the iris, as well as the sclera to see any signs of petechial hemorrhages. A common finding at this point is tache noire (Fig. 2.3) which is a drying artifact found on the eye. When present, it will appear as a brownish band on the eyes from exposure to the air. After the eyes have been examined it is time to move down to the neck.

The neck should be inspected and palpated to check for any signs of injury or deformities. Common injuries of the neck could be sharp-force injuries from a knife, or a pattern abrasion from a strangulation or hanging. Signs of

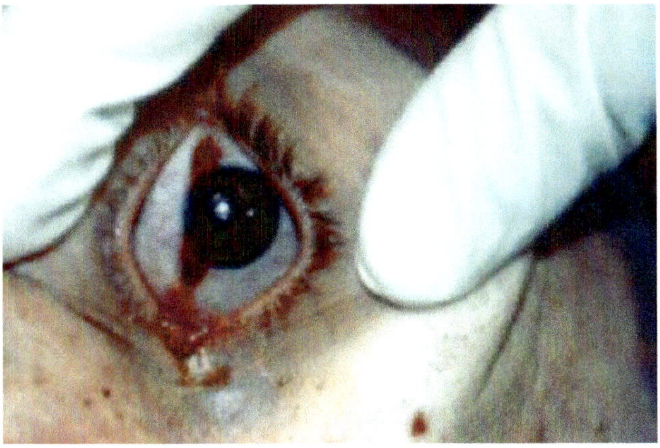

FIGURE 2.3 An example of tache noire.

natural disease or a medical event could also be present. An example of this could be the presence of a mass or tracheal deviation. This is why, in addition to palpating the decedent's spine, one should also take care to assess the lymph nodes and assess the trachea's midline position.

The decedent's upper extremities are next. Starting with the fingers and moving proximally toward the shoulder, special attention should be placed on inspecting for any signs of intravenous drug abuse. Signs of intravenous drug use would present in a number of ways. There could be a single, circular puncture mark in an area of skin overlaying a vein, or there could be track marks present. Track marks are a collection of scars from previous injections in a specific area where the user injected herself/himself many times. These are not always present, however. It usually depends on the type of syringe and needle used. Smaller needles, a needle used for insulin injections as an example, may not leave any easily visible marks. The medicolegal death investigator should also take additional pictures and document any signs of trauma to the hands and wrists which could indicate that an altercation or restriction could have taken place prior to death.

Following the upper extremities, the decedent's trunk should be thoroughly examined. The trunk includes the chest and abdomen. A simple visual inspection of this area can instantly reveal a number of chronic medical issues the decedent may have been dealing with. Examples of this could be a barrel chest which may indicate the decedent had emphysema, ascites could indicate the decedent abused alcohol, and obesity or excessive fat around the abdomen could indicate the greater likelihood of heart disease. Some findings might even lead the medicolegal death investigator to a probable cause of death. An example of this would be the presence of Cullen's sign. This finding is a discoloration found around the umbilicus that could indicate the possibility of an intraabdominal hemorrhage.

Special care should be taken to fully palpate across the decedent's clavicle and ribs. Deformities to the thoracic cavity may not be readily evident upon inspection, but upon palpation crepitus or deformities may be quite pronounced with even the slightest pressure. Often, a decedent will be either fully or partially clothed. So, it is prudent of the medicolegal death investigator, after photographing and examining the clothing, to lift up or remove the items to perform a proper examine. If this is not done, it would be quite easy to miss important clues or possible evidence of trauma.

The hips and external genitalia require an assessment for deformities or trauma. Common diseases that might be found upon examination in this area are important to note but unlikely to be the decedent's cause of death. The most common findings the medicolegal death investigator should be looking for would be evidence of a hip fracture or trauma to the genitalia. Upon inspection of the hips the medicolegal death investigator should look for any deformities, any signs of swelling, and that there is symmetry. For sexual trauma, to preserve evidence, only external trauma should be documented. If there is a need for an internal examination this should be handled by the forensic pathologist at autopsy.

The lower extremities are last but are still an important part of the examination. The lower extremities should be inspected for signs of injury as well as natural disease. If the decedent was involved in a pedestrian versus motor vehicle accident, the lower extremities will need to be documented accurately to note the location of possible impact points. Additionally, if one leg appears shorter than the other this would be a common sign of a possible hip fracture or dislocation. When palpating the legs, in addition to looking for deformities and the presence of crepitus, attention should be paid to the tissues around the distal end of the legs for edema. This could be an evidence of an underlying natural disease process such as congestive heart failure.

Once the anterior aspect of the decedent's body has been thoroughly and accurately examined, the decedent should be log-rolled onto his/her side or placed in a prone position so that the posterior plane can be examined. When the initial palpation was done on the head and extremities the posterior aspect of those body parts was likely already assessed. They now just need an inspection for anything that may not have been seen or palpated the first time. The decedent's posterior trunk, however, should be completely palpated to ensure no injuries are present only on the decedent's backside.

POSTMORTEM CHANGES

Postmortem changes are an important finding to document as they play an essential role in helping to develop a timeline since the decedent died. Some factors involve evidence around the place where the decedent was located. These could include activity on cell phone, meetings kept and missed, or witness statements regarding the decedent. Other findings used to determine time since death rely on the changes that a decedent's body goes through after they die.

The three main findings that every medicolegal death investigator uses to develop a rough timeline are the decedent's livor, rigor, and algor mortis. All three findings can vary greatly depending on the environment in which the decedent was found. Additionally, each finding on its own does not provide great depth to the understanding of postmortem interval, but the three together provide a picture about the general timeline since death. The medicolegal death investigator should, however, take great caution in providing too tight of a postmortem interval since there is not a scientific way to say, based on this information, this is the exact moment in which someone died. Providing inaccurate information, particularly about the postmortem interval could greatly affect a criminal investigation if the timeline is not accurate in comparison to a suspected offender's whereabouts.

Livor mortis is the pooling of blood depended with gravity. This pooling occurs in the blood vessels and can be moved to a different area of the body if the decedent is moved. This means that if a decedent dies on his/her back, or in a supine position, the blood should pool to the decedent's back, with the exception of areas of boney prominence where there is pressure from the body touching a hard surface. Fig. 2.4 is depicting a livor pattern that has pooled in the decedent's face whereas Fig. 2.5 reveals a livor pattern with some blanching. The blanching in this photograph was from the individual being seated in a chair with vertical spindles and a broad top to the chair. This pooling of blood in small vessels usually has a violet color to it and will become evident within the first 2 h after death. This finding can also be present in an individual who is in heart failure and has a prolonged death (DiMaio & DiMaio, 2001). After a period of time the livor pattern can become fixed, once

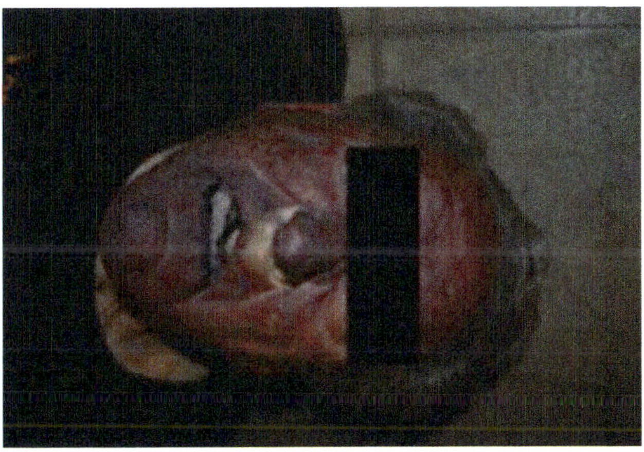

FIGURE 2.4 An example of livor pattern pooled in the face.

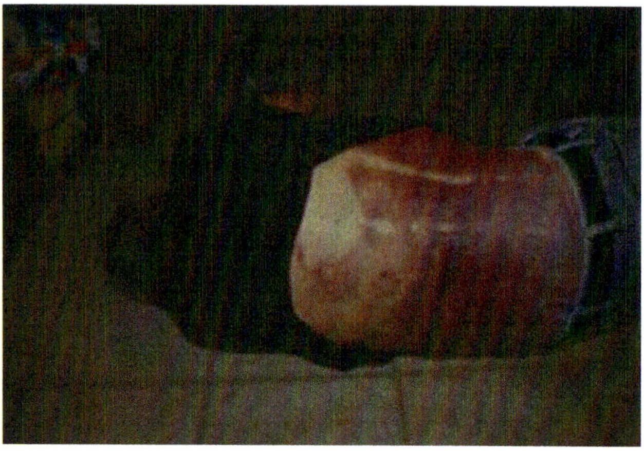

FIGURE 2.5 An example of livor pattern with some blanching.

the blood has hemolyzed, and if a decedent is placed in a different position after this point his/her livor pattern will not reposition.

Other factors can affect the presentation of livor mortis and could provide an initial indication for the medicolegal death investigator about what may have caused the individual's death. The most common change in livor mortis seen by investigators is the appearance of color from violet to cherry red. This is most often associated, although nonspecific, for carbon monoxide poisonings and hypothermia. In rare cases where a decedent may have cyanide poisoning, this finding may also be present.

Rigor mortis is another postmortem change that can assist the medicolegal death investigator in determining time since death. This is commonly known as the stiffening of a decedent's muscles. The process starts after around 2 h in the small muscles of the body, usually most evident in the hands and jaw, and progressing to the larger muscles. A body is considered fully fixed around 6–12 h depending on the environment in which the decedent is found. This change is caused by the absence of adenosine triphosphate, commonly referred to as ATP, which creates a "locking" of the actin and myosin filaments. After a period of approximately 24–36 h, rigor mortis will start to recede due to decomposition.

To distinguish whether someone's rigor mortis is progressing or receding, one must examine two things. First, is the decedent's livor pattern completely fixed? If it is not, due to the time it takes for a person, under normal room temperature, to have their livor mortis fixed the likelihood is that the decedent's rigor mortis is starting to fix instead of recede. Second, what muscles are you able to move more freely? Rigor mortis starts in the small muscles and progresses to the larger muscles, and when it recedes you will start to notice it in smaller muscles first, too. So, if you are able to freely move the jaw but not the extremities, the decedent is likely just starting to be in a state of early decomposition where rigor mortis is receding.

Algor mortis is the third common postmortem change that medicolegal death investigators look at when providing a window for how long it has been since an individual died. Algor mortis deals with the decedent's body temperature, and a number of factors determine the rate at which the body's temperature decreases. It is important to keep in mind that a decedent's decrease in body temperature does not change in a linear fashion, and the decedent's body temperature is greatly affected by internal as well as external factors (Henssge et al., 2002).

The major factors that affect a decedent's change in postmortem body temperature are the decedent's activity level and body temperature at time of death, the climate, and the environment one dies in. If a decedent was very physically active at the time of or just prior to his/her death, his/her body temperature would be elevated from that of a similar person who was not involved in a similar activity. Additionally, if a person has a higher percentage of body fat, he/she will decompose at a faster rate than someone who is thinner. This is due to the body fat insulating the body and keeping the decedent's core body temperature warmer, longer.

The climate and environment a person dies in play an important role in how a person decomposes over time. In a hot and humid region, the medicolegal death investigator is likely to find an individual who has a more bloated appearance, whereas someone who dies in a very dry, desert climate will more likely present with mummification, instead of going through a bloated, decomposing phase. In the event that there is advancing decomposition, the medicolegal death investigator will note skin and hair slippage, particularly when they are attempting to move the decedent, as well as blistering. If blisters are noted they will be filled with decomposition fluid. If a body is in a very dry climate there may be very little decomposition noted prior to mummification. There is exciting research coming out that may help medicolegal death investigators and forensic pathologists in determining a more accurate postmortem interval. The research has examined the microbes associated with decomposition of small animal cadavers as well as the gravesite soil. What the researchers found was that the microbial communities changed in a consistent, predictable pattern (Carter, Metcalf, Bibat, & Knight, 2015). This is exciting for the forensic community as it could provide a way to more accurately determine how long a decedent has been in an environment. Some additional findings commonly seen by the medicolegal death investigator include marbling, tache noire, and purge.

Marbling is a common finding usually found after at least 24 h since death occurred, and is a red, green, and black discoloration that follows the vessels of the body. Tache noir is a drying artifact of the eyes, the sclera specifically, where a dark brown line can be noted in areas where the eye lids were not completely shut and the eye was exposed to the ambient air. Lay people will at times confuse this finding with petechial hemorrhages. Purge is decomposition fluid that is commonly found in the mouth and nares of a decedent. It is important to become familiar with the differences between purge and blood, because many lay people will see the dark fluid and assume it is blood from a traumatic event.

DOCUMENTING SCENE FINDINGS AS A TEAM

Earlier in the chapter, scene photography was discussed when evaluating the scene, and is one of the essential functions to properly documenting scene findings. However, there are some basic steps the medicolegal death investigator should follow to successfully document and process a death scene. These include assessing the scene, thoroughly documenting how the scene presents, performing a detailed search, and documenting the collection of evidence.

When assessing a death scene, the initial steps taken by the medicolegal death investigator and the responding law enforcement professionals can determine success later on in the investigation or even at trial later on if the case is criminal in nature. It is the responsibility of the law enforcement agency to secure the scene and to make it safe prior to the arrival of the medical examiner or coroner office personnel. This includes setting identifiable boundaries, and mitigating as much as possible the potential hazards on scene. However, if this is not done when the medicolegal death investigator arrives on scene, he or she must insure that this happens before moving forward with the investigation.

Once the scene is safe, the next step is to start the collaborative process of documenting and processing a scene. It should be the goal of all individuals involved in the death scene investigation to take a team approach so that the work is handled in the most efficient, complete way possible.

The first step, as noted previously in this chapter, is to be briefed by law enforcement and other responders about what they heard, saw, and did when they initially arrived on scene. The informant at this stage could be a detective who responded after being called out, it could be the patrol sergeant who has command over the scene, or it could be one of the first arriving officers. Additionally, if the paramedics and fire department are still on scene they too may serve as an initial contact for the medicolegal death investigator. Regardless of who the informant is, this is an essential part of any investigation. The medicolegal death investigator will want to take special note of anything that was reported as having been moved or changed from the time the first responders got on scene until the arrival of the medicolegal professionals. This documentation is important in a variety of cases to help determine the cause and manner of death, but one example that is commonly encountered is when a gun is moved by the first responding units. Oftentimes, if law enforcement does not know if a person is alive or deceased, they may move a firearm and render it safe. This is obviously not the preferred method, but it does happen with some regularity. Knowing the position of the gun could be the difference between a case initially appearing as a suicide and a case that raises suspicion of foul play.

The last two items related to the initial assessment of the scene for documentation purposes are having an accurate scene log and knowing what additional resources you will need up front to properly document the scene. The scene log is regularly kept by the law enforcement agency but it is something the medicolegal death investigator should be aware of. There may come a time where a certain finding, such as trace evidence, is discovered and forensic investigators will want to know who had access to the scene so that they can exclude investigative and forensic professionals as the contributor of the piece of evidence.

As for assessing the need for additional resources, it is imperative that the medicolegal death investigator have the necessary tools and personnel to accurately process and document the scene findings. This may be something as simple as the right equipment such as a notepad, appropriate scene forms, personal protective equipment such as gloves and shoe covers, and a flashlight to name a few common items. It also might be identifying the need for a particular specialist on a scene. Common examples of this could be calling the fire department out to use their four gas meter to check for levels of carbon monoxide, or consulting with a forensic anthropologist if the medicolegal death investigator is confronted with skeletal remains. Once you have laid the initial groundwork to be successful at documenting the scene, it is time to enter the scene to do your initial walk-through.

The initial walk-through with the investigative team is an important opportunity to document the scene prior to it being significantly altered by crime scene investigators, detectives, and the medicolegal death investigator. The investigative team performing the walk-through should be a detective or law enforcement official, the crime scene investigator, and the medicolegal death investigator. This is not the time to open cabinets, drawers, or move the decedent. At this stage it is all about photographing, writing, and possibly even drawing how the scene initially presents. Is the residence neat and orderly, or disheveled? Do items appear where they should or are things out of place, damaged, or missing? Does it make sense for the decedent to be at this location or do the owners of the property not know who the decedent is? Are there items found on or near the decedent that may have played a role in their death, such as a weapon, illicit drugs, prescription medications, tobacco products, or alcohol? Are there any indicators that the individual was in poor health, such as oxygen tanks, assistive devices, or paperwork indicating recent physician office visits or hospitalizations? All are important to photograph and document as possible supporting evidence for the eventual certification of death.

After the scene is completely documented, including photographs, of how it presented initially to investigators and after a property body exam is performed, the area and/or property should be thoroughly searched. It is important to have an understanding of the applicable laws and statutes that stipulate when, what, and how something can be searched, but in general a search of the property should be performed for the medicolegal death investigator to form an initial impression as to what the cause and manner of death might be for the particular case. What is most commonly looked for when searching a scene from the medicolegal death investigator's perspective is the presence of prescription medications, illicit drugs, or other substances such as tobacco and evidence of excessive alcohol consumption that could give a more complete picture of the individual's health status and the time of his/her death. Additionally, if a decedent is not found by a close friend of family member a thorough search of a property is definitely warranted to find evidence of family members. This is usually accomplished by finding a contact list or book, or pieces of mail that could be from family members such as a birthday or holiday card. Lastly, a property search would be justified to find the decedent's health-care providers if this information was not already known. These providers, once contacted by the medicolegal death investigator, might be able to look in the decedent's chart for emergency contact information to assist with locating the decedent's next of kin.

The last step in the process of documenting a death scene is the collection of evidence. When processing a scene, particularly a suspected homicide, the majority of biological and trace evidence that is to be collected will be done on scene by the crime scene investigator from the involved law enforcement agency. However, there are a few common evidence collection basics that the medicolegal death investigator must be knowledgeable of. They are how to collect medications, biological and trace evidence, and how to further preserve evidence that will be collected at the time of autopsy.

The collection of medication by a medicolegal death investigator is quite common and is usually dictated by office policy. Some offices will indicate through their policies and procedures that all medications should be collected on every scene, others will not collect any medications but will instead document and count each on scene, and the majority of offices have policies somewhere in the middle such as collecting medications only on cases that are to be autopsied or there is a suspicion of overdose. Regardless of the specifics of the policy, all medications that are to be retained by the medicolegal office should be placed in a paper or plastic bag that can be sealed for transport. Once back at the office, all medications should be fully documented, including number dispensed, number of medication remaining, provider, dose, regiment, date the prescription was filled, and who it was prescribed to. This will not only provide information about how the medication was taken by the decedent, but since the agency is collecting it there must be an accurate paper trail to show that it was stored, retained, and disposed of properly. This documentation also discourages abuse or theft of medications by individuals who may have access to them.

Collecting biological evidence usually involves items covered in blood or other fluids that the medicolegal death investigator believes may be valuable for the forensic pathologist to examine at the time of autopsy. This could be a clothing item that has a defect in it from a possible gunshot wound. In this specific example, the evidentiary value is significant as it could help determine the range at which a gun was fired. Other forms of biological evidence, such as blood spatter on a wall, should be collected by the crime scene investigator from the law enforcement agency. Biological evidence is best preserved when it is appropriately dried in a sterile environment, such as a drying rack at the crime lab or autopsy facility, to avoid mold and degradation of the evidence. However, this is not feasible on a crime scene. So, there are two ways of addressing this issue. First, if the item is securely on the decedent, such as a blood-soaked T-shirt, the item should be left in place to be removed at the time of autopsy. Second, if the item is not secured to the decedent's body, such as a blood-soaked hat, it should be placed in a paper bag for transport back to the lab where it can then be appropriately dried. The paper bag allows the item to breathe, which is important. If biological evidence was placed in a plastic container, condensation would likely build up which could degrade the evidence.

Trace evidence is something that is generally recovered at the time of autopsy, but the medicolegal death investigator should still have a basic understanding of what and how things are collected. Trace evidence could be hair, fiber, paint chips, or fingernail scrapings, to name a few. Regardless of the item being collected, there is a general way in which trace evidence is collected. The item is either grabbed with clean, gloved finger or forceps (either cleaned stainless steel forceps or disposable plastic forceps) and placed on a piece of filter paper. The filter paper should then be folded at least twice to help retain the item in the middle of the paper. Once folded, the filter paper with the trace evidence can then be placed inside of an appropriately sized manila envelope and sealed. The envelope, as with any container for evidence should be marked with the case number, a few words regarding what the item is and where it was recovered from, and the date and time of collection. This is in addition to properly sealing the container with evidence tape and black marker with the collector's initials, date, and time along with black lines across the tape and container to show that it has not been tampered with. Lastly, as with any evidence collected, the items should be retained separately. So, if hair fibers were recovered from the decedent's upper left leg, that would be stored in a separate evidence envelope from hair fibers collected on the decedent's shirt. While some evidentiary items may be collected on scene, the vast majority of evidence is best left to be collected by the forensic pathologist at the time of autopsy.

There are a few basic steps that a medicolegal death investigator can take while on a scene to help preserve evidence for collection at the time of autopsy. First, the body itself is evidence and should be treated as such. This does not mean that family members should not be allowed to see and touch their loved one prior to the body being removed to the medical examiner or coroner office, assuming there is no suspicion of homicide. However, it does mean that each decedent that is going to become a medicolegal case, in other words an autopsy will be performed, should be placed in a body bag and that body bag should be sealed prior to transport. The reason for this is that it is a safeguard to show that the decedent was not tampered within any way from the time he/she left the sight of the medicolegal death investigator, until the forensic pathologist views the decedent in the autopsy suite. There are also certain death investigations that require additional procedures to preserve evidence.

It is a common practice when there is a firearm involved that a decedent's hands would be bagged. The bagging of the hands helps to contain any gunshot residue that might be found on the decedent's hands as well as preserve any evidence of blood spatter that may be present. It should be noted though that many offices do not do gunshot residue testing any longer due to the lack of value that the findings produce. One could fire a handgun and have no residue whatsoever, and someone else in the room that didn't fire a gun could test positive. Another instance where you would always want to bag the decedent's hands would be if they were involved in a confrontation prior to death. The bagging of the hands in this scenario would protect possible trace evidence that could be recovered at the time of autopsy. In particular, the concern would be if you did not bag the decedent's hands you could lose valuable DNA evidence that could be found by doing fingernail scrapings or clippings. Regardless of the reason, when the hands are bagged, the medicolegal death investigator will utilize new brown paper bags. Once the bags are over the hands, evidence tape is used over the bag near the opening to secure it onto the body. It should be noted that the tape should not be touching the skin at any point. It should be entirely secured over the paper bag. Exposed feet are sometimes covered with paper bags in the same fashion, particularly in homicide investigations, but this varies depending on the medicolegal offices' protocols.

Lastly, many offices utilize a commercially available evidence sheet to wrap the body in for homicide investigations prior to placing them in a sealed body bag. This is not a standard, but if the cost is reasonable for the office it should be considered. The benefit of having these sheets is the belief that it helps catch and retain any trace evidence that might shake loose from the body during transport. Once the scene has been processed and documented, and the body examination completed the next step is to obtain a detailed history on the decedent.

OBTAINING A MEDICAL, SOCIAL, WORK, AND FAMILY HISTORY

The vast majority of cases handled by the medicolegal death investigator are natural deaths and the best way to determine a preliminary cause of death on a decedent with no apparent signs of trauma or foul play is to get a proper medical, social, work, and family history. This is best obtained in two manners. First, the medicolegal death investigator can request medical records from the decedent's primary care provider or any facility where he/she had been recently treated. Second, and most expeditious, the medicolegal officer can interview a family member or close friend who is a good historian. If a family member or close friend is not a good historian or they only cursorily know the decedent's health history, extra care should be taken to document health history through other confirmatory means.

The medical history is very important to the medicolegal death investigator because it provides a general overview of the decedent's health at the time of their death. Was the individual generally healthy and active, or did he/she has a number of chronic health conditions? Many health conditions will be discussed later in this textbook, but a number of health conditions could lead to a sudden death. Knowing their documented medical history could be the difference between needing to bring that person in for an autopsy, and having their primary care provider sign the death certificate based on their history and releasing the decedent to a mortuary directly from the scene. The medical history can also reveal a recent change in the decedent's health status. A good example would be an individual who only went to his/her primary care provider's office once a year for a physical examination, but has recently gone in multiple times for an increase in a certain sign or symptom. All medical records collected by the medicolegal death investigator should be retained in the case file (Fig. 2.6) along with all other case documents so that they can be retrieved and referenced at any time. In addition to the medical history, a decedent's social history can provide indications for why an individual died.

FIGURE 2.6 Medical records collected by the medicolegal death investigator.

A decedent's social history includes a number of factors including substances he/she used and/or abused, as well as the lifestyle he/she lived. The three main social issues a medicolegal death investigator should know on every case are if the decedent used tobacco, drank alcohol, and abused prescription or recreational drugs. The use of any of these, particularly in excess, could have very negative consequences on a decedent's health.

Tobacco use has been linked to a number of chronic health conditions such as atherosclerotic cardiovascular disease, stroke, and lung cancer to name a few (US DHHS, 2015). Additionally, tobacco can have a negative impact on a family's ability to have a child because tobacco use has been shown to decrease male sperm counts as well as increase the risk of many birth defects and miscarriage (US DHHS, 2001, 2010, 2015). Due to this, if an individual does not have significant medical history or a well-documented medical history from not having regular physicals with a provider the history of long-term tobacco use in addition to their age could lead a medicolegal death investigator to suspect a death related to atherosclerotic cardiovascular disease. The excessive use of alcohol could also lead the medicolegal death investigator to suspect certain medical conditions.

The consumption of alcohol is a widely socially acceptable part of our culture. However, the excessive consumption of alcohol can lead to a number of health conditions. Alcohol is the most commonly abused substance and can play a significant role in a person; developing cardiac, hepatic, digestive, and/or neurologic conditions will be discussed later in the textbook that can be the result of chronic alcoholism. Family members or friends may be reluctant to describe the decedent as being an alcoholic or a "heavy drinker," but signs on scene such as excessive, empty containers of alcohol could be an indication that he/she was more than a social drinker.

It is important, as a part of a good social history, for a medicolegal death investigator to know about any prescription or recreational drug abuse. The abuse of prescription and recreational drugs can lead to respiratory failure, among other things, and death. Additionally, prescription medications that are not prescribed to the decedent could create an adverse reaction when taken with another prescription or substance. The combination of some substances can create a synergistic effect whereas the total reaction of the substances is greater than the sum of its parts.

In addition to medical and social history, family history can be an important factor when hypothesizing a possible preliminary clinical impression about what happened to a decedent. It is yet another piece of the puzzle when examining an individual and it can provide insight into what may have happened, particularly if the decedent has signs of contributing factors toward a disease. The perfect example of this would be a gentleman with morbid obesity who has a strong familial history of cardiovascular disease and stroke. The morbid obesity, in this scenario, would already predispose someone to cardiovascular disease and if there was also a genetic

Checklist for Interviewing Family or Co-Victims

- ✓ Introduce yourself
- ✓ Ask, "tell me about the events leading up to your loved one being found."
- ✓ Medical History
    - o Chronic health conditions
    - o Recent illnesses
    - o Psychiatric history
    - o Medications they were taking and did they take them as prescribed
    - o Primary care provider
    - o Specialists they have seen
    - o In-patient facilities where they have been treated
    - o Any recent changes in their health
- ✓ Social History
    - o Alcohol use and how frequently
    - o Illicit drug use, even if only remote or in the past
    - o Tobacco use: what, and how much per day
- ✓ Work History
    - o Where did they work
    - o What type of work they performed
    - o Any issues or conflicts at work
- ✓ Ask, "is there anything we have not discussed that you think would be important for me to know?"
- ✓ End the conversation by discussing what the next steps are and where their loved one will be

FIGURE 2.7 A sample template of questions to discuss with family members to help obtain a full medical record for the pathologist.

component at play the likelihood that this might be your cause of death is relatively high, especially with the absence of any evidence of drugs or trauma. Fig. 2.7 provides a quick reference to make sure that all important topics are discussed with family members so that the forensic pathologist has a complete record to review prior to autopsy, should one be required.

MAKING A POSITIVE IDENTIFICATION

Positively identifying a decedent is one of, if not the most, the crucial aspects of any medicolegal death investigator's job. This is not only because as a professional you want to be able to state definitively that the person you say is deceased, is in fact, deceased. There is also a large legal and estate component to this determination. One of the tasks that falls under the purvey of the medical examiner/coroner, as previously discussed in Chapter 1, is the signing of the death certificate. The death certificate is one of the ways that this identification is made official for the previously stated purposes.

The legal documentation of someone's death allows for the closing of business and personal accounts, the sale or transfer of ownership to another party, and allows for the payout of life insurance. There are many ways in which the medicolegal professional can identify the decedent. Some of these are considered scientific means of identification, while others are considered presumptive identifications.

Scientific means of identification are items that utilize a proven, documentable method for proving that the decedent is the person you say, and this form leaves no doubt about the identity of the decedent. The various scientific identifications include fingerprints, dental, DNA, and imagine comparison with antemortem radiography. Some of these means are utilized more frequently than others based on the quickness of the turnaround for identification as well as the cost associated with them to the medical examiner/coroner office. Fig. 2.8 is an example of an antemortem radiograph from a dental office that was used to make a comparison with Fig. 2.9 which is a radiograph obtained by the medical examiner's office.

Fingerprint identifications are the most common form of scientific identification utilized by medicolegal offices. This is because the information is often readily available and is very cost-effective as the comparison can be done by a certified fingerprint examiner likely at the local crime laboratory from whose jurisdiction the case originated from. Some larger offices may also

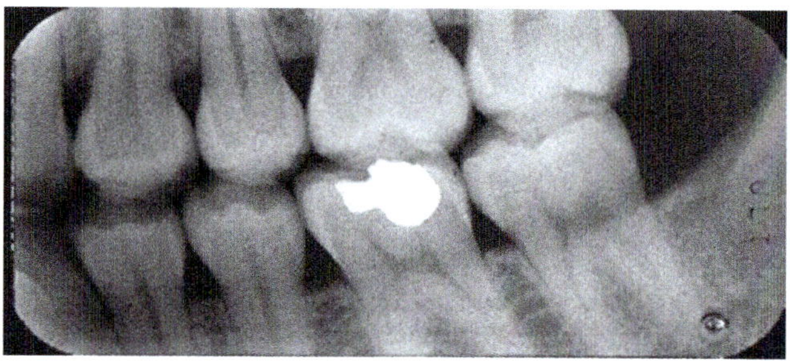

FIGURE 2.8 An example of antemortem radiograph obtained from the dental office.

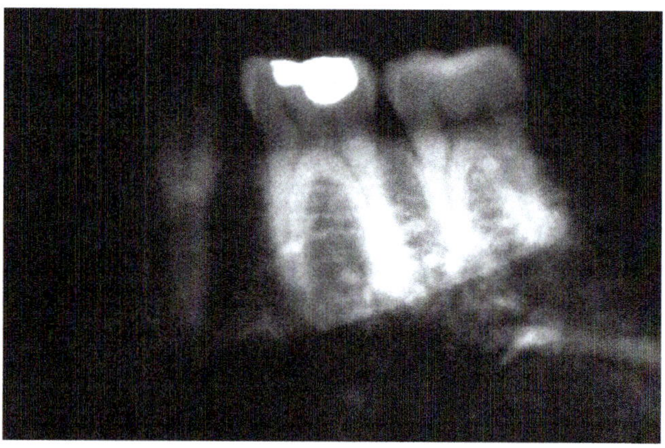

FIGURE 2.9 An example of antemortem radiograph obtained from the medical examiner's office.

have certified persons in-house. In order for this to be done properly the examiner needs proper postmortem fingerprints or moldings that can be compared to a known antemortem sample.

The most common way a medicolegal death investigator will collect postmortem fingerprints is with a ten-print card using some form of an ink pad to document the ridge detail for each finger. This is commonly done on every decedent taken into the medical examiner/coroner's office when there is a recent death and there is no substantial decomposition of the fingers. With this method the key is to obtain the widest, most complete print possible by rolling the inked finger side-to-side and then up on the specific finger box on the ten-print card. Another common fingerprinting method with nondecomposed remains uses powder and fingerprinting tape. With this method, the cleaned hand will be dusted with a wand utilizing powder to identify the ridge details of the fingers. Then small sections of tape are pressed over the dusted fingers to capture the ridge details of the individual fingers.

REFERENCES

Bledsoe, B. E., Porter, R. S., & Cherry, R. A. (2006). *Paramedic Care: Principles and Practice* (second ed.). Upper Saddle River, NJ: Pearson.

Carter, D. O., Metcalf, J. L., Bibat, A., & Knight, R. (2015). Seasonal variation of postmortem microbial communities. *Forensic Science, Medicine, and Pathology, 11*(2), 202–207.

DiMaio, D., & DiMaio, V. J. (2001). *Forensic pathology*. CRC press.

Henssge, C., et al. (2002). *The Estimation of the Time Since Death in the Early Post-mortem Period* (second ed.). London: Edward Arnold.

U.S. Department of Health and Human Services. (2015). *The Health Consequences of Smoking—50 Years of Progress: A Report of the Surgeon General*. Atlanta: U.S. Department of Health and Human Services, Centers for Disease Control and Prevention, National Center for Chronic Disease Prevention and Health Promotion, Office on Smoking and Health, 2014.

U.S. Department of Health and Human Services. (2010). *How Tobacco Smoke Causes Disease: What It Means to You*. Atlanta: U.S. Department of Health and Human Services, Centers for Disease Control and Prevention, National Center for Chronic Disease Prevention and Health Promotion, Office on Smoking and Health.

U.S. Department of Health and Human Services. (2001). *Women and Smoking: A Report of the Surgeon General*. Rockville, MD: U.S. Department of Health and Human Services, Public Health Service, Office of the Surgeon General.

Chapter 3

Cause and Manner of Death

Chapter Outline

One of the most important tasks assigned to medical examiner and coroner offices, one could argue the most important along with positively identifying decedents, is certifying the cause and manner of death. This information is crucial not only for the family to know what happened to their loved one but also for statistical data about what is causing death in a defined population.

In the first chapter, the importance of the death certificate was discussed in greater detail. It is important to understand that the cause and manner of death is only a small piece of the information that public health officials are interested in collecting, but being able to describe what happened to a decedent in a short, succinct fashion allows for the general understanding about what happened. A person may have been found unresponsive in the street lying next to his/her bicycle, but an autopsy revealed that he/she had a significant cardiac event that caused his/her accident and death, and urges the family and friends not to worry that he/she was involved in some sort of accident while biking. This information is placed usually at the beginning of an autopsy report under diagnosis and is then certified on a death certificate. The professionals who are allowed to certify the information on a death certificate is based on a particular states' statutes. Some coroner states allow for nonphysicians who are the coroner or their designee(s) to certify the death. Additionally, there is some variation as to the level of healthcare provider who can certify the death certificate. In some states, it is only an MD or a DO who can certify, while in others a physician assistant or nurse practitioner has the ability. Regardless, the information that is included in this certification is the cause, mechanism, and manner of death.

CAUSE OF DEATH

The cause of death relates to the natural disease or injury/injuries that cause a physiologic change that eventually leads to death. This can be from a chronic

Essentials of Medicolegal Death Investigation. http://dx.doi.org/10.1016/B978-0-12-803641-9.00003-3

condition or a very acute event. The general idea is, "but for" this happening the decedent would still be alive. In other words, if the decedent who the medicolegal death investigator is examining did not have a certain condition or injury they would not have died at that particular moment. The idea of "at that particular moment" is an important concept, particularly when trauma is involved. This also speaks of contributing factors.

A contributing factor is anything that hastens death in some fashion. Later on in this chapter, contributing factors will be discussed as they relate to the manner of death, but one example could be the presence of a drug in a decedent's system that exacerbates a decedent's underlying health conditions. An example of a contributing factor for a natural death could be the presence of multiple comorbidities such as diabetes or obesity. In this natural example, diabetes and obesity would be occurring along with the major condition, possibly atherosclerotic cardiovascular disease.

The cause of death can be from an acute event that just occurred or it could be from a prolonged, chronic condition or illness. The most common example of a chronic condition being a decedent's cause of death would be complications related to atherosclerotic cardiovascular disease. This condition will be discussed in greater detail in the natural deaths chapter, but in short, it is the narrowing of an individual's coronary arteries due to plaque deposits. These deposits and the eventual narrowing of the arteries build up over time, which creates the potential for a sudden natural death.

An example of a nonnatural delayed death could be an individual who was in a severe motor vehicle accident. This person may have survived the initial event but was a quadriplegic as a result of the injuries he/she sustained. If this individual dies of a complication related to being a quadriplegic, then the cause of death would include the injuries he/she sustained many years from the motor vehicle accident. An example of a condition that developed out of the chronic effects of trauma could be sepsis from sores related to being bedridden. In this example, the decedent's cause of death on the death certificate might read: Sepsis, due to bed sores, due to quadriplegia related to a motor vehicle accident. Some certifications of the cause of death are much simpler. It is up to the forensic pathologist to determine what was the greatest condition or illness that caused the irreversible changes in a decedent's body that could have led to the death.

In practice, the realization is that an individual may have had a number of conditions that could have caused his/her death. This is an example of how the practice of medicine, in this case determining the cause of death, is both a science and an art. The forensic pathologist must weigh the scene, autopsy, and ancillary test findings against the decedent's medical records and the pathologist's own knowledge and experience to determine the most significant condition that caused the individual's death. The cause of death is different from describing the mechanism of death, and even though the mechanism of death does not go on the death certificate it is still something that should be examined as part of the overall determination of what could have led to the decedent's death.

MECHANISM OF DEATH

The mechanism of death is the physiological imbalance that is caused by the overarching cause of death in the individual. It is important to note that this might not be specific to that exact disease or injury that caused the decedent's death. For instance, a person could suffer a catastrophic hemorrhage inside of his/her body from both cardiovascular disease as well as metastatic cells advancing into a vessel. Hemorrhage would also be the mechanism of death for any number of traumas including a gunshot wound to the head as well as from blunt force injuries sustained in a motor vehicle accident. The manner of death is the last piece of the certification that must be determined on each case in which the medical examiner or coroner takes jurisdiction.

MANNER OF DEATH

The manner of death is based on the circumstances surrounding the case and is broken down into five categories: natural, accident, suicide, homicide, and undetermined. This piece of the certification often times relies very heavily on the medicolegal death investigator to accurately capture the information at the scene, as well as information obtained through interviewing appropriate parties. The medicolegal death investigator's scene findings tell the complete story as to what happened to a decedent. Without this piece, the forensic pathologist is simply looking at a disease process or an injury without the story regarding what happened up to that point. Not having a thorough scene investigation and report would be like asking an internal medicine physician to determine the best clinical course of care without any clinical or social history that leads up to the current health issue. Not having the information would decrease the ability to make an accurate diagnosis and develop an appropriate course of care, and the same is true for the forensic pathologist when determining the manner of death of a decedent.

Natural

Natural deaths make up the largest percentage of any medicolegal office's caseload, usually around 50%. For a death to be classified as natural, the only reason attributed to why that person died can be a disease process. The most common causes of death associated with this manner of death would be cardiovascular disease, cancer, respiratory disease, hepatic disease, and neurologic conditions. All of these disease processes will be discussed in the natural deaths chapter. While natural deaths account for the largest percentage of cases handled by the medical examiner/coroner's office, it is important to understand that not all natural deaths are what are considered reportable.

Depending on the death investigation system, the jurisdiction's population, and the resources of the specific medicolegal office there could be a great number of natural deaths that are not seen by the medical examiner/coroner's office. A study by Clarke (2015) showed that jurisdictions that were smaller in total population served were more likely to respond to a greater number of natural deaths, whereas large, urban offices simply did not have the resources, likely due to a high call volume, to respond to death scenes where there appeared to be no foul play involved. Additionally, hospice deaths or inpatient hospital deaths rarely generate a scene response.

Deaths that occur under hospice care or natural inpatient deaths at a medical facility, particularly greater than 24 h after the decedent was admitted, do not generally receive much of an investigation by the medical examiner/coroner's office, if at all. The reasons for this are simple. It is often not realistic to generate a full response and investigation into the death of an expected death unless there is cause for concern when there is limited financial and human capital; however, this creates a reliance on other healthcare professionals to spot problems. Often times this is not an issue. However, nurses and physicians in a clinical setting lack the training to pick up on minor changes that might cause concern for a medicolegal death investigator. Additionally, nurses and physicians may not fully understand how a recent history of trauma could change the manner of death determination. If a decedent suffered a traumatic event, it is important to evaluate whether or not it played a role in why that person died today and not later in life. For this and other reasons, it is important for the medicolegal office to provide training to healthcare providers in the area about what events or findings need to be reported to the office at the time of death if a jurisdiction is relying on them to be a safeguard in the death investigation system. Another important factor to consider when investigating a suspected natural death is if the decedent had drugs in his/her system, even if they are prescribed to the individual, they should be counted and then evaluated by a forensic pathologist to determine whether or not they could have contributed to the death.

Accident

If a death is classified as an accident, this means that some external event or substance contributed to the decedent's death. The most common examples seen by medicolegal death investigators are falls where injuries occurred, motor vehicle accidents, or deaths related to substance abuse such as a drug overdose.

While a traumatic event such as a hip fracture from a fall on a cement sidewalk would likely not lead to death in a healthy younger adult, it might be too much stress for an elderly individual. The stress of the fracture and the body's response to the injury could put an elderly individual with chronic health conditions into heart failure (Perdue, Watts, Kaufmann, & Trask, 1998). This is important for the medicolegal death investigator to understand when he/she is taking a report on a suspected natural death. As discussed in the previous section regarding natural deaths, often times the perceived routine death of an elderly individual does not generate a full scene investigation. Therefore many offices will require that the attending nurse or physician call these deaths in if the death occurred at an assisted living, nursing home, or medical facility. The staff member reporting the death may not think of including a history of falls or injuries, particularly if the decedent was declining in health due to a chronic health condition, though, as stated earlier in this section, an injury can hasten an individual's death. If it is the medical opinion of the provider overseeing the care of a decedent who has died that an injury caused an individual's death even 1 day sooner, the death should be certified as an accident. It is proper for the medicolegal death investigator to ask, "if the injury had not occurred, would the decedent still have died at this particular moment".

Like falls, motor vehicle accidents account for a large percentage of deaths that a medicolegal jurisdiction will handle in a given year. In the chapter about blunt force injuries, this topic will be explored further. As it relates to certifying the manner of death, motor vehicle accidents are almost always certified as accidental death. The caveat to this is that some offices, although this has lost favor in recent years, will certify motor vehicle–related deaths as homicides if, just prior to or during the accident, the driver of the at-fault vehicle was committing a felony offense. Examples of this would be a drunk driver who causes a death, or the driver who hits and kills someone and then leaves the scene without calling for help. Again, however, this is not common and these deaths in the vast majority of jurisdictions would be classified as an accidental death. One important note here is that just because the medical examiner or coroner classifies a death as accidental, this does not limit any potential legal proceedings. The medicolegal office's determination is a medical one, not a legal determination. One additional situation that may arise and would have an effect on the manner of death as it relates to motor vehicle accidents is if there was evidence that an individual used his/her vehicle in a manner that suggests he/she attempted to end his/her own life. An example of this could be someone who has told friends and family that he/she intends to end his/her life and his/her vehicle is witnessed to be driving straight at a cement pillar at a high rate of speed. These circumstances would lead the medicolegal death investigator to suspect suicide as the manner of death and not accident. The intent is important when considering motor vehicle accidents, just as it is with prescription and illicit drug overdoses.

For individuals who abuse prescription and/or illicit drugs, a drug overdose is likely to be certified as an accident. This is due to the fact that even though the average person might never even consider injecting heroin due to the obvious health effects, as an example, the user in this scenario intends to achieve a high with his/her drug abuse, not death. The same could be said for the individual who routinely abuses prescription medications. Unless there was an intent to end one's life, these too are commonly signed out as an accident.

Suicide

For a death to be classified as a suicide, there needs to be the explicit or implicit intent by the individual to end his/her life, or the action he/she took would be one that a normal prudent person would understand as an event that would end his/her life. The most common deaths that are classified as suicides are ligature hangings, intentional gunshot wounds, or intentional prescription drug overdoses. It is also important to note that a suicide note need not be present for a death to be categorized as a suicide.

Depending on which study you read, there are varying percentages of suicides where notes are present. Many studies have examined whether the writing of a suicide note is a common occurrence and they have put the prevalence of a suicide note anywhere from 23.4% to 61.4% (Bennett & Collins, 2001; Cattell, 1988; Cattell & Jolley, 1995; Cheung, Merry, & Sundram, 2015; Juurlink, Herrmann, Szalai, Kopp, & Redelmeier, 2004; Karch, 2011; Purcell, Thrush, & Blanchette, 1999; Snowdon & Baume, 2002; Wanta, Schlotthauer, Guse, & Hargarten, 2009). Regardless of whether a suicide note is present or some other form of communication was present to outline the decedent's intent, it is important to always get a proper psychosocial background to see what events may have led up to this event where the decedent decided to end his/her own life.

Interviews with family, friends, and associates are important to see what was going on in the decedent's life. Did the individual have a history of mental illness or of previous suicidal ideations or attempts? Additionally, was there anything particularly different about the day(s) leading up to this event? There are a few commonly accepted stressors and conditions that predispose individuals to suicide such as a history of alcoholism or substance abuse, impulsive tendencies, history of mental illness, and a family history of suicide (CDC, 2015). However, there are some indications that individuals who commit suicide due to financial stressors need not have a history or mental illness or documented history of reaching out for mental health services (Coope et al., 2015). This is important for the medicolegal death investigator to understand because often times when there is a suicide, family members will deny that the decedent could have taken his/her own life because he/she was not depressed or did not see a therapist and did not take antidepressant medications. Those might all be very true, but research like the study noted above illustrates that those conditions are not highly predictive of someone committing suicide when one experience a financial stressor such as the loss of employment or another significant change in one's financial status occurs.

There need not be a note or a verbal statement about the desire to end one's life for the death to be classified as a suicide. The act itself is often an obvious indicator that the individual intended to end his/her life. Examples could be a secure scene with no signs of foul play and the decedent has an intraoral gunshot wound. In the first place, it would be difficult to place a gun inside of someone's mouth to execute this kind of a shot, and the absence of anyone else being present in the room would lead one to believe that the individual acted alone. The same is true for an individual who secures a noose to the rafter of a garage, places his/her head and neck through the noose and either partially or fully suspends his/her body with the ligature. A great number of suicides will fall into the category of "you will know it when you see it." However, some are not as easily discernable.

Prescription drug overdoses tend to fall into the category of less than obvious manners of death. A classic example that the medicolegal death investigator will be confronted with many times throughout his/her career is where a decedent has a medical history that is significant for depression and anxiety, has medications for such, and is found to have died from a prescription drug overdose. When this occurs, there must be a significant effort undertaken to determine what events lead up to the death, such as loss of employment or relationship, the findings on scene, and weighing them against the levels of substances found in the decedent's toxicology report. There is a big difference between the person who has borderline lethal levels of substances in his/her body and has no positive scene findings and the individual with completely empty prescription bottles that were recently filled and extremely high lethal levels of substances in his/her toxicology report.

Homicide

For a death to be classified as a homicide, the death must be due to the actions of another individual. What is important to note here is that the medical examiner or coroner is not placing blame or criminal charges on an individual with this certification. Often times lay people and professionals alike get the terms homicide and murder, a legal term, confused. An easy example to differentiate between the two is to consider a simple scenario. Let us imagine that an individual enters a store with the intent to rob the place. He/she has a gun and during the robbery he/she shoots and kills the cashier. The death of the cashier is both a homicide, because the decedent was shot by another individual, and a murder because a crime was committed. Let us use the same scenario but this time assume a police officer enters the store during the robbery. The offender points his/her gun at the officer, and the officer shoots and kills the offender. The death of the robbery suspect would still be classified as a homicide because he/she was shot by another individual, but the officer would not be charged with murder as the shooting was justified.

The majority of deaths that are classified as homicides are acute in nature. Meaning, the time from when the event or injury occurred is in close proximity to the pronouncement of death. However, this is not always the case. It would not be uncommon, however certainly not a regular occurrence, that a medicolegal death investigator would deal with cases like this throughout his/her career. An example of this would be someone who sustains a gunshot wound that leaves them with a chronic health condition, like scaring of the lungs if they were shot in the chest. This chronic lung condition ends up being a contributing factor in his/her death later in life, and since without that gunshot wound all those years earlier the individual would not have died when he/she did as a result of his injuries, the death would be appropriately classified as a homicide.

Undetermined

Sometimes, even after a complete autopsy has been performed, including appropriate studies like histology and toxicology, the reason for why an individual has died is not scientifically known. Additionally, if a cause of death is known but the circumstances surrounding the death are not known, it is best to classify these deaths as undetermined. A retrospective study from one medical examiner system showed that over a 10-year period 11.5% of all the medicolegal cases that were certified were signed out with an undetermined manner of death with much of the ambiguity leading to this certification related to not being able to rule out whether the death was accidental or not, particularly with toxicological cases (Advenier, Guillard, Alvarez, Martrille, & Lorin de la Grandmaison, 2015). This illustrates an important point regarding medicolegal death investigations.

The proper certification of death, as mentioned earlier in this chapter, is absolutely dependent on a thorough scene investigation as well as follow-up work done by the medicolegal death investigator. The documentation of the scene, the interviews with family and friends, and the collection and reviewing of medical records can be the difference between a death being certified as undetermined or as a definitive natural, accident, homicide, or suicide. The correct certification is not only important for statistical reasons like we discussed with death certificates, but also for families to have a complete picture as to what happened to their loved one and for certain criminal cases to move forward if the death is a homicide versus an accident or suicide.

It is important to note here that the cause and manner of death could both be undetermined, or only one could be ruled as such. An example of this might be the previously discussed case of someone with a mental health history who overdoses on his/her medications. If there is a disagreement or uncertainty in regards to the facts of the case the death may be ruled undetermined to reflect the uncertainty surrounding the case. Additionally, some skeletal remains will show no signs of trauma and with the absence of the body's tissues it is highly unlikely that a certification other than undetermined cause of death and undetermined manner of death will occur. Lastly, deaths involving children less than 1 year of age with no signs of natural disease or trauma that could have led to death will almost always be classified as sudden unexplained death in infancy as the cause of death and undetermined for the manner of death. These child deaths used to be classified as sudden infant death syndrome as the cause of death and natural as the manner of death. However, this is no longer the accepted classification as the new classification accepts the reality that after every accepted examination and testing was performed we still do not know with any degree of medical certainty what caused the child's death. Child death investigations will be discussed in great detail in Chapter 10.

CONTRIBUTING FACTORS

Often times on a death certificate as well as on the front page of the autopsy report, which shows the diagnoses made by the forensic pathologist, there will be any number of contributing factors listed. What a contributing factor is has been discussed briefly through various examples in this chapter, but what is important to understand about them is that they played a role but were not the main cause of death.

When reviewing the autopsy report, the contributing factors are generally listed after the actual cause of death. Again, it is important to remember here that the cause and manner of death are a medical opinion from the physician handling the certification. The physician, or in some jurisdictions the coroner, is making the judgment based on a degree of medical certainty. This is why it would not be uncommon to have slightly different opinions about the exact cause of death. At times, there are even disagreements about the manner of death that generally play out in a courtroom when, usually, the defense puts their own medical expert on the stand to give an opinion about what they believe happened in the case.

As for the presence of contributing factors on a death certificate or an autopsy report, the medicolegal death investigator is most likely to see them on an individual with significant natural disease or with an individual who died from a traumatic event. With the example of an individual with significant natural disease, it would be pertinent to list all of the chronic health conditions that played a role in making the main disease worse. An example of this would be the person who dies from complications related to chronic obstructive pulmonary disease (COPD). This was the main disease process that ended his/her life, but if he/she suffered from hypertension/coronary artery disease, and he/she were a chronic smoker these would all be important to list as they made the main diagnosis, COPD, worse and in the case a decedent, fatal. A similar reason exists for traumatic deaths.

When there is a traumatic death, it is often the compounding factors of all the injuries that make a particular event too severe for an individual to survive. Here are a few examples to illustrate the point:

- Motor vehicle accidents are an excellent example of how multiple injuries can compound the trauma experienced by a decedent from a single event. Often times, individuals who die in a motor vehicle accident have their cause of death signed out as being due to multiple blunt force injuries.

After this diagnosis, the forensic pathologist will then list all of the injuries that were noted during the autopsy. The vast majority of these injuries by themselves would not be enough to kill a healthy adult, but the totality of all the injuries cause the event to be one that was not survivable.

- When someone suffers one significant or multiple smaller stab wounds there are often many organ systems that are affected. In these situations, all of the injuries from the stab wounds are noted. Some of the injuries may have only played a small role in the death, but their mere presence dictates that the death was not natural and thus must be noted.
- Elderly individuals with multiple chronic health conditions are a different, yet important, group of traumatic deaths where the medicolegal death investigator is likely to find contributing factors listed. These, however, are not likely multiple traumatic injuries that are being listed but instead multiple, significant chronic health conditions that contributed. These chronic health conditions are listed because without the decedent having those conditions they might have survived the traumatic event. An even simpler way of describing this is if a 20-year-old person breaks his/her femur he/she is likely to survive that traumatic event if the proper care is provided. However, if an 80-year-old person breaks his/her femur and has multiple health conditions, the fracture alone would likely be enough.

REFERENCES

Advenier, A. S., Guillard, N., Alvarez, J. C., Martrille, L., & Lorin de la Grandmaison, G. (2015). Undetermined manner of death: an autopsy series. *Journal of Forensic Sciences, 61*(Suppl. 1). http://dx.doi.org/10.1111/1556-4029.12924.

Bennett, A. T., & Collins, K. A. (2001). Elderly suicide: a 10-year retrospective study. *The American Journal of Forensic Medicine and Pathology, 22*, 169–172.

Cattell, H. R. (1988). Elderly suicide in London: an analysis of coroners' inquests. *International Journal of Geriatric Psychiatry, 3*, 251–261.

Cattell, H., & Jolley, D. J. (1995). One hundred cases of suicide in elderly people. *British Journal of Psychiatry, 166*, 451–457.

Centers for Disease Control and Prevention. (2015). *Suicide: Risk and protective factors*. Retrieved from: http://www.cdc.gov/violenceprevention/suicide/riskprotectivefactors.html.

Cheung, G., Merry, S., & Sundram, F. (2015). Late-life suicide: insight on motives and contributors derived from suicide notes. *Journal of Affective Disorders, 185*, 17–23.

Clarke, S. (2015). Accreditation and certification in the forensic sciences. In *IACME conference, July 25, Las Vegas, NV.*

Coope, C., et al. (2015). Characteristics of people dying by suicide after job loss, financial difficulties and other economic stressors during a period of recession (2010–2011): a review of coroners' records. *Journal of Affective Disorders, 183*, 98–105.

Juurlink, D. N., Herrmann, N., Szalai, J. P., Kopp, A., & Redelmeier, D. A. (2004). Medical illness and the risk of suicide in the elderly. *Archives of Internal Medicine, 164*, 1179–1184.

Karch, D. (2011). Sex differences in suicide incident characteristics and circumstances among older adults: surveillance data from the national violent death reporting system-17 U.S. states, 2007–2009. *International Journal of Environmental Respiratory Public Health, 8*, 3479–3495.

Perdue, P. W., Watts, D. D., Kaufmann, C. R., & Trask, A. L. (1998). Differences in mortality between elderly and younger adult trauma patients: geriatric status increases risk of delayed death. *Journal of Trauma and Acute Care Surgery, 45*(4), 805–810.

Purcell, D., Thrush, C. R. N., & Blanchette, P. L. (1999). Suicide among the elderly in Honolulu County: a multiethnic comparative study (1987–1992). *International Psychogeriatrics, 11*, 57–66.

Snowdon, J., & Baume, P. (2002). A study of suicides of older people in Sydney. *International Journal of Geriatric Psychiatry, 17*, 261–269.

Wanta, B. T., Schlotthauer, A. E., Guse, C. E., & Hargarten, S. W. (2009). The burden of suicide in Wisconsin's older adult population. *Wisconsin Medical Journal, 108*, 87–93.

Chapter 4

Common Natural Diseases and Disorders

Chapter Outline

Having a strong education in common natural diseases and disorders that are encountered by a medicolegal professional is essential to being a successful medicolegal death investigator. Knowing how to collect evidence and interview witnesses are important. Also, since the majority of cases one will handle in his/her career deal with natural diseases this information is imperative to be proficient in. Additionally, having a solid education in common natural diseases can better allow the medicolegal death investigator to referee cases, determining what cases need to be brought in for further examination and what cases can be released directly from a scene to a mortuary.

When discussing the decedent's history with family and friends, medicolegal death investigators should do their best to get the most complete picture of the factors related to the decedent's health. So, in addition to information about their diagnoses, the decedent's family, work, and social history should also be taken.

Family history is important to understand because there could be a genetic component to why the decedent died today and not later in life. Multiple studies have shown a significant increase in the likelihood that individuals will suffer a cardiac event if one or both of their parents have had one (Lloyd-Jones, Nam, D'Agostino, Levy, Murabito, Wang, et al., 2004; Sesso, Lee, Gaziano, Rexrode, Glynn, & Buring, 2001). Yet, others found that environmental factors

Essentials of Medicolegal Death Investigation. http://dx.doi.org/10.1016/B978-0-12-803641-9.00004-5

played a larger role in determining how long an individual has lived (Ljungquist, Berg, Lanke, McClearn, & Pedersen, 1998). Knowing what medical history a decedent's family has, particularly siblings and parents, can provide medicolegal death investigators with a window into what may have occurred with the decedent they are currently investigating. It is also important to remember that if a parent or siblings of the decedent are not deceased the family on a death scene may not report any family history. If families deny any medical history, either for the decedent or their family members, a good follow-up question is "do they take any medications?" Family members may not think of their loved ones as having any medical history, but if decedents or their family members took medications for hypertension and high cholesterol it is clear that is not the case.

Work history is an important factor to consider when evaluating a potential natural death. The environment an individual works in can have a significant impact on the individual's overall health status. A specific example of this is the research that supports an increased incidence of lung cancer in laborers who work in the railroad industry (Garshick et al., 1988; Garshick, Laden, Hart, et al., 2014; Laden, Hart, Eschenroeder, Smith, & Garshick, 2006). The medicolegal death investigator need not know the specific increased risks for each element that might be present in a work environment, but it should be understood that the chemicals that people are exposed to on a regular basis, particularly in a confined space, can predispose individuals to certain health conditions. Additionally, some high-stress professions can also have negative effects on a person's health.

The concept of a stressful workplace environment has been thoroughly researched as it relates to psychological wellbeing. However, research has also shown that employees who viewed their workplace as a stressful one also reported lower levels of overall physical health (Nixon, Mazzola, Bauer, Krueger, & Sepctor, 2011). While the self-reporting of research participants should not be the definitive method for determining if this is in fact a significant factor in adults' overall health, it does provide a social consideration in someone's death if his/her family and/or friends report significant stress and he/she appeared to have died of natural causes at a young age.

Social history is also essential to understand. By social history, the basics that should be made known to the medicolegal death investigator are if the decedent used tobacco products and how frequently, use and frequency of alcohol, and use and frequency of recreational drugs.

Tobacco use, as we will discuss with many of the diseases in this chapter, can have significant health effects. The constant presence of a carcinogen on the body will greatly increase the likelihood that a decedent will have chronic health conditions. There are numerous reports that link heart disease and stroke to the tobacco use, and there is empirical evidence that since the United States government has made decreasing tobacco use a priority the incidence of tobacco use and heart disease have seen a significant decrease (Mozaffarian et al., 2016). Due to this, knowing the decedent's tobacco history is something that the medicolegal death investigator should note on every case. This could be the difference for a forensic pathologist who is on the fence as to whether there is enough medical history to perform an autopsy or if the decedents' death certificates should be signed out by their primary care provider based on their health history. Some states, Colorado as an example, even require the certifier of a death certificate to indicate whether or not tobacco use contributed to their death.

The use of alcohol is also an important factor to keep in mind when evaluating a decedent's likely overall health history. The use of alcohol is prevalent in our society. A recent study by Stahre, Roeber, Kanny, Brewer, and Zhang, (2014) showed that "From 2006 through 2010, an annual average of 87,798 alcohol-attributed deaths and 2.5 million years of potential life lost occurred in the United States." The problems can come when alcohol is used excessively or in a chronic, daily fashion. Research has shown that heavy alcohol use increases an individual's risk of heart disease (Briasoulis, Agarwal, & Messerli, 2012). Knowing this, obtaining the information related to alcohol abuse could provide a window for the medicolegal death investigator into what associated health conditions may be present.

Recreational drugs are often thought of as an indicator of a possible drug overdose, but it could also increase the likelihood of death from some natural diseases. As we have previously discussed and will continue to discuss in later chapters, the presence of illicit drugs in a decedent's system when he/she died will often cause the manner of death to be changed from natural to accident if it could have exacerbated the decedent's chronic health condition(s). Additionally, decedents who have a history of certain drugs of abuse could have associated chronic health conditions due to this. One example to illustrate the point would be the case of a former intravenous drug user who developed hepatitis as a result. The finding of hepatic disease, with the absence of drugs in the system when the individual died, would warrant the manner of death to be signed out as natural due to tradition even though an external factor, in this case illicit drug use, played a contributing role in the development of the disease.

The following information will discuss the most common natural diseases and disorders that medicolegal death investigators should be familiar with, as they will routinely be present in cases they investigate.

CARDIOVASCULAR

Even with a significant public focus on cardiovascular health, there is still an alarmingly high prevalence of cardiovascular disease in the United States. In 2013 there were over 220 deaths attributed to cardiovascular disease per 100,000 Americans (Mozaffarian et al., 2016). Knowing this, the medicolegal professional should be well versed in the common cardiovascular conditions he or she may encounter. The most prevalent of these are preventable when the general population lives a healthy lifestyle. This is mentioned because when a medicolegal professional is investigating the suspected natural death of an individual it is important to understand the overall health status of the decedent.

Some of the most significant risk factors include personal care factors that can be controlled such as the use of tobacco, low physical activity, and an unhealthy diet. These factors are likely to become evident when investigating the suspected natural death of an individual. Low physical activity is subjective depending on who you interview, but tobacco use and a poor diet can be ascertained simply by taking a good look around the decedent's living environment.

Hypertensive Cardiovascular Disease

The finding of hypertensive cardiovascular disease is a significant one because of it being a risk factor for coronary artery disease and stroke. The prevalence of hypertension varies depending on which study you read, but some data suggest that nearly 20% of individuals who have hypertension do not know it (Nwankwo, Yoon, Burt, & Gu, 2013). The effects of hypertensive cardiovascular disease, particularly when untreated, can cause an enlargement of the heart, particularly found in the left ventricle. The walls of the left ventricle become hypertrophied and less effective at pumping blood to the rest of the body.

Additionally, as will be discussed later in this chapter, hypertensive cardiovascular disease can increase the likelihood of a number of significant conditions such as an aortic dissection, nontraumatic intracerebral hemorrhage, and renal disease.

Coronary Atherosclerosis

The presence of coronary atherosclerosis is a common finding at autopsy the older a decedent is at the time of his/her death (Fig. 4.1). However, the degree to which someone suffers from the plaque buildups within his/her arteries varies from person to person. One important fact to keep in mind is that a large percentage of the cases the medicolegal death investigator sees where coronary atherosclerosis is the eventual cause of death will be asymptomatic prior to their terminal event.

As plaque builds up in the coronary arteries there may not be evidence or history of a previous myocardial infarct, however, this does not mean that there are not areas of ischemia due to a restricted flow of blood to the affected area. This could create a situation where a fatal arrhythmia occurs. In fact, while it is believed that greater than 75% narrowing of the coronary artery is fatal, there have been cases where this is less than 75% narrowing and the death was still a result of the coronary atherosclerosis. Some drugs can make an individual's coronary artery disease more lethal. An example of this would be the coronary artery spasms that can occur while using cocaine.

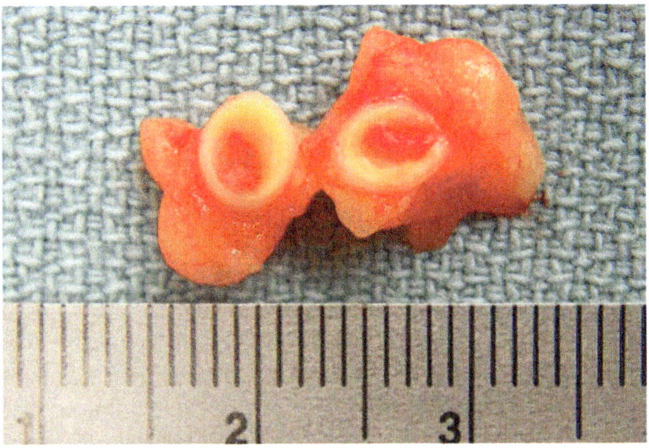

FIGURE 4.1 An example of coronary atherosclerosis.

Another common occurrence seen by the medicolegal professional with someone who has significant coronary atherosclerosis is a coronary thrombus. This is simply a blood clot that forms and becomes lodged in the already narrowed coronary artery. A complete blockage in a coronary artery will cause the cardiac tissue distal to the event to die from the absence of the oxygenated blood. This is depicted in Fig. 4.2 where a clear, patent coronary artery on the left allows blood to flow freely to the tissues of the heart, whereas the plaque buildup and

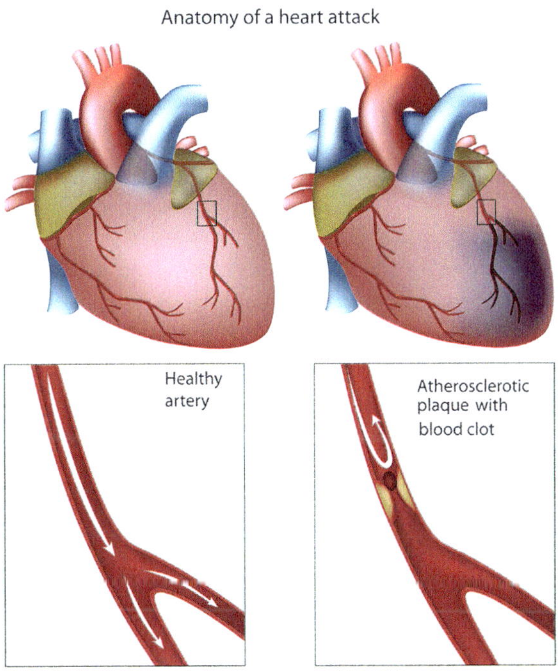

FIGURE 4.2 An example of coronary thrombus.

blood clot on the right do not allow blood to flow to the areas distal to this blockage. This results in what is commonly referred to as a heart attack. As with all cardiac-related deaths, it is important to screen for the risk factors associated with coronary atherosclerosis on every case, which include hypertension, diabetes, family history of heart disease, high cholesterol, and tobacco use.

Cardiomyopathy

The groups of diseases that make up the category of cardiomyopathies are diverse in their etiologies and require the medicolegal death investigator to have a basic understanding of these differences. The two basic categories that the medicolegal death investigator will encounter are dilated and hypertrophic.

The highest occurrence of cardiomyopathy and the number one inherited cardiac anomaly in children is found to be dilated cardiomyopathy (Maron, McKenna, Danielson, Kappenberger, Kuhn, Seidman, et al., 2013). For these children, there may be a strong documented history that the medicolegal death investigator can obtain. These children may even be on the heart donor list depending on how great an effect the condition has on the child's heart's ability to pump blood. If there is a strong medical history documenting this condition with a small child it would be unlikely that the decedent would be brought into a medicolegal office for an autopsy. However, this does not mean that a proper scene investigation should not occur. A full child death investigation, which is outlined in the special investigations chapter, should still be completed to rule out foul play or any other potential causes of death.

In adults dilated cardiomyopathy may be present in alcoholics. As with all dilated cardiomyopathies, all four chambers of the heart are dilated; however, it is more pronounced in the left ventricle, which is responsible for pumping blood to the whole body. When this condition is present in adults, the medicolegal death investigator may not have a documented history of the condition depending on the decedent's level of care with a primary care provider or cardiologist, but a history from the family might reveal signs of heart failure. The signs of heart failure include lethargy, shortness of breath, and edema of the lower extremities. It is important to note that heart failure is not only found in the presence of a dilated cardiomyopathy, but instead it could be caused by many different conditions.

When a decedent is found to have died from a hypertrophic cardiomyopathy the autopsy findings are quite different. Instead of dilated chambers, the heart has an obvious thickening of the left ventricle's myocardium. A decedent who has died from a hypertrophic cardiomyopathy may not know he/she even had the condition that is caused by a gene mutation. However, when talking with family and friends they may report to the medicolegal death investigation that the decedent had been feeling fatigued, experienced chest pain, or had pronounced chest palpitations. The presence of a hypertrophic cardiomyopathy may also be the cause of death in a young athlete who collapses during an athletic event without warning.

Dissection

Fatal aortic aneurysms are not all that prevalent, with a rate slightly over two per 100,000 in the world, according to the Global Burden of Disease Study (2015). An aortic aneurysm dissection occurs when the inner most layer of tissue of the aorta tears, and the blood being pumped out by the heart through the aorta fills the other two layers of tissue, which results in separation. If an aortic dissection is their cause of death, the forensic pathologist will see copious amounts of blood in the abdominal cavity as the dissection would have ruptured through the outer most layer of tissue. As stated above, this is an uncommon cause of death seen by the medicolegal professional as many who die from this are likely to be older individuals with other significant medical history that would preclude them from becoming a medicolegal case.

However, two things that may provide medicolegal death investigators with an idea that they may be dealing with a decedent who has had a dissection or the family reports that prior to death the decedent was complaining of a tearing pain up or down their back, or on examination an area of ecchymosis around the abdomen, scrotum, or upper thigh. The ecchymosis is an indication of possible significant bleeding in that area.

Congenital Heart Defects

There are many congenital heart defects, but this brief section will only talk about four that medicolegal death investigators are likely to encounter with some regularity in their career: aortic valve stenosis, atrial septal defect, ventricular septal defect, and tetralogy of Fallot.

Aortic valve stenosis is a condition where one particular valve leaks and does not open and then seal properly. Over time, damage to the heart can occur due to the poor outflow of blood. Surgical intervention might be indicated if a patient is experiencing significant negative effects from this condition, and there are some patients who are at high risk for surgery due to their overall health that they are having their aortic valve replaced through a transcatheter procedure, which has shown success is a large multinational study (Mack et al., 2015). There is great debate as to whether aortic valve stenosis requires surgical intervention, but the medicolegal death investigator should take particular care to obtain medical records that reflect the patient's ejection fraction to provide to the forensic pathologist for his/her review.

An atrial septal defect is a condition where the wall between the two atria (upper chambers of the heart) is not properly formed, and there is an opening. This opening allows blood from both sides of the heart to mix and blood can back up into the lungs causing damage. Children are unlikely to receive this diagnosis since individuals are generally asymptomatic until later in life when they might present with shortness of breath, a heart murmur, or edema of the lower extremities. The risk of a large septal defect that is not repaired either by surgical intervention or catheterization can increase a person's risk for stroke or heart failure. This particular condition is relatively common, found in more than 200,000 individuals a year in the United States alone (Mayo Clinic, 2014). For the medicolegal death investigator, the information one would want to collect if one was informed of this condition would be to ask questions related to the complications the decedent had from the condition, and if any medications were required or if the decedent had any surgical procedures to close the opening.

Like an atrial septal defect, a ventricular septal defect is an opening in the wall separating the two chambers of the heart but this time in the lower chambers. This opening is present in all of us during normal gestation but in normal development closes prior to the baby's birth. As previously noted with septal defects of the atria, when there is a ventricular septal defect deoxygenated and oxygenated blood mix due to the opening in the wall. This creates added pressure on the heart and can lead to damage of the cardiac tissue. This condition is rarer than an atrial septal defect and if found early in childhood and treated, there are generally no prolonged effects for the child as he or she progresses into adulthood.

Tetralogy of Fallot is a heart defect that has four key features according to the American Heart Association:

1. a ventricular septal defect,
2. there is a narrowing of the pulmonary valve,
3. the aorta improperly develops over the top of the ventricular septal defect,
4. the right ventricle is overly thickened, or hypertrophied.

This condition, while rare, will require surgical intervention and this is generally done within the first year of a child's life. Signs and symptoms that a child may have tetralogy of Fallot include blue discoloration of the skin and nail beds from poor oxygenation, shortness of breath, and general fatigue. If a medicolegal death investigator is investigating the death of a child with a history of tetralogy of Fallot, it is important to know if the child has had surgical intervention or not, which would be evident on examination due to the last midline chest scar. If the child has had surgical intervention and then dies, depending on the medicolegal office's policies, this child should be brought in for an autopsy to see if there were any complications with the surgery. Often times, a teaching hospital would gladly perform this autopsy as a way to evaluate and improve care for future patients.

RESPIRATORY

Even with smoking rates on the decline, currently in around 17% of Americans which is down from nearly 21% in 2005 (Centers for Disease Control and Prevention, 2015), respiratory disease is a common finding. However, not all respiratory disease is due to tobacco use. The following section will discuss

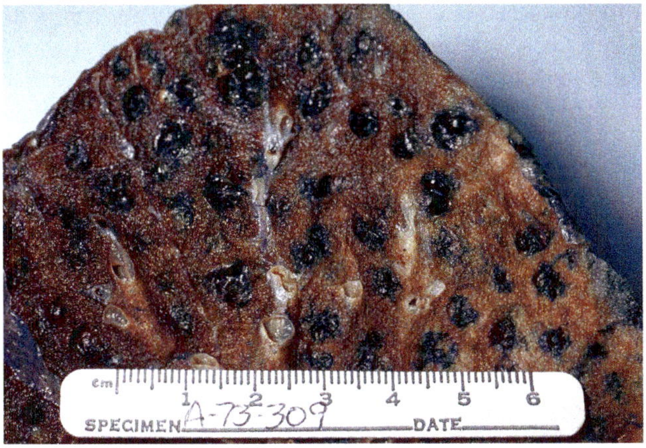

FIGURE 4.3 An example of emphysema destroying the alveolar walls.

the most common respiratory diseases the medicolegal death investigator is likely to encounter on a regular basis.

Emphysema

Emphysema and the next disease discussed chronic bronchitis are often referred to as chronic obstructive pulmonary disease. The disease is usually a result of environmental toxins or tobacco use and is a result of the destruction of the alveolar walls (the alveoli, or tiny sacs, are depicted in Fig. 4.3). Chronic exposures of the alveolar walls from a harmful substance decrease the productivity of gas exchange and air can become trapped in the lungs due to decreased recoil. The effects of this can cause some changes of the body that will be apparent to the medicolegal death investigator.

The most obvious signs that a decedent may have suffered from emphysema is the presence of a barrel chest. This is caused by the increase in diameter of the chest, both anterior and posterior. They will also have suprasternal retraction and accessory muscles, which are well developed. The disease will, over time, create the excessive production of red blood cells, polycythemia, which may also produce a pink appearance of the individual. This is why individuals with emphysema are often referred to as pink puffers.

Chronic Bronchitis

Chronic bronchitis is the increase in mucus secreting cells in an individual's lungs, which causes a filling of the airways which decreases gas exchange. However, unlike emphysema, there is no damage done to the alveolar walls. Like emphysema, this disease is usually caused by chronic exposures to cigarette smoke.

When discussing the decedent's health conditions with family and friends, they will likely report the individual producing excess amounts of sputum. Additionally, due to the increase in mucus production these decedents would have often suffered from multiple lung infections in life. While decedents who suffered from emphysema tend to be underweight, decedents who suffered from chronic bronchitis are often overweight.

Pneumonia

Pneumonia is a common lung infection that according to the CDC accounted for over 50,000 deaths in 2013 in the United States alone (Kochanek, Murphy, Xu, & Tejada-Vera, 2016). The infection causes an inflammation response from the body which in turn causes phlegm and fluid to collect in the alveoli of the lungs. At autopsy, the forensic pathologist will likely note heavy and dense lung tissue. It may surprise many people to know that pneumonia is not only a significant issue for the elderly and chronically ill, but it also accounts for approximately 15% of all childhood deaths in a given year worldwide (WHO, 2015). The infection can be caused by bacteria, virus, or fungi, and is highly preventable with proper care and the use of a vaccine. In the event that one does develop pneumonia, the infection is highly treatable with current antibiotics. Problems occur when an individual does not seek treatment or does not have access to treatment when he/she develops symptoms.

As the medicolegal death investigator responds to a possible natural death, there are a few indicators to look for that may cause one to suspect pneumonia. The family may report that in recent days or weeks the decedent had been having a productive cough, felt chest pain while coughing or trying to breathe deep, shortness of breath, and possibly a fever. It is also important to note here that while the infection is spread through airborne droplets, the medicolegal death investigator only needs to use the routine universal precautions when handling a decedent.

Lung Cancer

Lung cancer is number one in terms of cancer fatalities, accounting for almost 160,000 deaths in 2012 alone (Centers for Disease Control and Prevention, 2015). This is a staggering number considering a large number could be prevented by individuals by simply not smoking, but incidences of lung cancer have been decreasing since the early 2000s. For the medicolegal death investigator, the majority of lung cancer deaths do not fall under their jurisdiction. However, there are cases of lung cancer that are undiagnosed and could require a response from the medicolegal office.

Often times, even if there is not a diagnosis, warning signs are present to indicate that someone is ill. For the medicolegal death investigator, this could present as the family stating the individual had recently experienced unexplained weight loss, general weakness, and a persistent cough that would produce phlegm or blood. A history of smoking is, of course, a significant finding to record, but all lung cancer patients have a history of smoking.

According to the American Lung Association, smoking accounts for 80–90% of all lung cancer cases. However, outside of smoking or being exposed regularly to second-hand smoke, the other leading causes are exposure to radon and environmental exposures in a workplace setting. Radon is a gas that is naturally occurring in the soil and depending on where you live there could be a greater potential for exposure than in other areas. Areas in the upper Midwest and Northeast of United states have higher average radon levels, on average, than areas in the South and West (EPA, 2016). However, some studies (Cohen 1990, 1995) have suggested that radon levels in a residential environment present no increased risk for cancer. Various work environments can also create exposures to known carcinogens.

There are certain careers that may expose individuals to carcinogens during the regular commission of their duties. One of the many issues associated with understanding the risk to workers is that there is very little knowledge of the effects of the vast majority of the chemicals commonly used in American industries (President's Cancer Panel, 2010). Workers who do not smoke may not associate symptoms they may be experiencing with lung cancer. However, the medicolegal death investigator should consider this as a possibility if someone working in this industry is reported to have exhibited the previously mentioned signs and symptoms, including hemoptysis.

Pulmonary Embolism

One of the more common conditions seen by the medicolegal death investigator is a pulmonary embolism. This occurs when a blood clot, often times from the lower extremities, travels through the body's vasculature and becomes lodged in one or more of the arteries in the lungs. The treatment for pulmonary emboli can vary, usually done with blood thinners and preventative measures to reduce future clots forming like using compression stockings, but treatment can help reduce the risk of death.

Medicolegal death investigators should be aware of the risk factors associated with deep vein thrombosis (DVT) as it could provide an indication for why someone they are examining on a scene may have died. Individuals who have a very sedentary lifestyle, those with recent traumatic injuries, particularly of the lower extremities, and those who have recently had surgery would be at greater risk for developing a DVT. Signs that a decedent may have had a DVT prior to death include swelling, pain, and a warm sensation in the affected area, usually of the posterior aspect of the leg. If a clot becomes lodged in the lungs, the decedent may have experienced chest pain, weakness, and shortness of breath.

GASTROINTESTINAL

Diabetes

Diabetes mellitus can be broken down into two main categories—Type 1 and Type 2. A pregnant woman can also develop gestational diabetes where she has too high blood sugar during pregnancy; this will be briefly discussed shortly. The individual's ethnic background matters, too. American Indians and black patients have a higher incidence of diabetes when examining all ethnic and racial backgrounds (American Diabetes Association, 2014).

Type 1, or insulin-dependent, diabetes is sometimes referred to as juvenile diabetes because it usually develops in childhood. Type 1 diabetes is when the pancreas produces very little, if any, insulin. Individuals will generally report feeling lethargic, thirsty, and frequent urination prior to their diagnosis. The keys to proper treatment include an individual being physically active, maintaining a healthy diet, and using supplemental insulin to help their body maintain normal blood glucose levels.

Type 2 diabetes occurs when a person's body improperly handles the glucose in their system. In a number of instances, patients can manage their type 2 diabetes with healthy diets and exercise. Additionally, if an individual loses weight and maintains a healthy lifestyle, they are sometimes able to avoid any complications normally experienced by diabetics and do not need to regularly monitor their blood glucose. However, the majority of type 2 diabetics must actively monitor their blood glucose levels and take insulin injections to help their bodies process the sugars.

Diabetes, in general, has shown to increase the incidence of cardiovascular disease, stroke, and renal disease. This is important for the medicolegal death investigator to understand because if someone states that his/her loved one had diabetes, but does not know what other problems he/she may have had. Knowing these common complications can provide a greater understanding of the other overall health of someone, particularly if his/her diabetes was not well maintained.

One of the most significant conditions that can occur with diabetics is diabetic ketoacidosis. This occurs when there is a hyperglycemic emergency, meaning the body has too much blood sugar and there is a lack of insulin to process those sugars, and an individual's body starts to burn fatty acids. This process produces ketones that when they build up in your bloodstream produce an acidic imbalance in your body, which can cause fatal complications, most notably with cardiac arrhythmias. If diabetic ketoacidosis (DKA) is suspected, it would not be uncommon for the medicolegal death investigator to use simple test strips that can be dipped in a collection of the decedent's urine to check for the presence of elevated levels of ketones. This is an easy method to check to see if DKA is a potential cause of death because the body will try to remove the ketones through the urine.

Gestational diabetes can occur when a woman is pregnant and her body develops an inability to use insulin like it has in the past due to the increase in hormones and weight. This occurs in less than 10% of all women who become pregnant in the United States (DeSisto, Kim, & Sharma, 2014). This is traditionally seen in the third trimester, and if high blood glucose levels are noted earlier on in the pregnancy it is likely that the mother had diabetes prior to becoming pregnant. Additionally, the mother's health and weight prior to pregnancy are common predictors of the chances that she will develop gestational diabetes. For the medicolegal death investigator, it is important to understand how this could affect the unborn child.

If a mother has gestational diabetes, there is an increased risk of the child being born with low blood glucose levels, hypoglycemia, as well as an increased risk for fetal demise prior to birth. One study done in California showed an increased risk of stillbirth from the period of 36 weeks' gestation, through 42 weeks in mothers diagnosed with gestational diabetes (Rosenstein, Cheng, Snowden, Nicholson, Doss, & Caughey, 2012). Knowing that a mother had that specific diagnosis and there being a stillbirth does not mean that the fetus will become a decedent that the medicolegal office will need to bring in for examination. However, it is something important that the investigator should note and might be a question that is asked of the healthcare provider that reports the death, assuming the mother made it to a hospital.

Liver Disease

The telltale signs of an individual who has liver disease is a jaundice appearance. However, the cause of the liver disease could be from a number of diseases or conditions. Often times, if someone has a diagnosis of liver disease it is often assumed that they developed the problem from drug or alcohol abuse. However, this is not always the case. The three most common liver diseases, outside of fatty liver affects due to chronic alcohol abuse, are hepatitis A, B, and C. All three are caused by a virus, and hepatitis quite literally means inflammation of the liver. It is generally most helpful from an investigative standpoint, as well as a personal safety standpoint to understand how the viruses are generally spread.

Hepatitis A is generally thought of as less severe and less likely to affect Americans. This is due to the health standards that we have here in the United States. The virus is often spread through the handling of or eating of foods that have been handled by someone with the disease or from drinking contaminated water. Additionally, a vaccine is widely available for this virus.

Hepatitis B is more serious, as the virus over time can cause significant scarring of the liver or even cancer. The virus is spread through bodily fluids. So, those who have sexual contact with an infected person or sharing a needle with someone would put an individual at significant risk. A person may also be asymptomatic and still possess the virus and be able to pass it on to others. Special care should be taken by the medicolegal death investigator who has knowledge whether an individual has hepatitis B or is involved in high risk activities, such as intravenous drug abuse, or if the individual pays or is paid for sex. A vaccine is also available for hepatitis B.

Hepatitis C, like hepatitis B, can cause significant scarring of the liver as well as cancer. This specific virus accounts for just less than 20,000 deaths each year and the Centers for Disease Control and Prevention (2014) believes there are approximately 2.7–3.9 million Americans with the disease. Additionally, patients could have the infection throughout their entire life and not know it. An example of lifelong exposure without a person knowing they have the virus is with veterans. This particular patient population has significantly higher rates versus the general population, 5.4% versus 1.8%, according to the Veterans Administration (2015). This is only the rates for veterans who are actively receiving care with the Veterans Administration. The actual rates of those infected could be even higher.

Alcoholism

Alcoholism negatively affects the body in a number of ways. As alluded to earlier in this section, chronic alcohol abuse can have significant negative effects on the liver. However, during his/her career, a medicolegal death investigator will undoubtedly see many other negative health consequences to decedents who abuse alcohol. These include various neurologic changes, cancers, and hemorrhages of the gastrointestinal system.

Korsakoff's syndrome is the result of a significant thiamine deficiency and is routinely seen in severe and chronic alcohol abusers. These individuals will have a history of being unable to remember events that just happened to them, as well as difficulty recalling significant events from their past. The medicolegal death investigator may not get a diagnosis of Korsakoff's from the family, as they may only know that their loved one was an alcoholic. However, knowing the signs and symptoms of the syndrome is beneficial because it will illustrate the seriousness of the individual's disease. In addition to contributing to neurologic deficits, chronic alcoholism can increase an individual's likelihood of developing certain forms of cancer.

Cancers that are caused, at least in part, to an individual's chronic abuse of alcohol would fall under the category of preventable. There is research to support chronic alcohol abuse's impact on an individual developing the following cancers (Cogliano, Baan, Straif, Grosse, Lauby-Secretan, El Ghissassi, et al., 2011):

- breast,
- colorectal,
- areas of the upper airway,

- esophageal, and
- liver.

According to the National Institute of Cancer, depending on the type of cancer one is diagnosed with, alcohol can contribute in a number of different ways to the development of the disease. These include the chemicals that are produced when alcohol is broken down in someone's body, decreasing the ability to break down and absorb certain nutrients, and by increasing estrogen in a woman's body. Knowing the exact biochemistry is not important for the medicolegal death investigator. What is important is if the medicolegal death investigator knows that someone has a history of alcoholism, this should serve as a trigger to ask further questions related to the decedent's overall health. Additionally, if an autopsy is performed and one of these cancers are noted and the forensic pathologist believes they are related, the past medical history that was obtained is important as chronic alcohol abuse should be listed as a contributing factor on the death certificate.

Certain cancers that may develop in the presence of chronic alcoholism could undoubtedly cause chronic and acute hemorrhages, particularly in the esophagus and upper airway. However, chronic and acute hemorrhages can also occur in the gastrointestinal (GI) system as a result of significant, chronic alcohol abuse. This could be from ulcers that might not present an immediate risk of death to an individual but certainly indicate significant abuse, or it could be from a more serious and life-threatening issue known as esophageal varices. These varices, with an individual who is a chronic alcoholic, are usually present when there is cirrhosis of the liver. The liver cirrhosis causes an increased venous pressure that enlarges some of the veins found in the esophagus. When one of these varices ruptures, there is the possibility to have copious amounts of blood present on scene. When investigating the death of a chronic alcoholic and there appears to be a large amount of blood coming from the decedent's mouth, the medicolegal death investigator must resist the urge to assume it is a ruptured vein and instead take special care to rule out any signs of a traumatic event. Severe vomiting associated with chronic alcohol abuse can also bring about significant and life-threatening hemorrhaging. This occurs when there is a tear where the esophagus meets the stomach. This type of injury is known as a Mallory-Weiss tear.

Hemorrhaging can also occur further down in the upper gastrointestinal system as well as in the lower GI system. These GI bleeds are easy to identify by the seasoned medicolegal death investigator as the decedent will have what is commonly referred to as "coffee-ground" emesis or defecation. It would also not be uncommon if someone had a GI bleed that they would have evidence of emesis or defecation in or near a bathroom. They may simply feel like they want to throw up or have a bowel movement. These scenes can be quite messy depending on the acuteness or severity of the bleeding. When interviewing family members of a decedent where the medicolegal death investigator suspects a GI bleed, they may report that the decedent complained of previously vomiting blood as well as noticing blood in their stools.

Regardless of the disease or disorder that presents itself as a result of an individual's chronic alcohol abuse, the important things for the medicolegal death investigator to know are how to support the belief that an individual was an alcoholic. This would include, but is not limited to, excessive amounts of alcohol in the residence, numerous empty alcohol containers, a history of excessive binge drinking, and signs and symptoms consistent with withdrawal. Additionally, a history of social problems like difficulty maintaining relationships or employment in the presence of signs of heaving drinking could also be a strong indicator.

NEUROLOGICAL

Cerebral Vascular Accident

When an individual has a cerebral vascular accident or more commonly referred to as a stroke, they are experiencing a life-threatening emergency. There are two types of strokes—ischemic and hemorrhagic. An ischemic stroke is when there is a blockage in one of the vessels of the brain causing an area to not receive the nutrients needed. When a hemorrhagic stroke occurs, it means that there has been a rupture in one of the vessels causing bleeding. This bleeding could occur because there was an aneurysm or any number of malformations of a vessel, or it could be the result of effects from a chronic health condition such as diabetes, hypertension, or hyperlipidemia, which are some of the same risk factors for ischemic stroke. Fig. 4.4 illustrates the basic differences between a hemorrhagic stroke and an ischemic stroke.

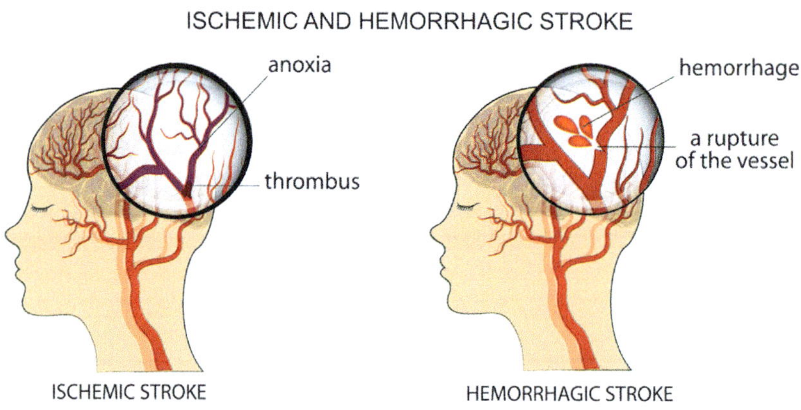

FIGURE 4.4 Differences between a hemorrhagic stroke and an ischemic stroke.

A commonly used acronym, FAST, is used to help people recognize when they witness or they themselves are having a stroke. FAST stands for:

Facial droop
Arm weakness
Speech difficulties
Time (Meaning, time is of the essence. So, get help immediately).

If someone is having these symptoms, they will often call for help immediately. This would, of course, present an ideal situation for anyone investigating a death if someone were to die a short time after calling for help with these signs and symptoms. However, someone might experience some or all of the above symptoms and they may not seek help, similar to a person who is having chest pain. A detailed interview with family, friends, and coworkers may reveal that the decedent had previously discussed having one-sided weakness, numbness in the face, or a period where their speech was slurred but simply dismissed it as being attributed to another issue.

Epilepsy

There are a number of reasons for why an individual could have a seizure disorder, and whenever a medicolegal death investigator is looking into the death of someone with this medical history, it is important to find out the etiology of their seizures. This is particularly true with individuals who have a seizure disorder after a traumatic event because it might be a significant determinant in determining whether or not a death is ruled as natural, or whether it is ruled as an accident, or homicide. If trauma is not the source of an individual's epilepsy, there are some common causes to be aware of.

Epilepsy does not always have a known etiology, or origin, and so family and friends of a decedent with a history of the seizure disorder may report that a cause was never determined. However, a few conditions are known to cause epilepsy. The first is a history of stroke or even a tumor that causes a change that affects the way signals are sent in the brain. The second is an infectious disease like meningitis, which we will talk about next, which has been shown to be a significant contributor to epilepsy. Studies have shown that areas where there is a higher incidence of meningitis infections they see an increase in the number of epileptics, with the majority of diagnosis of epilepsy within five years of the infection (Murthy & Prabhakar, 2008). A third believed cause for epilepsy is a genetic component since some family members have been shown to have similar seizure features such as the location of the seizure activity. It could be that one or a number of genetic markers could affect the normal developmental pathways of the brain (Guerrini, Marini, & Mantegazza, 2014). This is not an all-encompassing list and, again, there may not be a known etiology. For the medicolegal death investigator, a thorough history will need to be collected on every decedent with a seizure disorder to rule out trauma as a cause and to provide the forensic pathologist with a better understanding of the decedent's history related to his/her diagnosis. Additionally, if someone was being treated with medication for their seizures a toxicology workup could be performed to examine the levels of medication(s) in a decedent's system to see if he/she was properly taking their medications based on whether or not the results showed the levels in their system in a therapeutic.

Meningitis

There are many different strands of viral, bacterial, or fungal infections that cause meningitis, which is an infection of the meninges covering the brain and spinal cord (Fig. 4.5). Bacterial meningitis is the most dangerous form and requires early treatment. Powerful antibiotics are used to treat bacterial meningitis, as well as other treatments for supportive care. Treatment is important because meningitis can cause brain damage, hearing loss, and as we previously discussed the infection can cause the individual to develop epilepsy. Vaccines are available to treat a few of the common strands and are commonly given to school-aged children and those living in high risk environments where the infection could spread easily.

What is most important for the medicolegal death investigator to understand is how to identify a suspected meningitis case and to know the risk factors. When collecting medical history from the decedent's family, friends, and coworkers, the common symptoms that they may have meningitis are that they will have complained of feeling flu-like, being running a fever, and have a stiff neck. Additionally, some will report that the decedent seemed confused and disoriented prior to death. Being able to identify a case as possibly

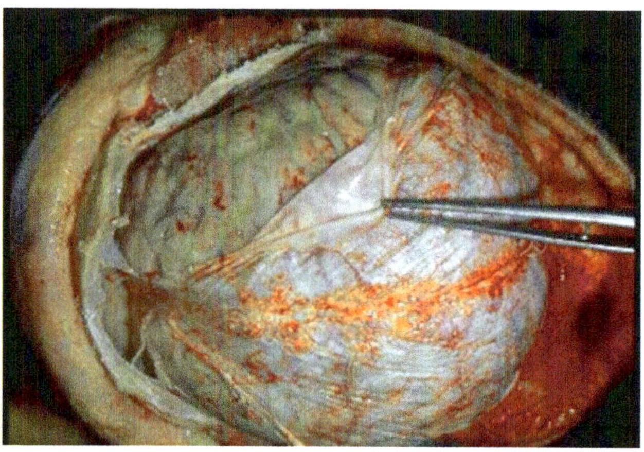

FIGURE 4.5 An example of meningitis infection of the meninges covering the brain and spinal cord.

meningitis is very important from a public health perspective. If the decedent lived in a dormitory, community housing, or had other people living with them inside of a single family home those individuals will need to be monitored and even prophylactically treated in some instances to ensure the infection does not spread.

CONCLUSION

This chapter has provided a brief overview of a number of common natural health conditions that medicolegal death investigators should be familiar with to be effective in their important public health and safety role. To function within a medicolegal office, it is essential that one can talk intelligently about the various common health conditions and have an understanding of what type of questions to ask based on the history given to them by family, friends, coworkers, or healthcare professionals who previously treated the decedent. Additionally, the understanding of the causes and mechanisms associated with diseases are constantly evolving as research continues. The same is true for medications as new treatments are constantly being brought to market. Staying up to date on this information and common treatments for the various diseases and disorders discussed in this chapter will ensure the medicolegal death investigator continues to be an integral, active professional in public health.

REFERENCES

American Diabetes Association. (2014). *National Diabetes Statistics Report, 2014. Estimates of Diabetes and Its Burden in the Epidemiologic Estimation Methods.* Natl Diabetes Stat Rep, 2009–2012.

American Lung Association. (2016). *Lung Cancer Fact Sheet.* Retrieved from: http://www.lung.org/lung-health-and-diseases/lung-disease-lookup/lung-cancer/learn-about-lung-cancer/lung-cancer-fact-sheet.html.

Briasoulis, A., Agarwal, V., & Messerli, F. H. (2012). Alcohol consumption and the risk of hypertension in men and women: a systematic review and meta-analysis. *Journal of Clinical Hypertension, 14*, 792–798.

Centers for Disease Control and Prevention. (2015). Current cigarette smoking among adults – United States, 2005–2014. *Morbidity and Mortality Weekly Report, 64*(44), 1233–1240.

Centers for Disease Control and Prevention. (2014). *Surveillance for Viral Hepatitis.* United States, Atlanta, GA: Statistics and Surveillance.

Cogliano, V. J., Baan, R., Straif, K., Grosse, Y., Lauby-Secretan, B., El Ghissassi, F., et al. (2011). Preventable exposures associated with human cancers. *Journal of the National Cancer Institute, 103*(24), 1827–1839.

Cohen, B. L. (1990). A test of the linear no-threshold theory of radiation carcinogenesis. *Environmental Research, 53*, 193–220.

Cohen, B. L. (1995). Test of the linear no-threshold theory of radiation carcinogenesis for inhaled radon decay products. *Health Physics, 68*, 157–174.

DeSisto, C. L., Kim, S. Y., & Sharma, A. J. (2014). Prevalence estimates of gestational diabetes mellitus in the United States, pregnancy risk assessment monitoring system (PRAMS), 2007–2010. *Preventing Chronic Disease, 11*, 130415. http://dx.doi.org/10.5888/pcd11.130415.

Environmental Protection Agency (EPA). (2016). *EPA Map of Radon Zones Including State Radon Information and Contacts*. Retrieved from: https://www.epa.gov/radon/find-information-about-local-radon-zones-and-radon-programs.

Garshick, E., et al. (1988). A retrospective cohort study of lung cancer and diesel exhaust exposure in railroad workers. *The American Review of Respiratory Disease, 137*(4), 820–825.

Garshick, E., Laden, F., Hart, J. E., et al. (2014). Lung cancer in railroad workers exposed to diesel exhaust. *Environmental Health Perspective, 112*(15), 1539–1543.

Global Burden of Disease Study. (2015). Mortality and causes of death collaborators. Global, regional, and national age-sex specific all-cause and cause-specific mortality for 240 causes of death, 1990–2013: a systematic analysis. *Lancet, 385*, 117–171.

Guerrini, R., Marini, C., & Mantegazza, M. (2014). Genetic epilepsy syndromes without structural brain abnormalities: clinical features and experimental models. *Neurotherapeutics, 11*(2), 269–285.

Kochanek, K. D., Murphy, S. L., Xu, J., & Tejada-Vera, B. (2016). Deaths: final data for 2014. *National Vital Statistics Report, 65*(4). (Centers for Disease Control and Prevention).

Laden, F., Hart, J. E., Eschenroeder, A., Smith, T. J., & Garshick, E. (2006). Historical estimation of diesel exhaust exposure in a cohort study of US railroad workers and lung cancer. *Cancer Causes Control, 17*(7), 911–919.

Ljungquist, B., Berg, S., Lanke, J., McClearn, G. E., & Pedersen, N. L. (1998). The effect of genetic factors for longevity: a comparison of identical and fraternal twins in the Swedish Twin Registry. *The Journals of Gerontology Series A: Biological Sciences and Medical Sciences, 53*(6), M441–M446.

Lloyd-Jones, D. M., Nam, B. H., D'Agostino, R. B., Levy, D., Sr., Murabito, J. M., Wang, T. J., Wilson, P. W., & O'Donnell, C. J. (2004). Parental cardiovascular disease as a risk factor for cardiovascular disease in middle-aged adults: a prospective study of parents and offspring. *Journal of American Medical Association, 291*, 2204–2211. http://dx.doi.org/10.1001/jama.291.18.2204.

Mack, et al. (2015). 5-year outcomes of transcatheter aortic valve replacement or surgical aortic valve replacement for high surgical risk patients with aortic stenosis (PARTNER 1): A randomized controlled trial. *Lancet, 385*(9986), 2477–2484.

Maron, B. J., McKenna, W. J., Danielson, G. K., Kappenberger, L. J., Kuhn, H. J., Seidman, C. E., Shah, P. M., Spencer, W. H., 3rd, Spirito, P., Ten Cate, F. J., & Wigle, E. D. (2013). American College of Cardiology/European Society of Cardiology clinical expert consensus document on hypertrophic cardiomyopathy: a report of the American College of Cardiology Foundation task force on clinical expert consensus documents and the European Society of Cardiology committee for practice guidelines. *Journal of American College of Cardiology, 42*, 1687–1713.

Mayo Clinic. (2014). *Diseases and Conditions: Atrial Septal Defect*. Retrieved from: http://www.mayoclinic.org/diseases-conditions/atrial-septal-defect/basics/definition/con-20027034.

Mozaffarian, D., et al. (2016). Executive summary: heart disease and stroke statistics—2016 update a report from the American Heart Association. *Circulation, 133*(4), 447–454.

Murthy, J. M. K., & Prabhakar, S. (2008). Bacterial meningitis and epilepsy. *Epilepsia, 49*(s6), 8–12.

Nixon, A. E., Mazzola, J. J., Bauer, J., Krueger, J. R., & Spector, P. E. (2011). Can work make you sick? A meta-analysis of the relationships between job stressors and physical symptoms. *Work and Stress, 2*, 1–22.

Nwankwo, T., Yoon, S. S., Burt, V., & Gu, Q. (2013). Hypertension among adults in the United States: National Health and Nutrition Examination Survey, 2011–2012. *NCHS Data Brief*, 1–8.

President's Cancer Panel. (2010). *Reducing Environmental Cancer Risk: What We Can Do Now*. Bethesda, MD: National Cancer Institute, National Institutes of Health, US Department of Health and Human Services, 2008–2009 annual report.

Rosenstein, M. G., Cheng, Y. W., Snowden, J. M., Nicholson, J. A., Doss, A. E., & Caughey, A. B. (2012). The risk of stillbirth and infant death stratified by gestational age in women and gestational diabetes. *American Journal of Obstetrics and Gynecology, 206*(4). http://dx.doi.org/10.1016/j.ajog.2012.01.014, 309.e.1-309.3.7.

Sesso, H. D., Lee, I. M., Gaziano, J. M., Rexrode, K. M., Glynn, R. J., & Buring, J. E. (2001). Maternal and paternal history of myocardial infarction and risk of cardiovascular disease in men and women. *Circulation, 104*, 393–398.

Stahre, M., Roeber, J., Kanny, D., Brewer, R. D., & Zhang, X. (2014). Contribution of excessive alcohol consumption to deaths and years of potential life lost in the United States. *Preventing Chronic Disease, 11*, 130293. http://dx.doi.org/10.5888/pcd11.130293.

Veterans Administration. (June 2015). *Hepatitis C: Information for Veterans*. Fact Sheet. Washington, DC.

World Health Organization. (November 2015). *Pneumonia*. Retrieved from: http://www.who.int/mediacentre/factsheets/fs331/en/.

Chapter 5

Asphyxiation

Chapter Outline

Deaths that involve asphyxiation could fall under a number of manners of death, and it is up to the medicolegal death investigator to fully document the scene findings in preparation for an autopsy so that these deaths can be accurately certified. Examples of accidental deaths by asphyxiation occur when an individual drowns, becomes wedged in an area that precludes them from being able to breath normally, or if they are in a confined space and are unable to get the oxygen they need. Common instances where a death could be ruled a suicide involve ligature hangings or displacement of oxygen by inert gas commonly done using helium tanks and a bag over a decedent's head. Lastly, asphyxial deaths could be ruled a homicide for the manner of death if an individual is strangled, as an example.

Asphyxia simply means not enough oxygen is reaching the cells and there are a number of ways in which a person could die in this fashion. The important thing for medicolegal death investigators to understand is their importance in documenting the findings at the scene to help properly certify these deaths. The findings, in a number of cases, could be something that could only be understood through a thorough scene investigation and would not be something that could be documented at autopsy.

For this very reason, the medicolegal death investigator should have an understanding of what to look for and what type of questions to ask by-standers. Often times a medicolegal death investigator will be presented with a scene that has been altered prior to his/her arrival. A family member may have cut down their loved one that they found partially suspended from a ligature prior to notifying emergency services, a caretaker may have removed an infant from an unsafe sleeping environment, or a fire fighter could have removed a

Essentials of Medicolegal Death Investigation. http://dx.doi.org/10.1016/B978-0-12-803641-9.00005-7

body from a confined space that did not have sufficient oxygen to support life. A thorough examination of the scene and proper witness interviews can help tease out this information that is vital to certifying the cause and manner of death.

The proper documentation starts with the photographs on scene. The routine photographs that were discussed in a previous chapter should be followed in these cases. However, additional photographs and possible sketches are required to fully understand the details of these cases. This could include multiple angles of the ligature around an individual's neck to document the difference between a near-circumferential ligature mark that follows the jaw line, which meets at a common point, and a more horizontal ligature mark that crosses in the back. It could be the photo documentation of a metal tank filled with a gas that was used to displace oxygen or certain aspects of a car that would support a possible carbon monoxide death. It could even be demonstrating through pictures how the environment in which someone was found would not support life. Lastly, the understanding of these findings could be the difference between an individual's death being a suspected suicide and a suspected homicide. Strangulation is the case with the first category of deaths that will be discussed.

STRANGULATION

A number of different causes of death could be attributed to strangulation, but ligature strangulations and manual strangulations are the two that the medicolegal death investigator must absolutely be knowledgeable about. Each instance will produce its own unique findings that will help the medicolegal death investigator generate a hypothesis regarding the death of an individual.

Ligature Strangulations

Ligature strangulations almost always fall into one of two manners of death categories—suicide or homicide. Each presents unique findings that help differentiate one manner of death from the other. Regardless of the manner of death, ligature strangulation occurs when an external object is placed around the neck and provides compression. The compression is usually applied to the neck by using the decedent's own body weight in what would generally be described as either a partial or complete hanging.

A partial ligature hanging simply means that part of the decedent's body is still touching the ground or another object. There are two common misconceptions related to ligature hangings. The first is that the cause of death associated with a complete hanging is a fractured neck. However, fractured vertebrae were only found to be present in 6 cases out of 761 hangings in a retrospective study (Uzun, Buyuk, & Gurpinar, 2007). The second common misconception is that a person cannot die from a ligature hanging if they are only partially suspending, either leaning forward or in a seated position. This, too, is simply not true.

Research has shown that it only takes 6 kg of force to occlude the carotid artery and only 7 kg of force to occlude the vertebral artery (Yamasaki, Takase, Takada, & Nishi, 2009). Due to this low threshold of force required to cause death in a ligature hanging, a decedent's body could be in a number of different positions to complete a suicide in this fashion.

Some of the more commonly seen body positions involve a ligature secured to an object above the decedents' head and their body simply leaning forward, decedents kneeling forward with a ligature secured to a door or door frame, or with their body in a seated position with the ligature secured above the decedents with their buttocks off the ground. This author has also seen less conventional presentations like an individual lying in a prone position on the ground with the head, neck, and chest only slightly elevated off the ground, as well as an individual in the middle of a room with a ligature secured above the decedent's head and only his/her heels slightly elevated off the ground. Complete ligature hangings, on the other hand, indicate that the decedent was found fully suspended with no part of his/her body touching the ground or any object.

Often with complete ligature hangings there will be an object or surface that was utilized to assist decedents in elevating their body prior to the act of hanging one's self. A common finding might be an overturned chair near the decedent or a ledge where the decedent could have stepped off from. Additionally, if individuals were to suspend themselves from a structure, like a bridge, or from a large tree that they climbed, these would be a complete ligature hanging. Regardless of whether the death is a complete or partial hanging, similar findings should be present.

The injuries present on the decedent's neck vary greatly depending on what type of material is utilized for the ligature. In general, the ligature around an individual's neck in a suspected suicide should include a near-circumferential ligature mark that follows the jaw line and eventually meets at a common point, usually behind the head. As for the material of the ligature, many individuals immediately think of a ligature as a robe with a true ligature knot. However, this is rarely the case.

The ligature utilized by decedents tends to be whatever they have available to them at the time they make the plan to end their life. While it could be a rope, often times it is a strap of some sort, a belt, shirt, and any other fabric they have available to them. One study showed that in 63% of all ligature suicides, the decedent used a nylon rope, with all other materials used each accounted for 10% or less of the remaining items. Of particular note, however, was that a large percentage of women who committed suicide via a ligature hanging used some type of scarf (Ambade, Tumram, Meshram, & Borkar, 2015). One might theorize that this is a vanity issue where women are trying to avoid the presence of an obvious injury if an open casket were to be part of a funeral service, though this would only be an assumption based on the ways in which women generally commit suicide versus the ways in which men generally commit suicide.

Being able to differentiate between a case being a suicide and a strangulation death being ruled a homicide can be difficult. A retrospective study from data over a 20 year period in a major European city showed that very few strangulation homicides showed no internal injuries, but greater than 50% of all suicides reviewed did not show evidence of internal injuries. In cases where the manner of death was classified as a suicide, the internal neck injuries were usually limited to the sternomastoid muscle, and in homicides there was a higher occurrence of hemorrhages of the laryngeal muscle as well as a much higher occurrence of fractures in the neck to the thyroid horns and to the hyoid bone. For the medicolegal death investigator, more importantly, when strangulation was the cause of death if the case were a homicide there would be a lot of additional trauma noted to the head and neck of the decedent (Maxeiner & Bockholdt, 2003). The ligature marks around the neck are also slightly different in most homicides when compared to suicides.

In this section it was previously discussed that ligature furrows are generally above the thyroid prominence and tend to slightly angle up along the jawline as seen in Fig. 5.1. However, in homicidal strangulations the ligature furrow can be either above or below the thyroid prominence and is more horizontal in nature as depicted in Fig. 5.2. Additionally, where the ligature furrow meets in the back of the head, in most cases, the furrow marks tend to come together at one point, whereas with a homicide, there appears to be a crossing of the ligature mark. This makes sense if you envision someone standing behind an individual, as an example, holding a rope at two ends and trying to pull tight.

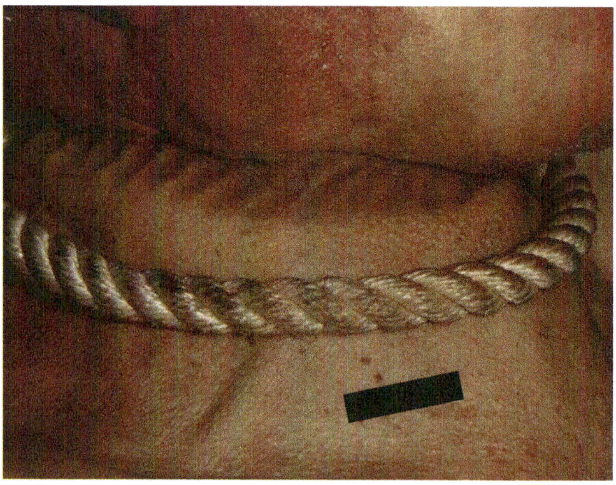

FIGURE 5.1 An example of a ligature furrow above the thyroid prominence and angled up along the jawline.

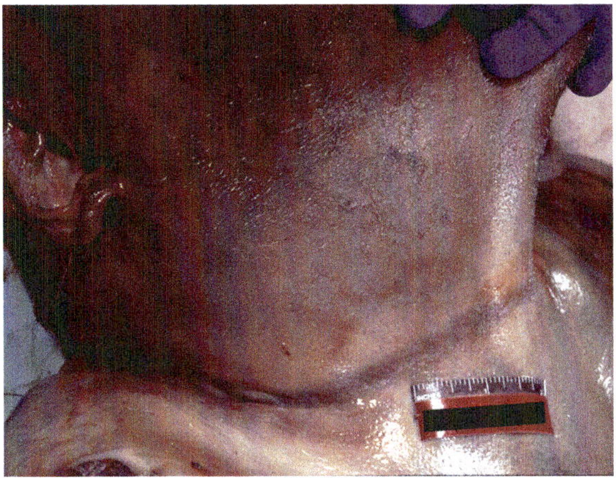

FIGURE 5.2 An example of a ligature furrow above the thyroid prominence and with a horizontal angle.

The presence of petechial hemorrhages can also differ between a suicidal strangulation and one that is homicidal in nature. It is the author's experience that there are generally more diffuse petechial hemorrhages with homicides than with suicides. This includes the face, conjunctiva and sclera of the eye, and even the eyelids. Just looking at manual strangulation, a study from one office's population in the southern United States showed that petechial hemorrhages were present in 89% of all cases reviewed (DiMaio, 2000). This illustrates that the medicolegal death investigator should be highly suspicious if there are diffuse petechial hemorrhages noted. However, the finding is nonspecific. You could have a suicide with or without petechial hemorrhages, and the same could be true for a homicide. The presence or absence of petechial hemorrhages is simply one finding at a scene that contributes to the overall picture. The medicolegal death investigator must weigh all findings: the scene and the decedent's medical, psychiatric, and social history; and the findings on the body are all part of the complete picture that help develop a suspected cause and manner of death.

SUFFOCATION

For the purposes of this chapter, we will discuss suffocation as it relates to confined spaces, smothering, and choking. Others will describe suffocation more broadly to include chemical and mechanical asphyxiation, but this text separates these two into their own categories.

Confined Spaces

Deaths that involve confined spaces are difficult to fully document in situ but also tend to fall into the category of "you know it when you see it." These deaths occur when a decedent has become trapped inside of a completely or near-completely air tight environment and they use up the oxygen that is available to them. Without any more oxygen to consume, the individuals die from asphyxia. Due to advancements in safety associated with consumer products these types of deaths are not generally seen in the home but instead are more common in a commercial environment.

The type of jurisdiction a medicolegal death investigator works in will likely play a significant role in the types of confined spaces they encounter. In a rural setting, it might be more common place to have a confined space death for someone who becomes trapped inside of a silo, grain elevator, manure pit, or a chemical storage tank. Compounding the issue in rural settings, there is often a lack of oversight in these structures to ensure that the workplace is as safe as it can be. That being said, confined space deaths can still occur in heavily monitored and regulated companies in a more urban environment.

There are areas inside of manufacturing plants that are designated as confined spaces due to the hazards they present and the idea that it is not healthy for individuals to have prolonged exposure in the particular environment. In commercial structures these could be storage areas for products or equipment, as well as working environments like inside of a manhole cover or in a dugout ditch. According to the United States National Institute for Occupational Safety and Health (1986), greater than 60% of all confined space fatalities are people who were attempting to rescue someone else. The purpose of this statistic in the report was to illustrate the need for companies to have specially trained professionals as well as a comprehensive program to prevent and respond to these incidents to reduce the likelihood of making a bad situation, worse. The same principle can be applied to the medicolegal death investigator. It is unlikely that someone from a medicolegal office is an expert in confined space rescue. As such, there should be a plan to have a specially trained team, usually from a fire department, make the removal.

Lastly, small children can become entrapped in a confined space and not have the ability to remove themselves from the situation. An example that while not common, could certainly be seen by the medicolegal death investigator is when a small child becomes entrapped inside of a container of some kind. Examples of this could be a plastic storage bin or a cooler. Often times when a child is found unresponsive he/she is quickly scooped up and attempts are made to revive him/her. Once someone from the medicolegal office arrives on scene to perform their investigation the child could be nowhere near the environment in which he/she was located. Later, in Chapter 10, proper investigation of a child's death will be discussed, but in short, the history about where the child was last seen and where he/she was found is critical in these cases. Asking the right questions about the environment in which the child was found may not seem significant to the family member or caretaker, but it could be the difference between knowing what happened to the child and having the death signed out as undetermined since confined space fatalities are so heavily reliant on a proper scene investigation for certification.

Smothering

When someone is told that his/her loved one died from smothering, he/she often times will associate that with a homicide. However, this is not always the case. Smothering simply means that a decedent suffocated by having their mouth and nares covered, restricting the ability of the decedent to breath in oxygen. Some have proposed calling blockage of everything above the epiglottis in the upper airway, as well as the external structures of the nose and mouth smothering deaths; everything from the epiglottis and lower would be considered choking (Sauvageau & Boghossian, 2010). If we are to accept the latter definition, the number of accidental deaths where smothering could be the cause of death would likely be expanded. If we accept the former definition, nonhomicidal smotherings would be mostly limited to someone who is incapacitated due to drugs or alcohol, or if they are disabled and unable to lift their head in a normal fashion as these individuals could be smothered by their own weight in a soft object, like a pillow. The same will be discussed later in Chapter 10, when we talk about child death investigations as this is another group of decedents, depending on their age, who might be unable to move their head to avoid a smothering situation. Children could also be smothered by getting their head entrapped in a plastic bag. The bag would cling to their face and block the child's ability to breath. All of the incidents discussed in this paragraph are examples of accidental deaths. However, smothering deaths can be suicides as well as homicides.

In one of the previous examples, the child that becomes entrapped inside of a plastic bag, the death would be ruled an accident. However, some individuals end their life via suffocation. While not a common method, some individuals will suffocate themselves with a clear bag with a draw cord that can be tightened around the decedent's neck. This type of bag will be discussed further a little later in the chapter when we discuss chemical suicides. Homicides tend to be a more prevalent manner of death associated with smothering as the cause of death.

Even if a homicide is attributed to a case of smothering, the case still generally requires a decedent who is incapacitated in some fashion. In children and the elderly, this incapacitation is usually attributed to their inability to deter a normal, healthy adult who is applying pressure over the mouth and nares. If a death is being investigated as a smothering and the decedent is a healthy adult, the medicolegal death investigator should pay particular attention to things that would restrict this type of a person from fending off the attack. As previously described, drug or alcohol intoxication could play a role and one would want to find supporting evidence of this. Another example could be documenting signs of severe physical trauma that could weaken a decedent during an attack.

Choking

To a lay person, the idea that someone died from a choking event might seem obvious and should not require a complete examination. They picture a person having something lodged in their throat and giving the universal sign for choking by putting their hands around their throat. However, this assumption is not always true. Some individuals might have something lodged in their airway and become unconscious shortly after the event, they might be trying to swallow something to conceal a crime, or it might simply be an unwitnessed event and choking is not fully considered because the person was of advanced age with chronic health conditions. One indication, however, that choking may have been an issue is if the decedent was given advanced life support care in the field or at a hospital, and a medical provider states that he/she had difficulty intubating the decedent because he/she was met with a lot of food or another foreign body. Choking can also occur by another individual applying external pressure to a decedent's neck.

Outside of the intentional choking of an individual with the intent to end his/her life, there are some reports of teenagers who have died as a result of something called the choking game. According to one small study, 19% of children aged 17–18 years reported playing the game at some point in their life (Williams County Partnerships for Success, 2007).

CHEMICAL

Asphyxial deaths that are due to a chemical component make up a wide range of manners of death that need to be considered. Since an external component is present in every situation listed in this section, none of these deaths would be considered natural. However, a thorough scene investigation will differentiate whether the death is an accident, suicide, or homicide. The vast majority of asphyxial chemical deaths will be signed out as a suicide. Additionally, with the rise in chemicals to assist in suicide, there are a number of chemicals that could cause an asphyxial death, but this section of the chapter will focus on three different scenarios that medicolegal death investigators is likely to routinely see in the course of their work. Knowing what to look for in each of these instances as well as how to safely investigate them is important.

Carbon Monoxide

The presence of carbon monoxide is routinely seen in suicides, but the medicolegal death investigator must be able to identify when it may have occurred in other settings. From a public health and safety standpoint, there is a great risk to the general public when there is a carbon monoxide leak in a commercial or residential structure because this could cause a number of deaths in a short period of time if people are not made aware of the risk.

Carbon monoxide is so dangerous because it binds with a higher affinity to hemoglobin than oxygen does, around 200–250 times more. This displacement of oxygen for carbon monoxide creates a hypoxic event since no oxygen is reaching the body's cells (Rodkey, O'Neal, Collison, & Uddin, 1974). Individuals with carbon monoxide toxicity will present with a cherry red lividity as opposed to the violet color that is usually exhibited. Identifying the source of the carbon monoxide is very important from a public safety standpoint and consultation with other professionals, usually a fire marshal, will help accomplish this goal.

If the death is a suicide and a motor vehicle was used, the source is quite obvious. However, this is not always the case. Searching for the potential source is important. It could be from a heating source of the structure where the death investigation is happening, which would include the boiler or furnace, a kerosene or gas space heater, generator, and how close it was to the decedent. Next, from a public health perspective, it would be pertinent to note whether or not a carbon monoxide detector was working in the residence. This may not seem like a big deal when writing up the scene report, but information like this can help public health officials determine risk factors and develop public awareness campaigns to prevent these types of deaths in the future. Sometimes the source of the carbon monoxide is obvious, though.

A motor vehicle as the source, as previously mentioned, is a common finding in a carbon monoxide suicide. This is less likely with newer cars since the catalytic converters are so efficient at filtering the exhaust. However, there have still been confirmed cases with new models as well as with hybrid vehicles. There have even been reports of individuals whose cars have a remote entry fob instead of a traditional key, and they have left their car running in the garage inadvertently, which allowed carbon monoxide to eventually fill their house causing a fatal event. If the medicolegal death investigator suspects a motor vehicle played a role in a death, there are a few things that should be checked regarding the car every time.

A scene report will need the following information related to a carbon monoxide death where a motor vehicle is the suspected source. The first is to note whether the vehicle was running at the time the decedent was located. If the vehicle was not running, were the keys in the ignition? If the keys were in the ignition and the car was not running, were the keys in the on or off position? It is possible that the car simply ran out of gas prior to the decedent being found. If a car's key is in the off position, at some point in the investigation the key should be moved to at least the battery-on position to check the gas levels. The gas level is particularly important to check if the car utilizes a keyless remote fob as it may not be immediately apparent if the vehicle was turned off or simply ran out of gas when the first responders arrive on scene. House fires are another scene where carbon monoxide could play a significant role.

If an individual died in a house fire, checking for carboxyhemoglobin, the complex formed when carbon monoxide binds to the hemoglobin molecule in red blood cells, is one of the methods used to determine whether or not a person was alive during or was dead prior to the start of the fire. This will be discussed later on in the textbook, but checking the carboxyhemoglobin is essential in every case where carbon monoxide intoxication is suspected.

Checking the level of carboxyhemoglobin is the quick and easy test that can inform the medicolegal death investigator and the forensic pathologist if carbon monoxide played a role in the death. Taking a complete medical history is important because smokers, as an example, can have a carboxyhemoglobin level of up to around 10% just walking around every day. In autopsy, there may be additional evidence that an individual was alive during a fire such as soot in their upper airway as depicted in Fig. 5.3.

Inert Gas

The use of inert gases, such as helium, has become more common as of late, likely due in part to it being listed as a method that is spelled out in the book, *Final Exit*. To carry out this form of suicide, an individual needs only a plastic bag or hood to cover the head with a drawstring feature that can be used to secure the bag around their neck, some form of tubing, and helium tanks. The helium tanks are not difficult to obtain as anyone can purchase them at party supply stores as part of balloon kits.

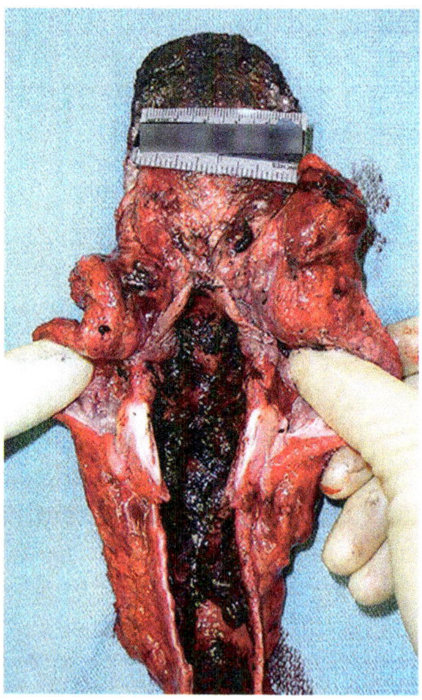

FIGURE 5.3 Soot from the fire in an individual's upper airway illustrating that they were alive during a fire.

Helium is not the only gas that can be used in these cases, nitrogen is also relatively common, but the proper documentation of the scene is one of the only ways to properly certify these deaths. The decedent dies as a result of the gas in the enclosed environment, in this case the bag or hood over a decedent's head, replacing oxygen. So, a decedent is breathing in a gas that is incompatible with life instead of oxygen. It is also difficult to test for the presence of some of these gases. So, without the scene findings an inert gas suicide could go undetected.

Hydrogen Sulfide Gas

In addition to a perceived rise in the use of helium as a method for committing suicide there has also been a perceived increased use of hydrogen sulfide (H_2S) gas suicides. This trend first started to appear in Japan when their Cabinet Office stated that in less than a 3-month period in 2008 there were 220 reported cases of hydrogen sulfide suicide, also commonly referred to as detergent suicide attempts. Since then, the method has been seen with increased frequency in the United States. Hydrogen sulfide displaces oxygen at the cellular level, thus creating an asphyxial death. The chemicals are easy to get too, as one only needs to mix hydrochloric acid with a sulfur-containing compound, usually lime sulfur, in a bucket and be in a relatively confined area so as not to let the gas dissipate easily. Common examples of a relatively confined area could be the inside of a car or in the bathroom of a residence. Scene safety should be of the upmost concern for the medicolegal death investigator, and it is common to allow a hazardous materials team to mitigate the environment first before the medicolegal office enters the scene. Usually, all that is required to make the scene safe is to allow the area to air out by opening windows and doors. Fig. 5.4 is an example of a hydrogen sulfide

FIGURE 5.4 An example of hydrogen sulfide suicide in a motor vehicle.

FIGURE 5.5 A closer range photograph of Fig. 5.4 that depicts the warning notes left on the window by the decedent to inform the first responders of the danger inside of the care.

suicide in a motor vehicle. Fig. 5.5 shows a closer range photograph that depicts the warning notes left on the window by the decedent to inform the first responders of the danger inside of the car. These warnings are not uncommon to see.

MECHANICAL AND POSITIONAL

The difference between mechanical and positional asphyxia is important for the medicolegal death investigator to understand. In general, mechanical asphyxia occurs when an object is compressing on a decedent and that compression restricts the normal breathing of an individual, and positional asphyxia is when a person's body is lying in such a fashion that normal breathing is not possible. Positional asphyxia usually occurs when an individual is incapacitated either from drugs or alcohol, or from a physical disability. This can also occur when someone falls.

Falls

A disabled or incapacitated individual falling down a flight of stairs is quite possibly the most common scenario where a medicolegal death investigator would find someone where it is believed that he/she died of positional asphyxia. If an individual falls down the steps and is incapacitated for whatever reason, and their head is in a severely flexed or extended position they will not be able to breath as they normally would, eventually dying in that position. The scene investigation is extremely important in these instances as proper documentation would be required for the death to be certified properly. Pictures from multiple angles would need to be taken to show the flexed or extended position of the individual. Additionally, pictures of the livor pattern will need to be taken as soon as possible, particularly if the decedent has not been deceased long and his/her livor pattern is not fixed. Particularly if the decedent was in a flexed position, the medicolegal death investigator is likely to see a blanched area around the midline of the decedent's neck, underneath the chin, and on the upper midline of the chest. The documentation of this livor pattern is critical to illustrating that there was pressure down on this area, making it difficult if not impossible to breath.

In Custody Death

Another example of a positional asphyxia death would be an individual in police custody who is being restrained in a prone position with an officer on top of them holding the individual down. The pressure being exuded on the decedent's chest wall and stomach can restrict normal breathing. If the decedent had a history of chronic health conditions, like cardiac or respiratory, those could exasperate this restrained situation and could cause death. In this scenario, a complete medical history as well as a complete history of the events leading up to death would be important to understand. In the previous example of an individual falling down the stairs it is more likely that the decedent would be found after a prolonged period of being down. Thus, there would likely be a livor pattern that would illustrate the areas of pressure. When someone goes unresponsive and it is witnessed, particularly by law enforcement, resuscitative efforts would begin almost immediately and there would not be a livor pattern to illustrate the decedent's position when he/she died as a result of their compromised position.

Motor Vehicle Accidents

Someone who dies in a motor vehicle accident generally dies from multiple blunt force trauma; however, a motor vehicle accident is also an example of a scene where the decedent could have died from mechanical or positional asphyxia depending on how his/her body is positioned in the car and the integrity of the vehicle itself after the accident. If the compartment in the vehicle where the decedent is found is compressed such that part of the vehicle is compressing against the decedent making normal respiration difficult or impossible, it is possible that the death would be due to mechanical asphyxia. An example of how the death following a motor vehicle accident could be caused by positional asphyxia is if the vehicle were to be rolled over onto its roof and the decedent's head and neck are overly flexed or extended, similar to what was discussed in positional asphyxial deaths after falls. As previously mentioned, the decedent's exact position will need to be fully documented to provide the forensic pathologist with the most complete picture of how the decedent was found in the vehicle. As with most asphyxial deaths, a complete autopsy will be needed to determine the exact cause and manner of death, and this is particularly true in these instances where an individual has been in a significant traumatic event and those injuries, if any, will need to be weighed against the possibility of a mechanical or positional asphyxia when determining the cause of death.

External Object

The classic example of a mechanical asphyxia death involving an external object is a car falling down onto an individual when the jack fails. Similarly, another example of a mechanical asphyxia from the author's own experience was a gentleman who was changing a tire on a recreational vehicle and the jack holding that particular section of the vehicle slipped out of position causing the large vehicle to fall down onto the decedent. In these particular cases, as well as all mechanical asphyxia deaths, the scene investigation is paramount to understanding what happened to the decedent.

Documenting these scenes involves extensive photographs of how the scene presented itself to investigators, and how the decedent was positioned in relation to the object. Knowing where the actual compression point was located is important to understand the likelihood that the event was a possible mechanical asphyxia or something else. If the object was resting on the decedent's chest or abdomen it is likely that the medicolegal death investigator could be looking at a mechanical asphyxia, but if the compression point is located somewhere else on the body it may be less likely. Additionally, once the object has been removed, documenting how the decedent presents is essential.

When the object is removed from the decedent's body, there should be a pretty well-defined livor pattern that shows exactly where the compression was located. This must be documented as soon as it is visualized to avoid losing this finding if the livor pattern is not fixed. Other signs of the compression may also be present, including congestion of the head and upper chest as well as diffuse petechial hemorrhages of the skin, conjunctiva and sclera of the eye, and even the eyelids.

REFERENCES

Ambade, V. N., Tumram, N., Meshram, S., & Borkar, J. (2015). Ligature material in hanging deaths: the neglected area in forensic examination. *Egyptian Journal of Forensic Sciences, 5*(3), 109–113.

DiMaio, V. J. (2000). Homicidal asphyxia. *American Journal of Forensic Medicine and Pathology, 21*(1), 1–4.

Maxeiner, H., & Bockholdt, B. (2003). Homicidal and suicidal ligature strangulation—a comparison of the post-mortem findings. *Forensic Science International, 137*(1), 60–66.

National Institute for Occupational Safety and Health. (1986). *National Institute for Occupational Safety and Health: Request for Assistance in Preventing Occupational Fatalities in Confined Spaces* (pp. 86–110). DHHS (NIOSH).

Rodkey, F. L., O'Neal, J. D., Collison, H. A., & Uddin, D. E. (1974). Relative affinity of hemoglobin S and hemoglobin A for carbon monoxide and oxygen. *Clinical Chemistry, 20*(1), 83–84.

Sauvageau, A., & Boghossian, E. (2010). Classification of asphyxia: the need for standardization. *Journal of Forensic Sciences, 55*(5), 1259–1267.

Uzun, I., Buyuk, Y., & Gurpinar, K. (2007). Suicidal hangings: fatalities in Istanbul retrospective analysis on 761 autopsy cases. *Journal of Forensic and Legal Medicine, 14*(7), 406–409.

Williams County Partnerships for Success. (2007). *Williams County Youth Health Risk Behavioral Survey, Fall 2006*. Bryan, OH: Williams County Partnerships for Success.

Yamasaki, S., Takase, I., Takada, N., & Nishi, K. (2009). Measurement of force to obstruct the cervical arteries and distribution of tension exerted on a ligature in hanging. *Legal Medicine, 11*(4), 175–180.

Chapter 6

Blunt-Force Injuries

Chapter Outline

The identification and understanding of the pathologic changes that can occur as a result of blunt-force injuries is essential to the everyday practice of a medicolegal professional. Blunt-force injuries are quite common, and a thorough understanding of the circumstances surrounding such injuries is important when it comes to classify the death; these deaths are mostly accidental deaths but could also fall under other classifications such as homicide or suicide.

When discussing blunt-force trauma with lay people they tend to think of incidents of homicidal violence such as being hit with a baseball bat. However, the reality is that some of the most common incidents of blunt-force trauma are much less criminal in nature. They tend to be the result of an elderly person falling or an individual being involved in a motor vehicle accident. Knowing that a person was involved in a fall with a fractured hip, as an example, can have a profound effect on the whole body and lead to the individual dying today as opposed to a later time in life. One such reason for this is that trauma can put an unusual stress on the body that exasperates a decedent's chronic health condition and can lead to heart failure (Roche, Wenn, Sahota, & Moran, 2005). Other signs of blunt-force trauma might not be the cause of death but can give an indication as to what happened to the individual prior to death. This chapter will focus on the different kinds of blunt-force trauma that are commonly encountered.

ABRASION

An abrasion is a very common finding for someone who has been suffering any number of blunt-force injuries. An abrasion is a form of soft tissue injury that involves the superficial layers of skin as a result of friction over the body (Fig. 6.1). This type of injury is found in a number of traumatic settings such as motor vehicle accidents, falls, and homicidal violence.

Essentials of Medicolegal Death Investigation. http://dx.doi.org/10.1016/B978-0-12-803641-9.00006-9

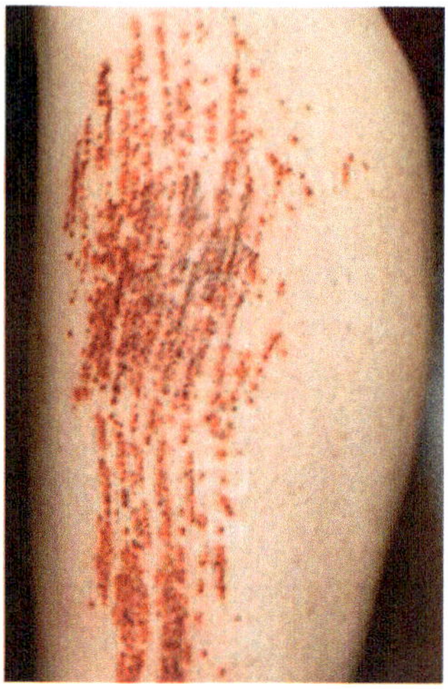

FIGURE 6.1 An example of an abrasion.

Motor vehicle accidents make up a large percentage of any medical examiner/coroner office's blunt-force trauma cases. Abrasions are often present due to the body's impact with the steering wheel, structural components of the vehicle, or from safety features such as an airbag or seat belt. Some injuries, such as the abrasion that could be created from a seat belt impact (Fig. 6.2), are pattern abrasions and provide an indication to the medicolegal death investigator as to where the decedent was located in the vehicle. Additionally, dicing injuries from the broken side window glass, which is tempered glass, can leave an abraded pattern on one side of the body revealing

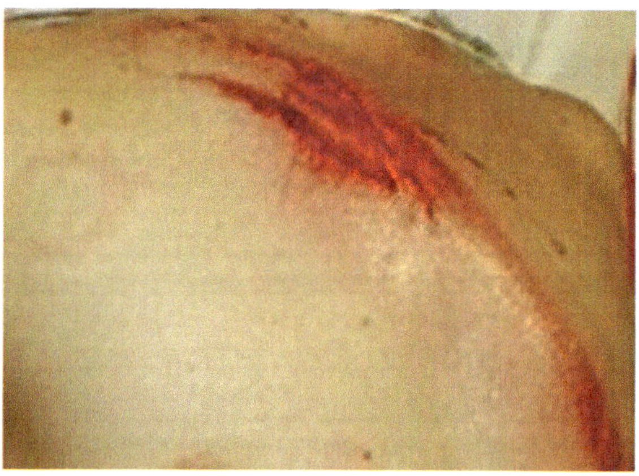

FIGURE 6.2 An example of an abrasion from a seat belt.

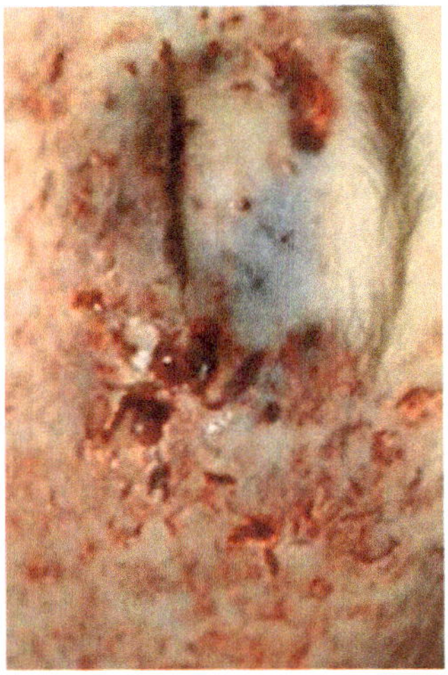

FIGURE 6.3 An example of a dicing injury.

the side of the car the decedent was on. The dicing injuries (Fig. 6.3) are caused when the small pieces of glass caused by the breaking of a tempered window make contact with the skin. In motor vehicle accidents, such as the one depicted in Fig. 6.4, the medicolegal death investigator is likely to encounter more than just one type of injury pattern. However, some abrasion evidence can also indicate a serious underlying problem.

In a large study examining children who were presented to an emergency department after a motor vehicle accident it was found that patients who were presented with signs of a seat belt injury were far more likely to have intra-abdominal injuries (Borgialli et al., 2014). Similar findings have also been

FIGURE 6.4 An example of a motor vehicle accident which can often times cause dicing injuries.

found in adult populations (Bansal, Conroy, Tominaga, & Coimbra, 2009). While this makes sense, as the injury is an indicator of a significant trauma, it is important for the medicolegal death investigator to understand this as it could provide an indication for a possible cause of death in this population. This would be especially true if there was a lack of other outward signs of trauma.

Falls are also a common occurrence where abrasions can be seen on examination. A fall could be the result of an individual losing his/her balance and his/her body making contact with the ground or another object on the way down. This could be the primary issue associated with a decedent's death, particularly in the elderly. An abrasion from a fall could also be an artifact of a terminal event such as someone losing consciousness after a myocardial infarction and the individual just happened to sustain an abrasion during the collapse. The important fact to remember with abrasions associated with a terminal event is that they must be evaluated to ensure they are simply an artifact or whether there is significant underlying trauma that would require further investigation.

The identification of abrasions is also important for the medicolegal death investigator when it comes to investigating a possible homicide. Research by Ambade and Godbole (2006) found that blunt-force head trauma was noted in 80% of the homicide victims in their retrospective study of 241 homicides over a 12-year period. This illustrates the need to be able to accurately identify and document this type of injury as it could be a patterned abrasion. This would provide further clues, just as it does for motor vehicle accidents that were previously discussed, as to a type of weapon that was used. This type of finding could very well be the piece of evidence that links an offender to a victim (Rao, 1986). Another form of trauma that is seen as a result of blunt-force trauma is a contusion.

CONTUSION

A contusion is commonly called a bruise and is the result of trauma to a specific area of the body. The trauma causes damage to the blood capillaries of the area causing blood to seep into the tissues (Fig. 6.5). Like an abrasion, a contusion is a sign that could provide the medicolegal death investigator with an indication of what may have happened to the decedent prior to death. The presence of a contusion could be from an acute incident or something that had happened some time prior to death. The color changes associated with the contusion could provide an indication to how long ago a traumatic event occurred.

One of the questions most commonly asked about contusions is to estimate how old a particular injury is. While there is not a scientifically accepted measure for dating contusions, multiple authors have noted that the color change observed can give a general frame of reference. An interesting study

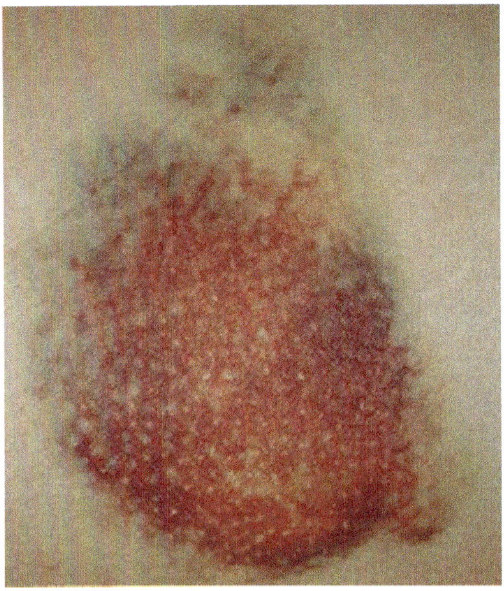

FIGURE 6.5 An example of a contusion.

that asked forensic experts to age pictures of bruises that were created in a laboratory setting revealed a high variability in the accuracy of a diagnosis (Pilling, Vanezis, Perrett, & Johnston, 2010). This illustrates the need to avoid dating contusions by all forensic professionals until there is a more precise way of dating contusions. A couple of studies have shown that the color of a contusion changes to yellow on the second day since bruising, but older studies that were referenced in these articles had the color change to yellow at least 7 days postinjury (Langlois & Gresham, 1991; Stephenson & Bialas, 1996). Again, since there is not a more accurate measurement the medicolegal death investigator should not guess. There are likely a number of factors that effect the change in color, including the decedent's age and overall health status, which includes medications they may be taking.

The presence of an acute contusion should cause the investigator to seriously suspect that trauma played a role in the death of the individual and the presence of purple–blue discoloration is essential. If there appears to be a mark on a decedent but blood has not perfused the area, then it might be a post- or perimortem injury. This simply means that the trauma to the body occurred around the time the individual died or after the individual died. This is a common finding that the medicolegal death investigator should become familiar with.

A common example of when there may be post- or perimortem injuries would be an individual who collapses during a terminal event, such as a stroke or heart attack. Another example could be the individual who dies while his/her body weight is pressing them against an object. There may be some brownish yellow discoloration, and possibly even an almost leathery appearance to the skin, but there is no purple–blue discoloration because when the event occurred the heart was no longer pumping properly, which would be needed for the blood to perfuse into the area.

If an event was acute in nature and contributed to death, the contusion would have color changes similar to any other blunt force the decedent had experienced earlier in his/her life. Additionally, the location of the contusion could provide an indication to the underlying organs that may be affected by the traumatic event. An area of contusion to the head may indicate the presence of bleeding around the decedent's brain, just as a large contusion to the decedent's chest may indicate the presence of bleeding in the thoracic cavity. The shape of the contusion may also provide clues as to what may have caused the injury.

Everyone has had a contusion at some point in his/her life and knows the marks that common accidents leave behind. The contusion patterns that common falls leave behind are generally localized to one area and are over boney prominences. Additionally, with the exception of an individual having multiple impacts within one incident such as falling down the stairs, contusions generally are found in only one region, if multiples are present from an event. Knowing these things, the medicolegal death investigator should be suspicious of any of the following contusions:

- Contusions that are very large and have a pattern to them. Examples of this may be a long, narrow pattern from the strike of a baseball bat.
- Contusions in areas of the body that do not have a boney prominence. An example of this would be contusions seen on the abdomen of an individual.
- Contusions in multiple regions of the body. Examples of this could be contusions of the head and chest, or of the chest and back.
- Any contusion that does not make sense when examined through the story being told by a witness to the death.

The presence of multiple contusions in multiple stages of healing could also be an indication about the events that led up to the death of an individual. This does not always mean that something criminal was occurring to the decedent prior to death. Instead, it may provide a window into another condition the decedent suffered from. The following two examples are quite common for medicolegal death investigators to see during the regular performance of their duties. They are signs that someone had suffered multiple previous falls, and the other could be supporting evidence that someone was using drugs or alcohol.

The presence of multiple healing contusions could be a sign that an individual may have suffered previous falls prior to his/her death. This does not mean that trauma is to be blamed for the death, but instead may indicate that the person's health was failing or they had a condition that predisposed them to falls if not properly cared for. It would not be uncommon for a nursing home to report to the medicolegal office that a decedent had fallen multiple times in the past few weeks leading up to the death. This would likely be the result of an individual who was becoming weaker and was unable to properly support his/her own gait. These contusions would likely be seen on areas of skin around the decedent's hips, buttocks, or extremities.

Contusions seen by individuals who abuse drugs or alcohol, on the other hand, are likely to be confined to their lower extremities. These injuries are caused when someone is under the influence of drugs and alcohol and frequently bumps into furniture or other objects due to his/her altered mental status. Additionally, alcoholics or drug users who have significant liver disease will also get contusions more easily due to their blood's inability to clot normally. So, a minor blunt-force trauma, such as bumping into a coffee table, may cause little-to-no evidence of the event for a completely healthy individual and may cause significant bleeding into the tissues of the affected areas. As these incidents happen with some regularity leading up to a person's death, the finding of multiple healing contusions would be obvious to the medicolegal death investigator. Sometimes however, signs of multiple contusions in various stages of healing can indicate that there was foul play involved.

The most common example of foul play associated with a decedent who has multiple contusions in various stages of healing is the individual who was abused over a prolonged period of time. This could be a child who was suffering abuse by a caretaker, or an adult who was the victim of domestic violence. In the United States alone, there are over 10 million victims annually of intimate partner violence (CDC, 2015). When dealing with someone who has been the victim of prolonged abuse, regardless of age, the contusions may be found in parts of the body that are easily concealable by clothing. A study of domestic violence victims revealed that in their population, the largest percentage of injuries were noted on the head and neck of the victims; however, this was followed closely by injuries to the upper and lower limbs with fewer injuries noted in the abdomen of the victims (Curca, Dermengiu, & Hostiuc, 2012). Conversely, a separate study of domestic violence victims showed 85% of victims had evidence of trauma to more than one region of their body (Reijnders, Van der Leden, & De Bruin, 2006). Regardless of whether trauma was easily visible, a thorough body examination should reveal evidence of repeated trauma.

The presence of near-healed contusions may also provide an indication for the medicolegal death investigator as to what happened to a decedent. If a decedent was found with significant near-healed contusions and it was known that the decedent had not sought out medical care recently, there could have been a slow progressing issue related to a traumatic event. An example of this would be someone who sustained head trauma, and there was a slow intracranial bleed associated with this. Undoubtedly, the decedent would have been experiencing headaches, possibly vertigo, associated with such a condition, but the decedent may not have shared that with anyone. A more common scenario would be where an individual previously suffered a traumatic event which caused a contusion, and later on a blood clot formed in the area of trauma.

The most common example of a blood clot forming in someone who previously injured themselves is when there is trauma to the lower extremities. The contusion may limit the blood flow in that particular area due to the swelling. Whenever there is decreased blood flow or stasis, there is an increased risk of a clot developing. However, it is important to note that any damage to a vessel can increase the risk of a blood clot, as can many other medical or health conditions. If a clot were to make its way up through the body and toward the heart and lungs via the vena cava, it can be a fatal event. For the medicolegal death investigator, they might suspect a thrombus if there was a reported history of a lower extremity injury with associated pain, redness, or swelling of the area.

One additional comment on contusions is that, to the untrained investigator, senile ecchymosis can look like a traumatic injury. This condition, also commonly referred to as senile purpura, is often seen in elderly individuals and is due to their decreased connective tissue in their skin as well as weakened capillaries. This is not due to any kind of traumatic event or assault the decedent may have suffered. Instead, it tends to be a benign phenomenon associated with the elderly, and research has shown that it is most commonly found in the upper extremities (Giles & Williams, 1994).

LACERATION

Lacerations are the result of blunt-force trauma that causes a shearing of the skin or organ. When examining a decedent, the presence of a laceration will almost always be over a boney prominence, usually the head. Many lay people as well as inexperienced medicolegal death investigators may have some difficulty differentiating between a laceration and a sharp-force injury. However, there are a few signs to look for to help easily identify a laceration.

The first sign that what the medicolegal death investigator is looking at is the presence of bridging. Bridging is the existence of connective tissue inside the wound that is being examined, which stretches from one side of the wound to the other, as seen in Fig. 6.6. There is literature that shows even with very

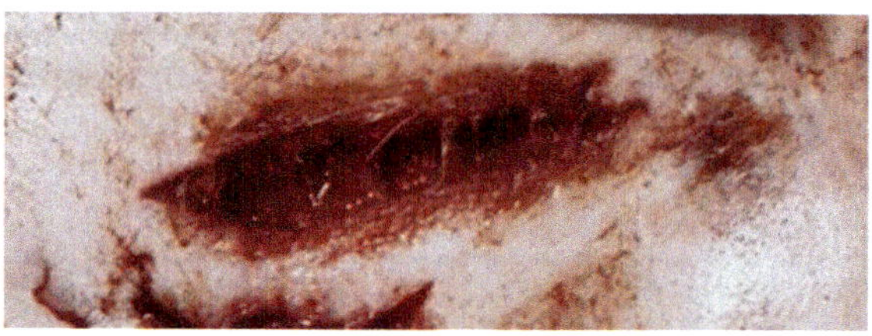

FIGURE 6.6 An example of bridging.

clean edges to a wound like that seen with some explosion-related injuries an examination of the wound still reveals the presence of bridging at deeper layers of tissue (Tiemensma & Wadee, 2014). This is also another reason why a thorough examination is so important. Without an understanding of what type of injury the medicolegal office is dealing with, there could be a delay in providing essential information to a law enforcement agency as to whether or not a death is suspicious in nature or not, or whether they should be looking for an object that caused a blunt-force injury or a sharp-force injury. However, some lacerations are relatively easily identifiable based on their outward appearance.

Irregular edges are not always present with a laceration, but certainly are quite common. Whereas a sharp-force injury is more likely to produce a wound with a regular pattern or edges. The shearing force associated with a blunt object hitting the surface of the skin, and then the affected area's tissues coming into contact with a bone generally will produce an irregular edge as well as a wound that is not linear but may appear to tear in multiple directions. The important thing for the medicolegal death investigator to understand is that the wound should be inspected to evaluate the appearance of the wound's edges. However, it would not be appropriate to insert a finger or tool into the wound to further explore it. Just as with any defect noted to the body, exploring the inside of the wound could cause damage or artifact that could negatively affect a forensic pathologist's autopsy. When examining the edges of the wound, the medicolegal death investigator may also find evidence of a contusion.

The presence of an associated contusion is also more commonly seen in a laceration versus a sharp-force injury. It is often the case that laceration size does not correlate with the object that caused in the injury. However, the surface area of the skin that makes contact with a blunt object is greater than the laceration itself. A simple example of this would be an individual who is struck in the head with a baseball bat. While a large laceration may occur as a result of this blunt-force trauma, it is not likely that the width of the laceration will be the same as the width of the bat that made contact with the skin. So, you would likely find a contusion in areas where there was not a laceration because you would still have the damage to the capillaries from the impact.

FRACTURE

The presence of a facture is a significant finding for the medicolegal death investigator, and it will always require further investigation to see what, if any, impact the trauma had on the decedent's death. The purpose of this section is not to provide a complete overview of all fractures, but instead to highlight a couple of important fractures as well as findings that the medicolegal death investigator might expect to see upon examination.

Starting with significant fractures, those fractures that occur to the head, chest, pelvis, and large long bones such as the femur should be fully investigated because they likely will play a significant role in how the death certificate is eventually signed. The text has already discussed how just the stress of one of these fractures could cause heart failure in an individual with significant chronic health conditions, but these types of fractures can also be a strong indicator of other significant trauma to the body.

The previously listed areas of the body where a fracture of one of the bones would be a significant injury also indicate a probable associated injury to the nearby organs. If there were a fracture to an individual's skull the medicolegal death investigator would be right to assume that there is likely an injury and bleeding associated with the brain, just as signs of multiple rib fractures could indicate the possibility of damage to the heart or lungs. In addition to the acute trauma to organs associated with blunt-force trauma that fractures a bone, there can be complications that are not realized until hours to weeks after the traumatic event.

While the initial impact of the blunt force trauma can certainly be enough to kill an individual, there are injuries to tissues that do not cause death until much later. The fracturing of a bone will cause swelling and tearing of nearby tissues which will increase the likelihood of blood clots forming, particularly with fractures to the bones of the lower extremities and to the pelvis. Additionally, fractures in the pelvis and lower extremities are going to greatly decrease an individual's ability to ambulate. This immobility creates a situation for blood stasis and it too will increase the likelihood that someone could produce a blood clot that could become fatal. Some fractures should also increase the suspicion of the medicolegal death investigator that something criminal may have been going on, particularly associated with children.

Any fracture in a pediatric death investigation should be treated with extra attention if it cannot be easily explained. This is because the younger an individual is, the more cartilage they would have in his/her bones. The cartilage makes a person's bones more flexible and less susceptible to fracture. This means that it takes a greater amount of force to cause a fracture. The following fractures have a high degree of suspicion for abuse (Flaherty et al., 2014, Table 1):

- Classic metaphyseal lesions
- Rib fractures and more specifically, posterior
- Scapular fractures
- Spinous process fractures
- Sternal fractures

Additionally, some research has indicated the specific type of fracture that is seen is suggestive of abuse.

Spiral fractures are a particular kind of fracture that occurs when there is rotational force applied to a bone. An example of when this could occur is when an individual is performing in a sporting event. The athlete could firmly plant his/her foot, but if another individual makes contact with the athlete and causes the planted foot to rotate without the athlete being about to pick up the planted foot, a spiral fracture could occur. This is, obviously, not a criminal example but one that is could be a child who is the victim of abuse by an adult. An example of how this could happen might be an adult that is grabbing a child's arm or leg and twisting it violently. This does not mean that a spiral fracture will always indicate abuse, however (Hui et al., 2008; Rex & Kay, 2000). It is, like everything else, something that the medicolegal death investigator should be aware of.

On scene, the medicolegal death investigator will not have radiologic studies available to them, unless of course the decedent made it to the hospital prior to death being pronounced, but they can perform a proper examination that may indicate to them that there is a fracture.

There are a number of indications that a decedent may have a fractured bone. In general, edema that is sometimes very firm, bruising, tenderness, deformity, and pain when bearing weight on the affected area. The chapter that discusses performing a body examination on scene goes into detail about how to generally perform this function; however, there are specifics that the medicolegal death investigator should be looking for as it relates to possible fractures.

When palpating, the medicolegal death investigator should be looking for any deformities or step-off (bones do not feel aligned), deformities to the chest wall, one leg shorter than the other for a possible pelvic fracture, and with the extremities the presence of deformities and crepitus (cracking sound). Certain evidence of blood in tissue, as noted in Fig. 6.7, can indicate a serious underlying fracture such as an orbital fracture. This is not an all-inclusive list, but does illustrate the most common findings.

It is important for the medicolegal death investigator to understand when evaluating blunt-force trauma that they are accurately identified and those

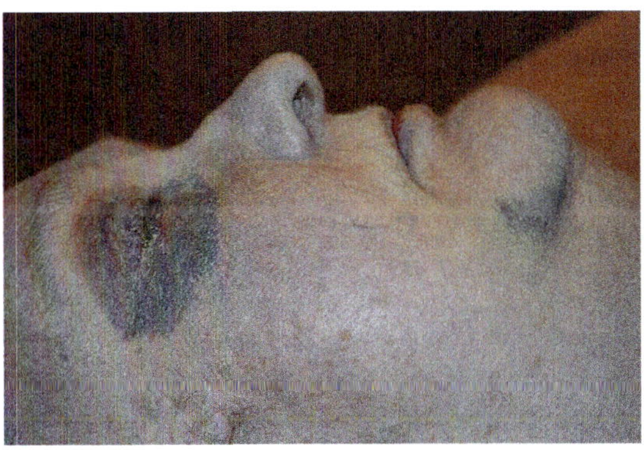

FIGURE 6.7 An example of blood in tissue indicating an orbital fracture.

injuries are used to help tell the story of how an individual died. They should always be asking themselves, does this injury fit with the story that I am being told. If not, what is different and could account for the changes. It is also important to differentiate between injuries that are old, injuries that are fresh but did not contribute to the death, and injuries that play a role in why the individual has died.

Oftentimes, the various traumas discussed in this chapter will be present together instead of in isolation. Someone that dies in a motorcycle accident will possibly have every injury discussed in this chapter, but prioritizing which ones contributed to the death and which ones helped tell the story is important. The abrasions might tell the story of how the individual was thrown from the motorcycle and slid across the concrete, the contusions and lacerations could illustrate points of impact or even give an indication of additional underlying injuries that might be present, and fractures might show the severity of the impact on the body from the accident and provide insight into areas of the body where there may be significant trauma that could be incompatible with life. Each injury tells a different, yet important, part of the story.

REFERENCES

Ambade, V. N., & Godbole, H. V. (2006). Comparison of wound patterns in homicide by sharp and blunt force. *Forensic Science International, 156*(2–3), 166–170.

Bansal, V., Conroy, C., Tominaga, G. T., & Coimbra, R. (2009). The utility of seat belt signs to predict intra-abdominal injury following motor vehicle crashes. *Traffic Injury Prevention, 10*, 567–572.

Borgialli, D. A., Ellison, A. M., Ehrlich, P., Bonsu, B., Menaker, J., Wisner, D. H., et al. (2014). Association between the seat belt sign and intra-abdominal injuries in children with blunt torso trauma in motor vehicle collisions. *Academic Emergency Medicine, 21*(11), 1240–1248.

Centers for Disease Control and Prevention. (2015). *National Intimate Partner and Sexual Violence Survey*. Retrieved from: http://www.cdc.gov/violenceprevention/nisvs/index.html.

Curca, G. C., Dermengiu, D., & Hostiuc, S. (2012). Patterns of injuries in domestic violence in a Romanian population. *Journal of Interpersonal Violence*. http://dx.doi.org/10.1177/0886260512438278.

Flaherty, E. G., et al. (2014). Evaluating children with fractures for child physical abuse. *Pediatrics, 133*(2), e477–e489. http://dx.doi.org/10.1542/peds.2013-3793.

Giles, T. E., & Williams, A. R. (1994). The postmortem incidence of senile ecchymoses. *The American Journal of Forensic Medicine and Pathology, 15*(3), 208–210.

Hui, C., et al. (2008). Femoral fractures in children younger than three years: the role of non-accidental injury. *Journal of Pediatric Orthopaedics, 28*(3), 297–302.

Langlois, N. E. I., & Gresham, G. A. (1991). The ageing of bruises: a review and study of the colour changes with time. *Forensic Science International, 50*, 227–238.

Pilling, M. L., Vanezis, P., Perrett, D., & Johnston, A. (2010). Visual assessment of the timing of bruising by forensic experts. *Journal of Forensic and Legal Medicine, 17*(3), 143–149.

Rao, V. J. (1986). Patterned injury and its evidentiary value. *Journal of Forensic Sciences, 31*, 768–772.

Reijnders, U. J., Van der Leden, M. E., & De Bruin, K. H. (2006). Injuries due to domestic violence against women: sites on the body, types of injury and the methods of infliction. *Nederlands tijdschrift voor geneeskunde, 150*(8), 429–435.

Rex, C., & Kay, P. R. (2000). Features of femoral fractures in nonaccidental injury. *Journal of Pediatric Orthopaedics, 20*(3), 411–413.

Roche, J. J. W., Wenn, R. T., Sahota, O., & Moran, C. G. (2005). Effect of comorbidities and postoperative complications on mortality after hip fracture in elderly people: prospective observational cohort study. *British Medical Journal, 331*(7529), 1374.

Stephenson, T., & Bialas, Y. (1996). Estimation of the age of bruising. *Archives of Disease in Childhood, 74*, 53–55.

Tiemensma, M., & Wadee, S. A. (2014). Blast-induced lacerations—more examples of the diagnostic entity. *The American Journal of Forensic Medicine and Pathology, 35*(3), 222.

Chapter 7

Sharp-Force Injuries

Chapter Outline

Sharp-force injuries are the result of the body coming in contact with a pointed or sharp-edged object, which creates a tearing of the tissue. These are often thought to be caused by knives but can include a large number of objects from a piece of glass to a propeller on a boat engine. There are three types of wounds that fall under the category of sharp force injury: incised, stab, and chop. Each has its own unique characteristics, and the proper identification of the specific wound can assist law enforcement in determining possible objects used in the event, and if the cause of the wound is criminal in nature.

It is also important to note that the damage and depth of the injury is dependent on the location of the injury. An injury occurring in the chest wall would have to contend with the ribs and thus might not be able to create as deep of a wound when compared to the same type of wound on the abdomen. The location of the sharp-force injury can give a general impression to the medicolegal death investigator as to what organ systems may be involved that could have led to the individual's death, but this is not always the case.

A journal article examined a large number of patients who were presented to a particular urban trauma center with thoracoabdominal stab wounds. The researchers found that solid organ injury occurred in over 50% of the patients who made it alive to the hospital, and the most frequently involved organ was the liver (Berg, Karamanos, Inaba, Okoye, Teixeira, & Demetriades, 2014). Having an understanding of the different organ systems that could be involved in a type of injury based on location, and the mechanism that could lead to death, in the case of the liver it is bleeding, can help reconstruct likely events associated with a death. The location could also provide a window into whether an injury was caused by an assailant or was self-inflicted.

While the totality of scene findings will provide a more complete picture of the possible manner of death associated with a sharp-force injury, some research tends to support the location of injury as a possible indicator, as well. Sharp-force injuries associated with homicides have been found to be associated with the chest and back as well as the head, whereas suicidal sharp-force injuries are most

Essentials of Medicolegal Death Investigation. http://dx.doi.org/10.1016/B978-0-12-803641-9.00007-0

commonly found in the extremities (Karlsson, 1998; Kemal, Patterson, & Molina, 2013). Multiple studies have also shown that homicides on average have a greater number of sharp-force injuries present versus those deaths that were categorized as suicides (Brunel, Fermanian, Durigon et al., 2010; Scolan, Telmon, Banc et al., 2004; Gill & Catanesem 2002).

Sharp-force injuries, in general, are less prevalent as a means for suicide when compared to other methods such as the use of a firearm, a ligature, or medications (Karlsson, Ormstad, & Rajs, 1988; Watanabe, Kobayashi, & Hata, 1973). However, understanding how they can cause death and identifying what their presence may indicate, even if the wound is not fatal, are essential to the investigation of these deaths. Each of the following sharp-force injuries presents with unique features that should be understood by the medicolegal death investigator.

INCISED WOUNDS

An incised wound is longer than its depth, and it is rarely a fatal wound. Instead, incised wounds tend to tell part of the story as opposed to being the cause of death in an individual. The presence and location of an incised wound could show that an individual was trying to fend off an attacker, whether someone went through a window or not, and could even be an indication that someone intended to hurt themselves.

Common incised wounds in a nonfatal setting tend to be those individuals who cut themselves while cooking, or a sharp edge from a broken piece of glass cuts someone's skin if an extremity goes through a glass window. In these instances, as well as others where someone suffers this type of sharp-force injury but lives, they are easily treated by a medical provider and other than a scar does not produce long-term consequences.

When there is a fatality, however, incised wounds can generally add to the conversation as to what happened, or even be the exact cause of death. First, however, it is important that an incised wound can be differentiated from a laceration. When examining a laceration, it is the result of blunt-force trauma that causes a shearing of the skin or organ. The most obvious sign that the medicolegal death investigator is looking in a laceration is the presence of bridging. Bridging is the existence of connective tissue inside the wound that is being examined, which stretches from one side of the wound to the other. However, when examining an incised wound, there will not be any presence of bridging because no shearing has occurred. Instead what the medicolegal death investigator will see are clean edges.

These clean edges produced from an incised wound will also be free of any signs of contusion or abrasions associated with the injuries. This is because the sharp edges of the object being used to make the wound, usually a knife, do not affect the surrounding tissue. This is true regardless of the weapon that was used to create the injury. The only difference the medicolegal death investigator might see would be the cleanness of the cut. If a less sharp object was used there might be a less smooth appearance to the wound, but there would still not be any of the characteristic findings associated with a laceration.

Incised wounds are also most common in suicides than they are in homicides. The location of the incised ones seems to be more prevalent in the wrist or throat area as opposed to the antecubital fossae or the forearm (Mazzolo & Desinan, 2005). This would make sense for someone who does not have much medical or anatomical knowledge, as an individual would be likely trying to cut a major artery; though most do not cut deep enough, particularly in the neck, to reach a major vessel.

Certainly there are times when incised wounds are fatal, but there may be other incised wounds that accompany the fatal one to help tell the story about what happened to the individual. This is most prevalent when there is the presence of a hesitation mark. A hesitation mark is a superficial wound that is a "practice" injury of sorts done prior to the decedent eventually cutting deep enough to inflict serious injury. As noted in Fig. 7.1, multiple superficial sharp-force injuries can be seen around the eventual deeper wound.

Defensive marks are oftentimes incised wounds and can help the medicolegal death investigator to differentiate a potential homicide from a suicide or accidental death quickly. Defensive marks are generally found on the palms, the back of the hand, or on the forearms. They are created when an individual is trying to fend off an attacker either by trying to deflect the knife as it is being thrust toward them or by grabbing it.

One last commonly seen incised wound is found on individuals who go through a glass surface such as the window of a house or motor vehicle. The severity of these wounds will greatly depend on the kind of glass and the size

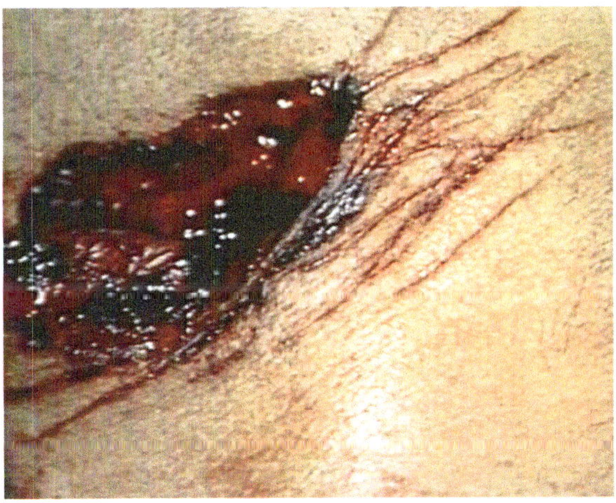

FIGURE 7.1 An example of multiple superficial sharp-force injuries around a deeper wound.

of broken pieces that come in contact with the body. The incised wounds created from the body going through a glass medium might also produce a less clean wound than that of a sharpened knife, but the damage can be just as serious. Oftentimes, however, the injuries serve as another piece of the puzzle that was the decedent's last moments of life. It can help identify, as an example, an individual's path as they were thrown from a motor vehicle that was involved in a high-speed accident. Lastly, depending on the type of glass, if there were small enough pieces the medicolegal death investigator might be able to appreciate some glass pieces in the incised wound. This would help differentiate wounds as being caused by going through glass from ones that may have been caused by an offender.

STAB WOUNDS

Unlike incised wounds which are longer than their depth, stab wounds are deeper than their length. When the medicolegal death investigator is examining an individual with a possible stab wound, the emphasis on scene should be to correctly identify the wounds and fully document the scene to determine if the death is a suicide or a potential homicide. These deaths are almost always homicides, as stated at the beginning of the chapter, sharp-force injuries make up a very small percentage of the total suicides in a given year, and very few of those are stab wounds, generally less than 3% (Byard, Klitte, Gilbert, & James, 2002; Karger & Wennemann, 2001). Even though only a small percentage of stab wounds are self-inflicted, a full scene investigation will help determine whether a death was criminal in nature or not.

In the United States, fatal stab wounds are not as common as they are in other parts of the world. Much of this has to do with the prevalence of firearms in the United States compared to other developed countries. However, research has shown that sharp-force injuries usually involve the chest and abdomen, which is in contrast to blunt-force injuries that generally involve the head (Ambade & Godbole, 2006). Additionally, in general, more stab wounds will be present if someone is killed at the hands of another versus someone who ends their own life. The depth of the stab wound and the size of the sharp object used to cause the injury are not always equal.

As a part of the scene investigation of a potential stabbing death, one of the inevitable questions is what type of weapon was used. With a stab wound, most people will assume a knife was used; however, this is not always a given. Any item that is sharp could potentially be used to stab an individual. These include daggers, switchblades, metal pieces, and broken pieces of glass, to name a few. It would be impossible to include or exclude an object as the weapon in these cases just simply on the scene findings. This is due to a number of issues.

First, it would be impossible to know the depth of a stab wound when examining it on scene. To know the exact depth of a particular stab wound, a complete autopsy would need to be completed to measure the depth at each level of evisceration. If a stab wound was located in the chest, a Y-incision would need to be made and the skin and muscles reflected off the ribs. Once at this level, there would be an inspection to see if the injury penetrated at this level. Then, the ribs would be cut to remove the sternum and anterior ribs to reveal the thoracic cavity. Once this step has been completed, the forensic pathologist would be able to see which organs were impacted and at what depth each organ was impacted. If a medicolegal death investigator were to place a probe within the stab wound at the scene, there would likely be a great distortion of the actual wound, and this artifact could make the more precise measurements taken at the time of autopsy impossible.

Second, multiple knives or other sharp objects could have been used just in one case. Fig. 7.2 shows multiple stab wounds to a victim. You can see the slight differences in sizes of wounds even though they were created from the same knife. It is important for the medicolegal death investigator to understand that it might not ever be understood what knife was used for a specific wound. An example from the author's own experience was a white male in his mid-50s who was stabbed over 30 times by a family member. The family member, it appeared, used every knife that was in a knife block in the family's kitchen. The knives ranged from utility and paring knives, to steak knives, as well as a large chef knife. In these situations, it is most prudent to collect every knife as possible evidence, and allow the forensic pathologist to examine each knife at the time of autopsy while they are examining the individual wounds.

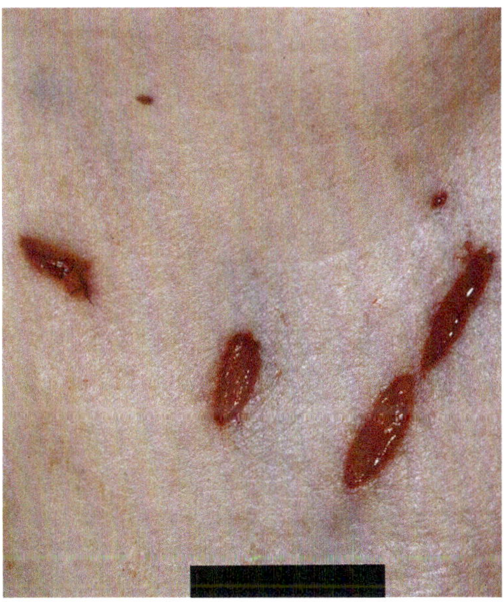

FIGURE 7.2 An example of multiple stab wounds to the body.

The location of the stab wound is important to document for the simple fact that it is the best indicator for the organs that may be involved in the fatality. A prospective study in a large urban area in Europe, where sharp-force violence is more prevalent, found that the vast majority of fatalities were noted with individuals who had a stab wound(s) to the chest and head, whereas stab wounds to the abdomen and extremities were much more predictive of survival (Webb, Wyatt, Henry, & Busuttil, 1999). This should make sense due to the vital organs contained in the thoracic cavity. Additionally, significant and deep stab wounds of the head are often fatal. Fig. 7.3 is an example of this where a large chef's knife became lodged in a decedent's head after the decedent was attacked by another individual. The location on the body will also speak how predictive the depth of the wound is when compared to possible weapons.

Depending on where an individual is stabbed will greatly influence the depth of the wound. Since the abdomen has less skeletal structure compared to other areas of the body, such as the thoracic cavity, there could be a very deep stab wound and the weapon used could be something as simple as a small pocket knife. The skin pattern would need to be assessed to see whether there are any identifying marks if the weapon used were questioned. Proper photographs of the possible stab wound, particularly close-range photographs, should always be obtained. This is because if the body begins to decompose or if there is insect activity, the detail of the injury pattern might be lost in the time from when the medicolegal death investigator examines the individual on scene until the decedent can be examined at autopsy by the forensic pathologist.

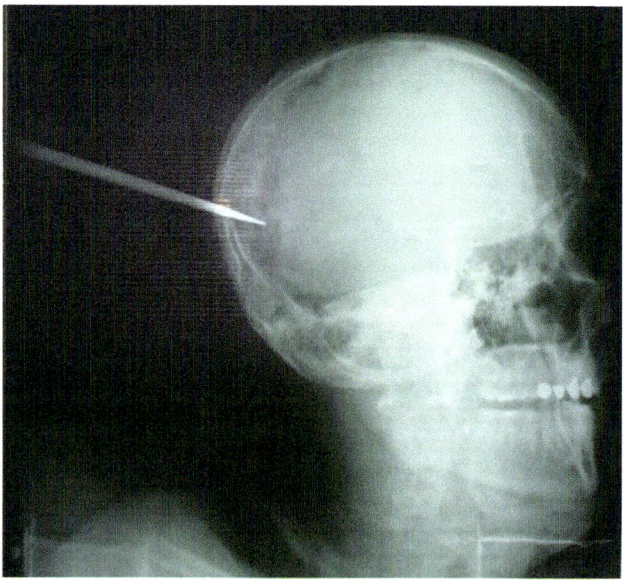

FIGURE 7.3 An example of deep stab wound to the head.

One last thing to consider when examining a possible stab wound on a decedent: depending on the weapon used to produce the sharp-force injury, there could be a hilt mark present. The hilt is essentially a safeguard as part of the handle of knife, dagger, or sword that protects the user's hand from sliding down onto the blade. However, this guard has been known to produce an abrasion and/or contusion where it made contact with the decedent's skin. While not all that common of a finding, they could speak to the type of knife that was used in an assault. Other specialists can also play a pivotal role in helping identifying injury patterns caused by sharp-force objects.

Anthropologists can be extremely useful in the identification of sharp-force injuries when the weapon used creates a defect, or injury, in bone. Molds using Mikrosil or other similar products can be utilized to show the detail of the particular defect. This material sets rather quickly and will provide great definition of the particular defect that you are examining. It can even be viewed under a microscope to help identify minute details. These details can then be compared to a particular weapon to see if there are identifiable characteristics shared between the two. This is no different than a tool mark expert looking at defects left by an object against a surface.

An unusual case involving sharp-force injuries was an instance of multiple nails fired from a nail gun into the decedent's chest and head. The individual was found in his residence by his wife after he left work for the day and did not return. The individual had been experiencing some financial as well as legal problems associated with his company. The decedent had multiple nails in his chest around the area of his heart, and one additional nail in the center of his forehead. The scene and follow-up investigation is important in this instance because if someone was simply presented with a body with these injuries there would be significant concern that the decedent may have been the victim of foul play.

However, the scene findings consisted of the nail gun next to the decedent in his vehicle where he was seated in the garage of his family home. There was also tubing from the exhaust of the vehicle that was feed through the back window of the truck. Lastly, a search of the inside of the home revealed a suicide note. Additionally, interviews with family and colleagues informed investigators of an ongoing investigation into the decedent and his company. All of these findings, in addition to the lack of other identifiable injuries on the decedent that may lead investigators to become concerned about foul play, allowed the manner of death to be properly certified as a suicide.

CHOP WOUNDS

A chop wound is caused when a heavy, usually large, object with a sharp edge creates a wide and deep injury. The object will oftentimes be an axe, machete, or a meat cleaver. These injuries will generally cause significant damage and likely will leave cuts into the bone, if it does not cut completely through the bone. A 10-year retrospective study of homicidal chop wounds revealed that the most common location for this type of injury was to the neck, followed by the head (Ong, 1999). Similar results were seen in a separate retrospective where the most common location of injuries from all sharp-force injuries was the head, face, and neck (Au & Beh, 2011). In areas where there are large bodies of water, the medicolegal death investigator will likely see an atypical chop wound periodically throughout their career.

Boat propellers are also known to cause chop wounds. These are considered chop wounds due to the broad, sharp edges of the propeller and the significant amount of force that they exude from the boat engine. These can cause devastating injuries and even fatalities. They generally appear as a series of wide, deep sharp-force injuries on a decedent's body (Fig. 7.4). An interesting, small, case study done in the Northeastern United States reviewed fatal injuries from boat propellers. They were able to identify common injury patterns and locations on the body that were likely to be life threatening (Semeraro, Passalacqua, Symes, & Gilson, 2012). The findings of this study are important for the medicolegal death investigator to understand because even though some in the research population did not die from their injuries, it outlines which type of wounds is likely to be fatal. Fatal wounds were most common in the head and torso regions. As noted when discussing stab wounds, anthropologists can also be beneficial in determining these types of injuries too when trauma to the skeletal system is present.

As a medicolegal death investigator who is confronted with a scene involving a decedent who has large, deep sharp-force injuries, the knowledge of this type of injury can help identify possible weapons that should be

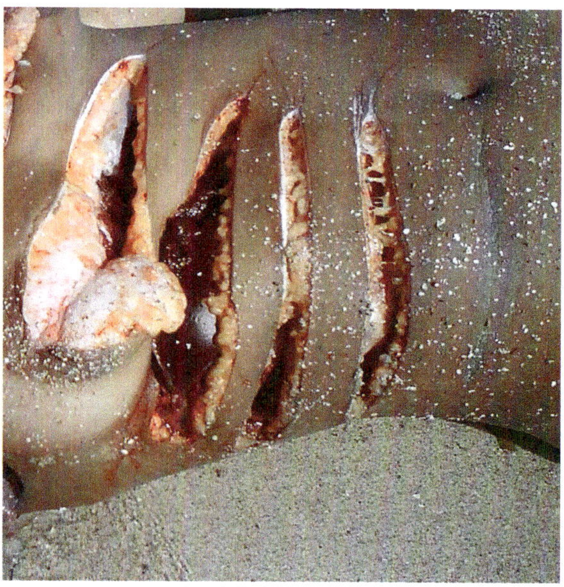

FIGURE 7.4 An example of deep sharp-force injuries.

retained for evidentiary reasons. If the decedent is cared for in a hospital setting prior to death, there is even some information that three-dimensional computed tomography may be a significant tool for forensic pathologist to have at their disposal to help evaluation characteristics of a wound prior to changes caused by medical interventions (Wittschieber, Beck, Vieth, & Hahnemann, 2016). The cause and manner of death can vary greatly with chop wounds depending on the circumstances of the case.

Chop wounds generally cause death by creating significant damage to underlying organs where the injuries are present. As noted above, the most common location for fatal chop wounds is the head and neck. So in these instances, it would be bleeding and damage to the brain, or structures or vasculature of the neck that would cause death. The manner of death in these types of cases is usually either accidents or homicides, with a very rare number being suicides. The individuals who die from objects falling on them or coming into contact with a boat propeller are going to have their manner of death classified as accident. However, a large number of chop wound fatalities are likely homicides.

As with other types of homicides that require the offender and victim to be within a close proximity to one another, the fatal chop wound(s) is not likely to be the only injury present. There will likely be other injuries that demonstrate a struggle on the decedent's hands and arms. Also with homicides, there will likely be multiple, significant injuries to the decedent which are not compatible with life. If the death is a suicide, there may also be multiple defects or injuries noted, but they are generally to the same area. With the exception of a fatal chop wound, the other injuries may have been "practice" wounds similar to a hesitation mark seen with incised wounds. Again, however, it is worth noting that committing suicide with a chop wound is not a prevalent type of case encountered by the medicolegal death investigator (Fig. 7.5).

Quick Reference for SFIs

Incised Wounds

- ✓ Longer than it is deep
- ✓ Rarely fatal
- ✓ Often seen with hesitation marks

Stab Wounds

- ✓ Deeper than it is long
- ✓ Do not examine depth on scene
- ✓ Usually associated with homicides

Chop Wounds

- ✓ Caused by a heavy, sharp object
- ✓ Wound is wide and deep
- ✓ Could be homicide (Axe, machete) or accident (boat propellers)

FIGURE 7.5 A quick reference on the differences between the various types of sharp-force injuries.

REFERENCES

Ambade, V. N., & Godbole, H. V. (2006). Comparison of wound patterns in homicide by sharp and blunt force. *Forensic Science International, 156*(2), 166–170.

Au, K. I., & Beh, S. L. (2011). Injury patterns of sharp instrument homicides in Hong Kong. *Forensic Science International, 204*(1), 201–204.

Berg, R. J., Karamanos, E., Inaba, K., Okoye, O., Teixeira, P. G., & Demetriades, D. (2014). The persistent diagnostic challenge of thoracoabdominal stab wounds. *Journal of Trauma and Acute Care Surgery, 76*(2), 418–423.

Brunel, C., Fermanian, C., Durigon, M., et al. (2010). Homicidal and suicidal sharp force fatalities: autopsy parameters in relation to the manner of death. *Forensic Science International, 198*, 150–154.

Byard, R. W., Klitte, A., Gilbert, J. D., & James, R. A. (2002). Clinicopathologic features of fatal self inflicted incised and stab wounds: a 20 years study. *American Journal of Forensic Medicine and Pathology, 23*, 15–18.

Gill, J. R., & Catanese, C. (2002). Sharp injury fatalities in New York city. *Journal of Forensic Science, 47*(3), 554–557.

Karger, B., & Wennemann, B. (2001). Suicide by more than 90 stab wounds including perforation of the skull. *International Journal of Legal Medicine, 115*, 167–169.

Karlsson, T. (1998). Homicidal and suicidal sharp force fatalities in Stockholm, Sweden. Orientation of entrance wounds in stabs gives information in the classification. *Forensic Science International, 93*, 21–32.

Karlsson, T., Ormstad, K., & Rajs, J. (1988). Patterns in sharp force fatalities: a comprehensive forensic medical study (Part 2), suicidal sharp force injury in the Stockholm area. *Journal of Forensic Science, 33*, 448–461.

Kemal, C. J., Patterson, T., & Molina, D. K. (2013). Deaths due to sharp force injuries in Bexar County, Texas, with respect to manner of death. *American Journal of Forensic Medicine and Pathology, 34*(3), 253–259.

Mazzolo, G. M., & Desinan, L. (2005). Sharp force fatalities: suicide, homicide or accident? A series of 21 cases. *Forensic Science International, 147*, S33–S35.

Ong, B. B. (1999). The pattern of homicidal slash/chop injuries: a 10 year retrospective study in University Hospital Kuala Lumpur. *Journal of Clinical Forensic Medicine, 6*(1), 24–29.

Scolan, V., Telmon, N., Banc, A., et al. (2004). Homicide-suicide by stabbing study over 10 years in the Toulouse region. *American Journal of Forensic Medicine and Pathology, 25*, 33–36.

Semeraro, D., Passalacqua, N. V., Symes, S., & Gilson, T. (2012). Patterns of trauma induced by motorboat and ferry propellers as illustrated by three known cases from Rhode island. *Journal of Forensic Science, 57*(6), 1625–1629.

Watanabe, T., Kobayashi, Y., & Hata, S. (1973). Harakiri and suicide by sharp instrument in Japan. *Forensic Science, 2*, 191–199.

Webb, E., Wyatt, J. P., Henry, J., & Busuttil, A. (1999). A comparison of fatal with non-fatal knife injuries in Edinburgh. *Forensic Science International, 99*(3), 179–187.

Wittschieber, D., Beck, L., Vieth, V., & Hahnemann, M. L. (2016). The role of 3DCT for the evaluation of chop injuries in clinical forensic medicine. *Forensic Science International.*

Chapter 8

Gunshot Wounds

Chapter Outline

Deaths associated from gunshot wounds are almost always classified as suicide or homicide. As with many types of death investigations, the medicolegal death investigator should work collaboratively with other experts on scene and back at the lab to fully examine the findings associated with the scene investigation. These would include, but are not limited to, examining the striations on the projectile(s) and the firing pin, as examples. These findings will be discussed further later on in the chapter. These deaths must also be fully investigated to ensure the scene findings align with the autopsy findings.

A body in a morgue with gunshot wounds does not tell the complete story of the death. Where was the gun located? Was the scene secure when the decedent was found and was the location where the decedent was found orderly? Does it make sense that the decedent was found in this particular location? Were there any findings that would support a possible suicide such as notes or psychiatric medications? There are also cases reported in the literature where there were multiple self-inflicted gunshot wounds to the head (Arunkumar, Maiese, Bolino, & Gitto, 2015). For this reason, the scene findings, in addition to knowing what areas of the body were involved through the autopsy findings, will provide the needed information to determine whether a gunshot wound was self-inflicted or the result of another person's actions. The damage to a decedent's body leading to death relies greatly on a number of factors including the ammunition and firearm type that was used, and the range of fire.

EXAMINATION OF PROJECTILES

For expert opinions on guns and projectiles, the medicolegal death investigator should always consult with a firearms examiner. These individuals are tool

Essentials of Medicolegal Death Investigation. http://dx.doi.org/10.1016/B978-0-12-803641-9.00008-2

mark professionals who focus on firearms and will be able to provide a breadth of information related to deaths that resulted from the use of a firearm. Some of the characteristics that they look at include the caliber, lands, and grooves.

The caliber of a bullet is the diameter of the projectile portion of a cartridge. This corresponds with the diameter of the gun barrel the individual is using. If the projectile is too large for a barrel, it is unlikely that the round would be able to load and be fired. If it did, there would likely be some damage to the barrel. If the round is smaller than the barrel, the round will not fire effectively due to the gap between the cartridge and the inside walls of the barrel. When a proper round is fired from a firearm, except smoothbore firearms which will be discussed shortly, there will be resulting lands and grooves present from the projectile traveling down the length of the barrel.

Lands and grooves on a projectile are created by the rifling of the gun. The rifling is important as it assists the bullet through the barrel by creating spin and improves the accuracy of the gun. Rifling is present for all fired projectiles except for those fired from a smoothbore firearm. In normal medicolegal work, the majority of smoothbore weapons encountered by the investigator are shotguns. For all other firearms regularly encountered, the barrel will have rifling. To understand rifling, you must first understand the difference between class and individual characteristics.

The class characteristics related to the rifling of a gun are the basic features of the lands and grooves of the barrel. A series of barrels made at a particular plant will have very near identical rifling. The lands and grooves will have the same width and twist, which is the direction the rifling turns and the rate at which a projectile rotates in the barrel. This is important to understand from an investigative perspective because if a law enforcement agency is unable to recover the specific firearm they believe was used in a crime, they could compare the class characteristics of the same make and model of a firearm from the same plant that was manufactured around the same time. This is due to the common tool used (there are other methods to creating the barrel) to create the rifling in the barrel. There would be minor differences, but there could at least be a comparison to note whether the firearm the investigators believe was used could still be considered as a possibility. These minor or individual differences are known as the individual characteristics of a firearm's rifling.

The individual characteristics of a firearm's rifling are the minor differences that differentiate one firearm from another, even when it is the same brand and caliber of gun. This could be from the changes over time with the tool used to create the barrel, changes due to use of the firearm, or from intentional destruction. The manipulation of the barrel is not always effective as the underlying rifling marks are likely to remain after a foreign object is introduced into the barrel, such as steel wool, but what the firearms examiner is likely to see is additional markings created by this action. Another way in which a fired projectile can be compared to a gun that potentially fired is by examining the firing pin.

The firing pin leaves a distinct mark on the primer at the bottom of a cartridge. This marking's size and alignment on the primer is consistent across all bullets fired from a particular firearm. This mark is formed when the firing pin, which is a hard metal, makes contact with the primer, which is a softer metal. Another artifact of firing a gun is the breech face marking.

A breech face marking occurs when the cartridge makes contact with the breech face, the area around where the firing pin comes out in the block where round is held in the chamber. When the trigger of the gun is pulled, the bullet is sent down the barrel and out of the gun, but the shell casing fires back against the breech face, thus leaving the mark. It is worth noting here that the breech face marking is not always completely imprinted. So, this particular marking may not always be available for comparison purposes. To understand and speak professionally to the firearm expert, the medicolegal death investigator needs to understand some basic features of a cartridge or bullet.

The specific parts of a bullet can vary to some degree, but the basic features of an unspent cartridge include the following:

- Casing: The outer shell of the cartridge.
- Bullet or projectile: The tip of the cartridge that ends up being the fired product that travels to its intended target. Rifling will be noted on the projectile as a result of traveling through the barrel of the gun.
- Primer: The aspect of the cartridge that creates the necessary energy to ignite the gunpowder when struck by the firing pin.
- Gunpowder: The propellant inside of the cartridge that is ignited by the primer when it is struck by the firing pin. The gunpowder can be in the shape of a ball, flakes which are disklike or rodlike in nature.

There are a number of common types of projectiles that the medicolegal death investigator will encounter, and each has specific features depending on the intended use. The most commonly seen projectiles are lead, semijacketed, full-metal jackets, wadcutter, and semiwadcutter. Some of these are better options if you are looking to cause significant tissue damage such as those who would be using the firearm for hunting, while others are better designed for firing in a range setting.

A lead projectile is a very simple forged bullet that generally has other metals as part of the bullet to improve the functionality. These metals, including tin and antimony, increase the strength of the lead projectile and many are covered in a thin amount of copper to help avoid any deformities from heat when firing the projectile. There are many common types of lead projectiles, and there are two specific variations that are commonly owned by private gun owners.

If an individual is an avid target shooter, it would be very common for them to have what is called a wadcutter round. This particular lead bullet has a flat nose and usually has one or more circumferential grooves around the base of the bullet. These bullets are excellent for making clean marks in the paper targets at a shooting range, but they do not travel well past short ranges. Additionally, the round is not as likely to penetrate as well as a rounded tipped bullet and would not cause the same type of tissue damage as other types of bullets, like hollow points. Similarly, there are semiwadcutter bullets that have similar features but some important differences.

A semiwadcutter bullet could easily be confused for a wadcutter, but there are slight structural differences. There is a flat nose just like a wadcutter, but with a semiwadcutter bullet there is an actual nose even though the tip is not rounded. Due to this slight difference, the bullet travels a little better and might be more likely to be used for hunting purposes. The blunted nose still makes it a common round for shooting at a range, particularly with revolver-style handguns. A more common round encountered by the medicolegal death investigator is that of a hollow-point bullet.

Hollow-point bullets are particularly dangerous and are not even legal in a number of settings. This, however, is not the case in the United States as very few types of hollow-point ammunition and in very few jurisdictions is this particular bullet illegal. A hollow point has a hollowed out aspect to the tip of the bullet that allows it to expand when it comes in contact with a target. The important things for the medicolegal death investigator to understand about this type of ammunition include the following:

1. When it makes contact with an individual, the hollowed out tip mushrooms open.
2. This mushrooming causes significant tissue damage.
3. The mushrooming also decreases the distance the round can travel.
4. As a result of this inability to perforate the body, many of these rounds will have the potential to be recovered inside of the decedent's body at autopsy.

When a hollow-point bullet is fired into either a gel or a water chamber in a laboratory setting, the bullet will still mushroom when it makes contact with a surface. Many rounds of ammunition today, including ones that are hollow point, are jacketed.

There are two types of jacketed bullets, full-metal and semijacket. A full-metal jacket is simply a complete covering of a bullet, usually lead, to provide it greater strength and higher velocity as it is loaded and fired compared to a nonjacketed lead bullet. A semijacketed round is usually associated with hollow-point ammunition and in addition to helping improve velocity, they can also be designed to aid in the mushrooming. Shotgun ammunition has different characteristics due to the smoothbore nature of this type of firearm.

Shotgun ammunition is measured differently than ammunition used in a handgun or rifle. Instead of measuring the diameter of a barrel or projectile, the gauge of shotgun is measured by the number of lead spheres of a particular bore diameter that would equal one pound. The specific parts of a shotgun round are also different than those of a cartridge. A shotgun round consists of the following:

- Casing: the outer shell of the round which is usually made of a paper tube or plastic.
- Projectiles: the spheres that are contained within the shotgun casing. Additionally, with a shotgun there could be a solid shell instead of the multiple spheres.
- Primer: the bottom center aspect of the shotgun round that creates the necessary energy to ignite the gunpowder when struck by the firing pin.
- Gunpowder: the propellant inside the shotgun round that is ignited by the primer when it is struck by the firing pin. The gunpowder can be in the shape of a ball, flakes which are disklike or rodlike in nature.
- Wadding: a component that separates the gunpowder from the spheres or slug. This is an important feature that protects the projectile(s) from the blast to ensure proper firing. The wad can be made of cotton, felt, paper products, or plastic.

There are a few types of shotgun shot that the medicolegal death investigator should be familiar with. They are birdshot, buckshot, and slugs. Each has their own intended use as well as unique features.

A birdshot, as the name suggests, is used mostly for hunting various fowl as well as smaller mammals. The small, round shots within the shotgun's shell travel well and are usually made of lead. However, some are made of steel, tungsten, or bismuth. Regardless of the shot's metal, if it is used against a decedent, one will likely find many of the pellets within the decedent's body. Fig. 8.1 shows the components of one particular type of birdshot shotgun shell. If the decedent is shot from a distance, the medicolegal death investigator will likely see a pattern of multiple, small circular defects on the individual's body. Distance from the shooter and the victim is important with birdshot. If an individual is shot at close range, the injuries can be severe and similar to those seen with a rifle if the shot is concentrated. If there is greater distance between the shooter and the victim, the injuries will likely be less severe (Ordog, Wasserberger, & Balasubramaniam, 1988). Buckshot is different in that even if there is more of a distance between the shooter and the victim, there is still likely to be significant trauma.

Buckshot ammunition is similar to birdshot in that there are multiple, round pellets inside the shotgun shell, but buckshot is a much larger pellet with an accompanying filler to help improve the shot pattern once the round has been fired. The filler is important not just for the improved accuracy of the shot, but for the medicolegal death investigator. This filler could be found on a decedent and could produce stippling (DiMaio, 1999). Like birdshot, when there is very little distance between the shooter and the victim there will likely

FIGURE 8.1 Components of one particular type of birdshot shotgun shell.

be a single, large circular defect for an entrance wound. Unlike birdshot, if there is a greater distance between the shooter and the victim there will still be multiple, circular defects but they are more likely to be deadly due to the sheer size of the shot. Lastly, slug ammunition for a shotgun is a less common round and has different injury patterns from that of the shots previously discussed.

A shotgun slug is commonly utilized for hunting larger animals and would create significant damage if used against a human. Instead of the area above the wadding having pellets, there is a slug which is usually made of lead or steel (Fig. 8.2). This slug has grooves in it that resemble rifling marks but instead are designed into the round to improve its reliability in flight toward its intended target. The result of an individual being struck with this type of a round is a circular defect noted on the skin where it entered, and there is usually an abraded area around the entrance wound. The internal damage is significant for any tissues that happen to be in the path of the projectile. This can be made even more severe if the particular slug is also a hollow point. Another type of slug to consider is the one that is commonly used by law enforcement, the less than lethal shotgun slug.

Less than lethal shotguns utilize a slug but instead of the round being made of lead or steel, it will be made of rubber. Even though this is considered a less than lethal round, it can still be fatal. Multiple articles have illustrated that these rounds can be fatal, particularly when they are fired from a close range, involve the head, or cause trauma in the area of the

FIGURE 8.2 A wadding made of lead or steel.

heart (Hiss, Hellman, & Kahana, 1997; Kobayashi, & Mellen, 2009). The findings that the medicolegal death investigator will see on scene are often large, circular abrasion.

One additional point of emphasis regarding the wadding that has previously been mentioned is the presence of this component with a shotgun wound. If the range of fire was contact or close, the wadding will likely be found within the wound track and should be documented and recovered. Additionally, some slug shotgun round are secured to the wadding so that these too will likely be located even if the range of fire were greater.

TYPES OF FIREARMS

Understanding the different types of firearms is an important study as each can present their own unique findings on scene and at autopsy. Firearm purchases in the United States are currently at a feverish pace. In 2015 alone there were 23 million National Instant Criminal Background Check System (NICS) checks performed for firearm purchases (Lynch, 2016). Making this more impressive of a number is that this does not account for the total number of sales in the United States as many ways in which a firearm could be sold do not require a background check. The types of firearm used in fatal events can vary greatly depending on the jurisdiction. In a rural area where hunting is prevalent, the majority of cases encountered will likely involve shotguns and revolvers, and the medicolegal death investigator might have a low incident of handgun fatalities. Conversely, if a medicolegal death investigator works in an urban environment, they may see a significant number of handgun-related fatalities, and they may rarely come across a shotgun- or rifle-related death. Regardless of the prevalence, there remains a need to be knowledgeable in all types of firearms. The four types of firearms that this text will explore are handguns, revolvers, rifles, and shotguns.

Handguns

Depending on where one lives, handguns could be very prevalent. It is estimated that there are at least 14 million handguns that are privately owned in the United States (Krouse, 2012). The majority of Americans buy handguns for personal protection and to target shot. They are designed to be concealable and portable. Due to this function, handguns are designed to be lightweight. Handguns as a class of firearm can be broken down into multiple subgroups, one of which is revolvers which will be discussed in the next section. Two others which we will discuss in this section are single-shot and semiautomatic handguns.

Single shot simply means that after each round is fired from the chamber another round must be manually loaded before another round can be fired. For this reason, single-shot handguns are not a popular commercial product. If the purpose of purchasing a handgun is for self-defense, it stands to reason that a firearm that has to be manually reloaded would not be a popular option.

Semiautomatic handguns, unlike a single shot, will eject the spent cartridge from the chamber and load another round. While this is a better self-defense option for obvious reasons, it does create a situation where the user would likely need more experience with the firearm to properly use it.

Revolvers

A revolver is a subtype of handgun. Instead of a magazine, the bullets are loaded into a cylinder which will usually hold either five or six bullets at one time. While the revolver is a simpler setup which is relatively easy for the user to learn, it does limit the number of shots that can be quickly fired.

When the cylinder rotates, the chamber with a loaded bullet aligns with the firing pin. There are multiple types of revolvers that are sold, but the most common that the medicolegal death investigator will encounter is one that swings out to allow for loading and unloading. There is a cylinder latch that when pressed will allow for the swing action. Two important things to note regardless of the type of revolver is the location of the spent round compared to the cylinder space that is lined up with the firing pin, and know whether the cylinder rotates clockwise or counterclockwise. The rotation of the cylinder is dependent on the brand of firearm. If it is a commonly used revolver, a firearms examiner should be able to tell you on scene which direction the cylinder rotates. If not, it can be easily looked up through the manufacturer once back at the office.

Rifles

A rifle has a longer barrel, most commonly utilizes a bolt action, and is more accurate than handguns. The vast majority of rifles are used for hunting; however, there are military-style semiautomatic or automatic rifles like the AK-47 that the medicolegal death investigator will undoubtedly encounter at some point in their career. Most rifles that will commonly be found on a scene will not be of the semiautomatic or automatic variety, also called assault rifles, but instead will be a single shot that requires the shooter to manually load another round as opposed to the rounds being magazine feed. From this author's experience, if a single-action rifle is found to have been used in a death investigation, it is almost always to commit suicide.

Shotguns

A shotgun, like a rifle, is a long barrel firearm. Unlike a rifle, a shotgun has a smoothbore barrel. The use of shotguns in homicides and suicides is common depending on the area of the country one works. The location of injury tends to also be dependent on the manner of death, to some degree. If the death is a suicide, the injury is almost always to the head. If the death is a homicide, the injury could also still be to the head but is also common to the chest and abdomen (Molina, Wood, & DiMaio, 2007). As with all firearms, there are a number of different types or actions of shotguns.

The three most common types of shotguns that are encountered include the break action, pump action, and semiautomatic. The break action is a very common type of shotgun where the barrel hinges open near the stock end of the gun. There are usually two barrels with this type of shotgun, and they can either be side by side or stacked. The pump action and the semiautomatic differ in that there is a tube magazine built into the gun that is manually loaded by the user.

For the pump action, these shotguns tend to have shorter barrels and are used by hunters as well as by many law enforcement agencies. To rack another live round into the chamber, the user must manually pull back on the pump action of the shotgun to load the next round. For the inexperienced user, there could be issues with not fully pulling back on the pump action which would result in a round not being chambered, and the inexperienced user is also likely to be slower at using this type of shotgun versus a semiautomatic one.

A semiautomatic, like we already mentioned, has a built-in tube magazine that allows for multiple fired rounds before the shooter must manually reload. Unlike the pump action that requires the shooter to manually perform a movement to load another round, the semiautomatic shotguns load the next round through the action of the gun being fired. The only exception to this is to manually chamber the first round.

One last comment regarding firearms is that there are basic identifiers that need to be recorded on every scene of investigation where a firearm is used and is present. The brand, caliber, serial number, and ammunition information will need to be recorded. The information on the ammunition should include how many spent shell casings there are, how many unspent rounds are in the gun still, and what ammunition is found on the scene. If the box with the ammunition information is present that is helpful, but most ammunition that is encountered will have a stamp at the base of the cartridge (Fig. 8.3), which traditionally identifies the caliber of ammunition as well as who the manufacturer is.

FIGURE 8.3 An example of the stamp at the base of the cartridge.

RANGE OF FIRE

One of most important questions associated with firearm deaths is what was the range of fire. There is not an exact measurement, as it varies depending on the type of firearm used. However, there are some basic findings associated with each category that help identify the specific range. The four basic ranges that will be discussed will be contact, close, intermediate, and distant.

Contact gunshot wounds are those in which the end of the barrel, or muzzle, is touching the skin when it is fired. This will cause the formation of a circular defect on the skin, and there may also be an impression or abrasion that is left on the skin from the muzzle. Depending on the type of gun there may also be a pattern on the skin consistent with other features of the muzzle. This can be seen in Fig. 8.4 where the outline of the muzzle can clearly be

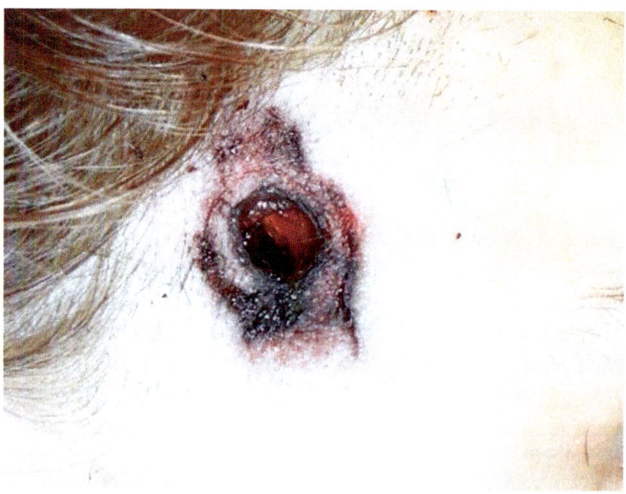

FIGURE 8.4 An example of patterns on the skin consistent with other features of a firearm muzzle.

seen. These markings, in some instances, can aid in identifying the firearm that was used. All of the soot from the fired projectile will be located within the circular defect, and the circular defect itself will have a slight abrasion around the edges of the wound. Additionally, there may be tearing of the skin outward from the circular defect. It is sometimes referred to as a star shaped laceration which is caused from tearing due to the gas expansion from the gun. With a gunshot wound that is not in contact with the skin, these gases simply dissipate into the ambient environment. However, when there is a contact gunshot wound these gases are forced into the body and the expansion, particularly when up against a boney surface, will cause the tearing as there is nowhere else for it to go.

Close-range gunshot wounds will have a circular defect with slight abrasions around the defect from the projectile forcing itself through the skin just like a contact gunshot wound; however, there will not be an abraded pattern from the muzzle as the gun was not touching the skin at the time it was fired. Additionally, the soot patterns are slightly different. Like a contact gunshot wound, there will be soot within the wound but there will also be soot around the outside of the wound on the skin. It is important to note there that the shoot and gunpowder markings on the outside of the wound will be concentrated, and there will not be markings consistent with stippling, which is the classic finding of an intermediate-range gunshot wound.

Intermediate gunshot wounds are unique in that stippling is present on the body surfaces around where the entrance wound is found. This is formed by the cone of gunpowder that exits behind the bullet as it is fired, which can be seen in Fig. 8.5. The presence of this gunshot powder can be checked on a decedent or suspect's hand by doing a gunshot residue test (Fig. 8.6) but this is

FIGURE 8.5 An example of the cone of gunpowder after a gun is fired.

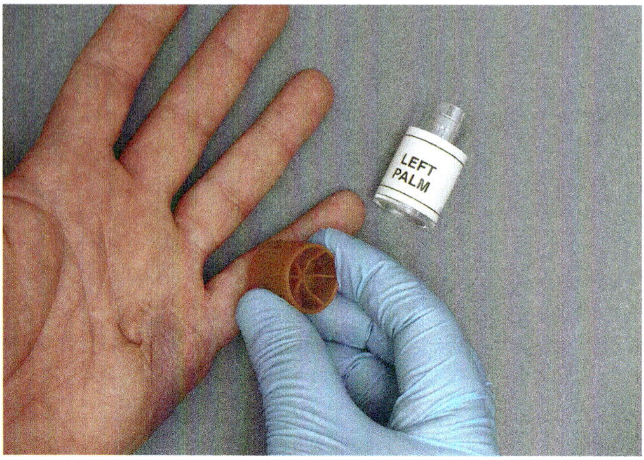

FIGURE 8.6 An example of gunshot residue test.

not routinely done anymore by crime labs for various reasons. When the gun is sufficiently far enough away from the decedent when it is fired this powder can spread out causing this powder tattooing. With a close-range gunshot wound there is not enough distance from the muzzle to the skin to cause these small, spots on the skin. This stippling does not easily wash off of the surface of the body as it is not simply a powder, but a small abrasion from the particles hitting the skin (Fig. 8.7). Lastly, soot is quite a bit less likely to be present,

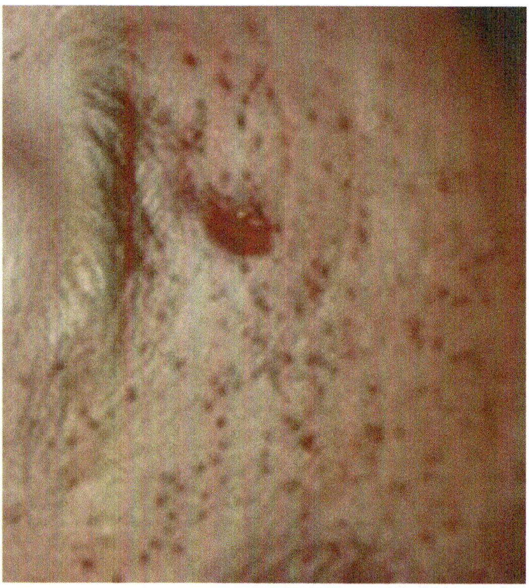

FIGURE 8.7 An example of small abrasions from the particles hitting the skin.

particularly as the spread of the stippling increases. Stippling would not be present when there is too great of a distance between the muzzle and the entrance wound, as the powder particles can only travel so far.

Distant gunshot wounds are identifiable for what is not appreciated by the medicolegal death investigator. Meaning, there will be a circular defect for the entrance wound with the slightly abraded edges, but no soot or stippling will be present for the reason already stated. The logical question to ask at this point is what distances make up each range. The answer is, it depends. The distance from which a wound is considered a close, intermediate, or distant range of fire depends on the type of firearm as well as how well as the manner in which the gun is cleaned and maintained. Because of this, it is better for the medicolegal death investigator to know the hallmarks of the different ranges, and leave measuring the distance in which the muzzle of a gun was from the skin to a firearms examiner who could attempt to recreate the patterns noted by the medicolegal death investigator and the forensic pathologist in a laboratory setting (Fig. 8.8).

The discussion so far has focused on entrance wounds, but it is quite common that multiple gunshot wounds are present on a decedent and in different areas of the body. When this occurs, the discussion on scene will inevitably turn to determining the entrance versus exit wounds. The easiest way to determine on scene (there are other methods that the forensic pathologist will employ while performing the autopsy, such as looking at beveling) what is an entrance and what is an exit wound is to look at the defect itself.

Quick Reference for Entrance Wounds

Contact

- ✓ Abraded edges
- ✓ Soot is inside the wound
- ✓ Possibly an abraded injury pattern from the muzzle of the firearm

Close

- ✓ Abraded edges
- ✓ Soot is inside the wound as well as on the skin around the wound
- ✓ No stippling

Intermediate

- ✓ Abraded edges
- ✓ The identifying feature is the presence of stippling

Distant

- ✓ Abraded edges
- ✓ No soot in or around the wound
- ✓ No stippling present

FIGURE 8.8 A quick reference on the differences between the various types of entrance gunshot wounds.

Entrance wounds, unless the projectile is entering the skin at a very low angle, will have a nice circular defect. This defect, if the investigator were to put pressure on the skin around the wound would not cause the opening to close. With an exit wound, the shape is generally irregular or has a slit-like appearance. When pressure is put on the skin around an exit wound the tissues will generally line up and the wound will "close." The irregular shape is caused by the yaw and tumbling of the bullet as it passes through tissue. Additionally, the entrance wound will have the abraded edges that have already been discussed, and exit wounds will not have this feature. There is, however, one exception to this and that is when there is a shored exit.

A shored exit occurs when a projectile is attempting to exit a decedent's body, and the area where the projectile is exiting is pressed up against a firm surface. This causes an abrasion around the wound but unlike an entrance wound that has a slight abrasion around the defect caused by the projectile, this abrasion pattern is often larger and irregular.

One last point to make regarding identifying the range of fire on scene is that often times there will be blood that is covering and sometimes has dried over and around the entrance wound. This should never be cleaned and the wound or the inside of the wound should not be palpated to aid in the identification of the range on scene. This may destroy or distort evidence. So, if the medicolegal death investigator is unsure as to the range of fire it is the best practice to allow the wound to be examined and cleaned at the time of autopsy by the forensic pathologist.

REFERENCES

Arunkumar, P., Maiese, A., Bolino, G., & Gitto, L. (2015). Determined to die! Ability to act following multiple self inflicted gunshot wounds to the head. The Cook County Office of the Medical Examiner experience (2005–2012) and review of the literature. *Journal of Forensic Sciences, 60*(5), 1373–1379.

DiMaio, V. J. M. (1999). *Gunshot Wounds: Practical Aspects of Firearms, Ballistics, and Forensic Techniques* (second ed.). Boca Raton, FL: CRC Press.

Hiss, J., Hellman, F. N., & Kahana, T. (1997). Rubber and plastic ammunition lethal injuries: the Israeli experience. *Medicine, Science and the Law, 37*(2), 139–144.

Kobayashi, M., & Mellen, P. F. (2009). Rubber bullet injury: case report with autopsy observation and literature review. *The American Journal of Forensic Medicine and Pathology, 30*(3), 262–267.

Krouse, W. J. (November 14, 2012). *'How Many Guns Are in the United States? – Number.' Gun Control Legislation* (pp. 8–9). Washington, DC: United States Congressional Research Service.

Lynch, L. (January 20, 2016). *Senate Appropriations Committee*. Washington, DC.

Molina, D. K., Wood, L. E., & DiMaio, V. J. (2007). Shotgun wounds: a review of range and location as pertaining to manner of death. *The American Journal of Forensic Medicine and Pathology, 28*(2), 99–102.

Ordog, G. J., Wasserberger, J., & Balasubramaniam, S. (1988). Shotgun wound ballistics. *Journal of Trauma and Acute Care Surgery, 28*(5), 624–631.

Chapter 9

Toxicology Deaths

Chapter Outline

The general public's awareness of toxicological deaths has increased dramatically with the rise in prescription drug abuse and in particular, heroin deaths. This is especially concerning as deaths from illicit drugs have increased in populations that do not traditionally see high incidents of abuse. Drugs were often thought of as a city problem, but are making their way into normal life in rural America. The average heroin user, as an example, now tends to be a nonurban Caucasian male (Kuehn, 2014). Much of the increase seen in heroin usage is believed to be the result of previously seen increases in opioid abuse (CDC, 2011). This could be seen as an unintended consequence of medical systems viewing pain management as the best way to improve patient care ratings.

The heroin example, much like other drugs of abuse that we will discuss in this chapter, illustrates that these types of deaths do not occur within a vacuum. Oftentimes the medicolegal death investigator will encounter a history of environmental, socioeconomic, criminal, or medical factors that may increase the likelihood that an individual began to abuse drugs of any kind in the first place. These examples of supporting information are essential to identify and record as factors that lead to the decedent's death today from an overdose. Like suicide, there is often a stigma associated with these types of deaths. To provide a covictim with all of the information associated with why a death was ruled a particular way, these supporting pieces of information will be paramount as many family members may struggle with the idea that their loved one was abusing drugs. For these reasons, a thorough scene investigation is essential in the determination of cause and manner of death associated with toxicological deaths.

SCENE INVESTIGATION

The scene of a toxicological death will yield many clues, in particular, as to the manner of death. An autopsy and blood work alone can easily reveal the

Essentials of Medicolegal Death Investigation. http://dx.doi.org/10.1016/B978-0-12-803641-9.00009-4

cause of death for a decedent, but without a proper scene investigation it will be difficult to fully understand the circumstances surrounding an individual's death. This includes doing a thorough body examination to look for signs of repeated abuse, searching for all medications, illicit drugs, and drug paraphernalia, and obtaining a detailed past medical and social history.

The body examination of the decedent can reveal a number of clues about the individual's overall health status and signs of abuse. When performing a body examination on anyone, but particularly someone who is suspected for drug overdose, there should be special attention paid to areas where individuals traditionally inject illicit drugs. This includes the neck, the arms particularly in the antecubital fossa region, and the dorsal aspect of the hands. What medicolegal death investigators are generally looking for are puncture marks, which sometimes are accompanied by minor contusions, and track marks. Track marks are simply old puncture marks that are discolored and scars have formed. The track marks depicted in Fig. 9.1 is an obvious sign to the medicolegal death investigator that someone was a chronic intravenous drug user. The decedent's overall health appearance can also provide insight into how someone lived their life.

When examining someone who is a chronic drug abuser, their overall health presentation can provide an initial indication that someone may have been abusing drugs. While certainly not always the case, individuals who are chronic drug abusers can present quite thin or gaunt and have signs that they have lived an unkempt lifestyle such as poor dental hygiene. Their skin could also appear jaundice from liver disease as hepatitis is a common disease associated with intravenous drug use. Their living environment is also likely to appear unkempt due to the user's need for constantly seeking drugs to feed their addiction. A search of the living environment is an essential piece of the

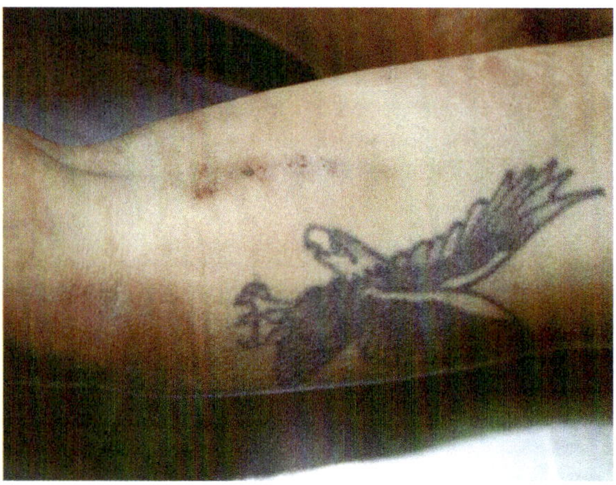

FIGURE 9.1 An example of track marks left by drug use.

scene investigation to continue to build support for or against an individual abusing medications of illicit drugs.

When searching the residence of a suspected drug user, particularly one that is known to abuse drugs intravenously, the medicolegal death investigator must have their own safety as a priority. This is only made a more difficult task if the decedent did have an unkempt living environment. Family members and other covictims can sometimes be a good resource to ask about where someone generally kept their medications or drugs of abuse. This is more likely the scenario with prescription medications as people will generally keep those together in one location. Areas such as the bathroom cabinet, night stands, and the kitchen generally are locations where these type of drugs are found. If the medicolegal death investigator is searching for illicit drugs and drug paraphernalia, this may be a more difficult task especially if the decedent lived with others. One such case from the author's experience was a married man in his early thirties that was using heroin intravenously. His wife knew that he had previously abused prescription pain medications, but was completely unaware when the topic of intravenous drug use was broached. Their apartment was neat and orderly with no signs of illicit drug use. However, a detailed search of the decedent's personal clothing closet revealed multiple syringes with needs and multiple, small bags of heroin in a tennis shoe box. Conversely, this author has also been to multiple residences where the decedent's drug use was widely known and was even at a scene where the decedent's bedroom floor was nearly completely covered with used syringes. The need to do a detailed scene search is even more important as more and more older adults are abusing medications and drugs. Without finding possible evidence of abuse, some of these cases could be signed out as a natural death and no autopsy with toxicology would be performed.

If possible drugs or drug paraphernalia are recovered on scene, they should be stored and inventoried as previously described in this text in the event that testing ever needs to be completed on a substance or item. Many people will remember the Conrad Murray trial regarding the death of Michael Jackson, and how everything related to the propofol found on scene was tested, including fingerprinting the individual vials. This is not likely the case; however, the evidence should still be collected in case it ever became necessary to test it. Additionally, there is a public health and safety aspect to collecting these items to help remove them from the general public. Once the medicolegal death investigator has completed a body examination and a search of the scene has been completed, there needs to be a detailed and focused interview of the family members and covictims present.

Performing a detailed medical and social history is essential to understanding the decedent's history with using and/or abusing drugs. Previously in the text it has been mentioned that knowing a decedent's documented medical history could be the difference between needing to bring that person in for an autopsy, or having their primary care provider sign the death certificate based on their history and releasing the decedent to a mortuary directly from the scene. The medical history can also reveal a recent change in the decedent's health status. This includes a social history regarding alcohol, drugs, and tobacco, but should also include their psychiatric history which could speak to the manner of death.

It has also been discussed that a decedent's social history includes a number of factors including substances they used and/or abuse, as well as the lifestyle they lived. The three main social issues a medicolegal death investigator should know on every case are if the decedent used tobacco, drank alcohol, and abused prescription or recreational drugs. If there is a known or suspicion of substance abuse, more pointed questions about this issue should be asked. They include how long the decedent has been abusing the substance, the various substances that they were known to use, and whether the decedent had sought treatment for their substance abuse and if they had, where specifically were they treated at. Lastly, the family and covictims should be asked if the decedent had ever overdosed before, and if they had, was it an intentional act. The family and covictim statements should be collected, but the decedent's full medical records from providers as well as treatment facilities should still be collected to have a more complete picture of the decedent's health and history of substance abuse.

As the investigation into a decedent's death draws to a conclusion, it is important to understand that this history is only one piece of the puzzle. The forensic pathologist will eventually have to weigh the scene findings, medical history, and autopsy findings including the toxicology report to determine the cause and manner of death. It is the function of the medicolegal death investigator, as with any death, to provide the most complete picture possible of the death of an individual.

COLLECTION OF SAMPLES

While certain cases necessitate further blood or tissue samples, there are a series of generally accepted standard items that should be collected on every autopsied case. Multiple blood samples are generally collected and the preferred site is from the femoral vessels. This has to do with how certain substances are dispersed postmortem. Specifically, the femoral vessels are not in close proximity to other organs and are not likely to be as easily affected by contamination. If blood is not feasible from the femoral vessels, subclavian blood is the next best option, then heart blood. At times, it might be not possible for blood to be collected from a traditional site. Pooled blood in the thoracic cavity can be collected, but the quality is not ideal for interpretation by the forensic pathologist. Regardless of the site drawn, blood and all other samples that will be collected must be properly labeled with where the sample was drawn from, by whom, and the case it is associated with. Some medicolegal offices track this manually while other, larger offices may take

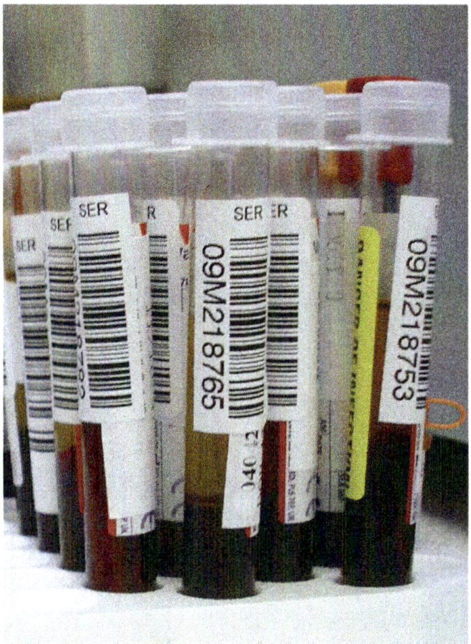

FIGURE 9.2 An example of barcode tracking system for screening and tracking blood.

advantage of a barcode tracking system like what is shown in Fig. 9.2. If blood from any source is not an option, tissue from the liver of skeletal muscle could be used, particularly if the body has been badly damaged due to trauma or from advanced decomposition. In addition to blood, urine and vitreous humor should be collected on every case.

Urine is traditionally measured for a total volume count on cases that are autopsied. Of this, some will need to be collected for analysis. The analysis of urine is generally a qualitative one; meaning the testing of the urine is simply looking for the presence of certain drugs of abuse. Some offices will use quick dip stick tests to see if certain drugs are present prior to sending blood for full toxicology testing. This is not a best practice as some substances may not be present in the urine or the test might not be sensitive enough to detect it. Thus, possible cases that involve toxicology as a possible contributing factor could be overlooked. Some offices will also use the dip sticks to give them a presumptive cause of death while they await the full toxicology workup. Dip sticks are also sometimes done to test for the presence of ketones in individuals with diabetes.

Lastly, vitreous humor should be collected on all cases, when practicable. Obviously, if a decedent is decomposed the chances of recovering this sample are minimal. However, it can provide useful information. Certain drugs, such as cocaine, will remain in the vitreous humor after they are no longer present in the blood or urine. Additionally, vitreous levels are often used for comparison for ethanol levels if the person was believed to be drinking around their time of death. The levels in the vitreous will be compared to the blood and urine to determine if they were drinking at the time of their death or a period before their death. As an example, blood alcohol levels that are lower than urine levels may indicate that the decedent had stopped drinking prior to his death, but had drank around the time of his death. If levels are still elevated in the vitreous humor but lower in the blood and urine, it could indicate that the decedent had drunk a few hours prior to their death, but the individual had not drunk in the perimortem period. Lastly, vitreous humor is used if there is a concern that the individual had an electrolyte imbalance. If this is the case, the vitreous humor can be tested for chloride, creatinine, glucose, potassium, sodium, and urea nitrogen.

The medicolegal death investigator's role in the performance of autopsies and collecting toxicological samples at the medical examiner or coroner office depend greatly on the jurisdiction in which they work. Regardless, it is important to understand what samples are collected and why. One example of a blood test that medicolegal death investigators will often do prior to the autopsy is to test for carbon monoxide.

The blood sample is generally taken from the femoral vessels or the subclavian vein, and a quick test for the presence and levels of carboxyhemoglobin is done. The resulting percentage of carboxyhemoglobin must be weighed against the individual's health. Research has shown that smokers can have at least 6–7% at all times (Hill, Haley & Wynder, 1983). Levels less than 30% tend to only exhibit neurologic symptoms (DiNenno et al., 1995), but these levels could be fatal in someone with continuous exposure and a history of severe chronic health conditions such as chronic obstructive pulmonary disease (COPD).

If a decedent receives an external examination instead of being autopsied, there still should be similar items collected. Femoral blood, urine through a suprapubic stick utilizing a long needle, and vitreous humor should still be collected, tested, and stored. That being said, a complete autopsy should always be the gold standard for a suspected drug overdose. The reason being, if the toxicology comes back negative or the results are borderline between toxic and fatal, the body has long been released and the opportunity to evaluation and the possibility of other causes of death are gone. One of the only reasons why an autopsy should not be performed in these instances is if there is a strong religious objection. Even then, the topic of an autopsy should still be discussed in detail with the family and why it is important for the procedure to be completed.

ILLICIT DRUGS OF ABUSE

Illicit drug abuse is a significant public health issue in the United States. While many drugs are abused, the text will focus on three street drugs that the medicolegal death investigator is likely to see on a regular basis. They are heroin, cocaine, and methamphetamine.

Heroin has become an epidemic in some parts of the United States. It has even increased in demographics not traditionally accustomed to such drug abuse such as women and higher-income individuals. In fact, individuals who use abuse opioid pain medication are 40% more likely to use heroin, and individuals who use cocaine are around 15% more like compared to the general population (NSDUH, 2014). The problem has become so bad that it is not uncommon to find Naloxone kits being carried and used on the streets by law enforcement officers. For the medicolegal death investigator, they should be aware of what the substance looks like, how it is used by the individual, and what other heath issues the individual may have as a result of their drug use.

Heroin on scene will generally appear in one of the three ways. Depending on how it is made, heroin can appear as a light brown powder, a white powder (Fig. 9.3), or as a black viscous substance. Additionally, there will generally be paraphernalia present for those who use the drug intravenously. In addition to a small needle and syringe (possibly multiple on scene), a spoon and lighter will likely be recovered too. This is due to the fact that the heroin is melted on the spoon. The drug is oftentimes crushed into a finer powder if it is not already and mixed with water. Once this is heated up the heroin becomes easier to draw into the syringe for injection. In addition to using heroin intravenously, it can also be smoked or snorted. However, these are less likely to be the route of choice due to the difference in the rush felt by the user.

There are a number of health concerns for individuals who use heroin. In addition to the obvious, which is that heroin is an opioid drug that is highly addictive, there are a number of infectious diseases that a heroin user could likely have as a result of their intravenous use. These include HIV and hepatitis. Additionally, there is the risk of serious blood infections due to multiple

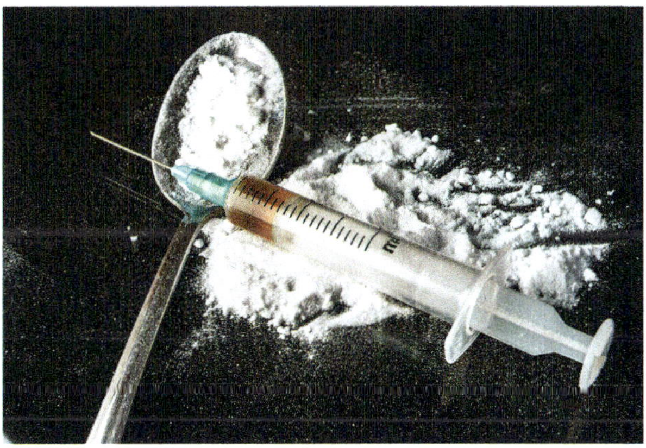

FIGURE 9.3 An example of heroin.

injections with a needle that is highly unlikely to be sterile. Knowing these complications associated with heroin abuse, the medicolegal death investigator should be careful when examining a decedent with a known drug history for their own safety.

Cocaine has also had resurgence as of late; there was a steady decrease in cocaine related fatalities until 2010 when the trend reversed and since that time cocaine deaths have been on the rise (CDC, 2015). This is in contrast to drug abuse patterns associated with other common drugs of abuse, both street drugs and prescription drugs. As such, knowing what cocaine looks like and how is it used is important.

Cocaine is a fine, white crystal powder substance that can be injected like heroin, but is usually snorted. Its use is often associated with higher-income individuals although crack cocaine is a less pure form of the drug, generally cut with baking soda, which is cheaper to purchase and is oftentimes smoked with a pipe. Regardless of how it is used, cocaine can have significant health effects for those who use it.

While cocaine generally does not cause significant damage to organ systems the way other substances do, it still can cause changes and be deadly. Snorting of cocaine damages the blood vessels in the nose and over time can create a septal perforation. As a result, many individuals will experience persistent nose bleeds. More than the issues associated with where the drug enters the body, cocaine can cause significant issues that could lead to death including coronary artery spasms which could restrict the blood flow to the heart. In individuals with atherosclerotic cardiovascular disease this could be fatal due to the already restricted blood flow due to plaque buildup. Lastly, cocaine and alcohol in an individual's body at the same time creates cocaethylene which has the potential for a prolonged high, but evidence has shown that it can cause greater toxic effects on the heart than just cocaine alone (Wilson, Jeromin,Garvey, & Dorbandt, 2001). For these reasons, as have been previously discussed in the cause and manner of death chapter information, individuals who test positive for cocaine or more commonly a metabolite of cocaine, benzoylecgonine, will have their death certificate signed out as an accidental death instead of a natural one.

Methamphetamine is a central nervous system stimulant that comes in a couple of different forms, crystal and powder. Crystal meth is commonly referred to as a rock and has an off-white appearance. The other form is that of more of a powdery substance, which is an off-white or light tan color. The drug is generally snorted, smoked, or injected. Regardless of the route, the effects are the same on the body.

Complications of methamphetamine abuse ranges from evidence of poor hygiene such as poor teeth to cardiovascular complications. While the poor dentition might be a first sign of drug abuse for the medicolegal death investigator, understanding the effects on the body internally is even more important. Methamphetamine as a stimulant is known to increase the breathing, heart rate, and blood pressure in individuals who abuse the drug; additionally, it can cause hyperthermia. The increases seen in an individual's heart rate and blood pressure can be the catalyst for the development of an arrhythmia which of course could be fatal if not addressed. Additionally, the increased body temperature could cause seizures, which too could be fatal. These individuals can go on prolonged binges where they do not eat or drink properly due to loss of appetite, and they might also be awake for multiple days at a time.

PRESCRIPTION DRUG ABUSE

Prescription drug abuse is on the rise in the United States, just as it is with illicit drug abuse. There are a number of reasons for why prescription drug abuse could be on the rise, but a lot of it could be the result of a cultural shift where we take a pill every time there is a "problem." Additionally, with an increased focus on patient satisfaction surveys many health-care systems support the notion that if their providers control pain with medication and write a prescription they are likely to see better satisfaction numbers (Zosel, Bartelson, Bailey, Lowenstein, & Dart, 2013). The three medications that medicolegal death investigators are most likely to encounter are opioid pain medications, sleeping medications such as Ambien, and benzodiazepines which are used to treat anxiety.

Opioid drug abuse has steadily been increasing in prevalence as well as fatal incidences since the early 2000s and has contributed, in part, to the increase in heroin usage. Oftentimes what starts out as an opioid prescription drug addiction will shift to a heroin addiction because it satisfies the same addiction, and it is often a lot less expensive. There are a number of opioid painkillers on the market, including codeine, fentanyl, hydrocodone, hydromorphone, meperidine, and morphine. Each presents their own unique properties and uses. It is outside the scope of this chapter to discuss the individual properties of all of these; however, there are commonalities that are important for the medicolegal death investigator to understand.

This class of medications binds to the opioid receptors in the body to reduce pain. When used appropriately, they are highly effective against pain. But when they are abused, opioids can be highly addictive and cause respiratory depression. This respiratory depression causes an anoxic event and if prolonged can most certainly be fatal. The methods of use are generally oral; however, some do crush the pills to inject them. Additionally, fentanyl has presented a unique challenge for the medicolegal community.

While fentanyl can be prescribed orally, a patient could also have a prescription for a transdermal patch. These patches are designed to release a small amount of the medication over time. The issue comes into play when people place multiple patches on their body or even worse, they chew the patches to get a lot of the medication at one time. The key to catching this as a possible cause of death is for the medicolegal death investigator to do a complete and thorough body examination on scene, especially if it is known that the individual has a fentanyl prescription. Proper placement tends to be in the upper arm, but someone who is abusing will likely place them anywhere on their body, usually under clothed areas to hide the abuse. If they are chewing the patches, this will likely be seen in their mouth when the investigator is examining the decedent's teeth.

Sleep medications are also something that should be on the medicolegal death investigator's radar. Studies have found that while the rate at which sleeping aids are prescribed has gone down in recent years, the incidents of individuals reporting using them in a nonprescribed manner has stayed relatively the same (Johnston, O'Malley, Bachman,& Schulenberg, 2013; McCabe, West, Teter, & Boyd, 2014). Their use, particularly in a great amount than prescribed fashion or in combination with other drugs is why they can be so dangerous.

If not taken properly, sleep medications can cause respiratory and cardiac depression which could lead to death. This is dangerous enough alone, but when you add other drugs to the mix, especially alcohol, it can be quite fatal. Another medication that is commonly found to be abused along with sleep aids is benzodiazepines.

Benzodiazepines, a class of antianxiety medications, are also a common drug that is overdosed on. The problem with this class of medications occurs when it is taken with other drugs or alcohol. The combination of benzodiazepines and a sleep aid such as Ambien can be fatal. The number of deaths attributed to benzodiazepines has been steadily rising since the early 2000s, mirroring overall deaths due to prescription medications (CDC, 2015). The common benzodiazepines that are prescribed currently are diazepam, alprazolam, clonazepam, and lorazepam. Rates of abuse appear to be associated with individuals who have a substance abuse problem on top of their mental health diagnosis which necessitated the need for the antianxiety medication (Cook, Chavez, Carmona, & Alegria, 2016). This fact should not come as a surprise that those who abuse one type of addictive substance are likely to abuse another. For the medicolegal death investigator, the take home message is that if someone has evidence that they may be an alcoholic, there should be great care taken to ensure that all medications on scene are collected and documented to ensure that they were taken as prescribed.

POISONINGS

While the term poisoning could be the result of any number of substances, many of which we have already discussed in this text such as alcohol, carbon monoxide, prescription and illicit drugs, there are some that are more commonly found if the manner of death is a homicide. These include arsenic and cyanide and are likely overlooked more often than they are found. Part of the problem has to do with testing for the compounds.

Substances Generally Tested for When Toxicology is Ordered

- ✓ Basic Drug Screen
- ✓ Amphetamines
- ✓ Barbiturates and its metabolites
- ✓ Cannabinoids
- ✓ Cocaine and its metabolites
- ✓ Fentanyl and its metabolites
- ✓ Methadone and its metabolites
- ✓ Methamphetamine and 3,4-Methylenedioxymethamphetamine (MDMA)
- ✓ Opiates
- ✓ Oxycodone and oxymorphone
- ✓ Phencyclidine

FIGURE 9.4 An example list of traditional drug screen. *Retrieved from NMS Labs.*

With both cyanide and arsenic, blood from the decedent can be checked for the presence of either as well as get a quantitative level. However, only arsenic is able to be examined in other samples by most labs. These other samples could include hair, nails, urine, and tissue samples. The reason they are overlooked, however, is that neither of these are on a traditional drug screen (Fig. 9.4). To test for these poisons, the medicolegal office must specifically request the examination. So, if a person overdoses on an opioid, as an example, but there is not any evidence on scene it would still be caught assuming that a toxicology screen was performed. If there was no evidence on scene that an individual was poisoned prior to their death, that would not be screened for.

REFERENCES

Centers for Disease Control and Prevention. (2011). *Policy Impact: Prescription Painkiller Overdoses*. Atlanta, GA: US Department of Health and Human Services, CDC.

Centers for Disease Control and Prevention. (2015). *CDC Wonder*. Atlanta, GA: US Department of Health and Human Services, CDC.

Cook, B., Chavez, L., Carmona, R., & Alegria, M. (2016). Assessing Comorbidities and service use among patients with benzodiazepine abuse. *European Psychiatry, 33*, S295.

Toxicity assessment of combustion products. In DiNenno, P. J., et al. (Eds.), *Handbook of the Society of Fire Protection Engineering* (second ed.), (1995).

Hill, P., Haley, N. J., & Wynder, E. L. (1983). Cigarette smoking: carboxyhemoglobin, plasma nicotine, cotinine and thiocyanate vs self-reported smoking data and cardiovascular disease. *Journal of Chronic Diseases, 36*(6), 439–449.

Johnston, L. D., O'Malley, P. M., Bachman, J. G., & Schulenberg, J. E. (2013). Monitoring the future national survey results on drug use, 1975–2012. In *College Students and Adults Ages 19–50* (Vol. 2)Ann Arbor, MI: Institute for Social Research, The University of Michigan.

McCabe, S. E., West, B. T., Teter, C. J., & Boyd, C. J. (2014). Trends in medical use, diversion, and nonmedical use of prescription medications among college students from 2003 to 2013: connecting the dots. *Addictive Behaviors, 39*(7), 1176–1182.

National Survey on Drug Use and Health (NSDUH).(2014).

Kuehn, B. M. (2014). Driven by prescription drug abuse, heroin use increases among suburban and rural whites. *JAMA, 312*(2), 118–119.

Wilson, L. D., Jeromin, J., Garvey, L., & Dorbandt, A. (2001). Cocaine, ethanol, and cocaethylene cardiotoxity in an animal model of cocaine and ethanol abuse. *Academic Emergency Medicine, 8*(3), 211–222.

Zosel, A., Bartelson, B. B., Bailey, E., Lowenstein, S., & Dart, R. (2013). Characterization of adolescent prescription drug abuse and misuse using the researched abuse diversion and addiction-related surveillance (RADARS®) system. *Journal of the American Academy of Child & Adolescent Psychiatry, 52*(2), 196–204.

Chapter 10

Special Death Investigations

Chapter Outline

This chapter is a catchall of sorts meant to provide the medicolegal professional with a basic understanding of the intricacies associated with each of these types of deaths. Each death in this chapter will touch on a topic that requires its own unique additions to the basic death scene investigation. Every death scene should be approached the same way whether the decedent is an elderly individual with chronic health conditions found dead in bed or a possible homicide victim who is found in the street. The basics are the same, but it is hoped that the specific challenges of each of these death investigations will be addressed in this chapter.

It is also recognized that this is not an exhaustive review of the material for each of these types of deaths. Each of these deaths could easily be made into its own book and many have. The first of these special death investigations is likely one of the most common of the group depending on your jurisdiction. The investigation of a child's death tends to be the most challenging emotionally for the medicolegal professional.

CHILD DEATHS

Working With the Family

The first and foremost concern of any child death investigation should be to find answers for the families and covictims who are affected. Too often law enforcement and medicolegal death investigators treat every child death like it is a homicide. This is not to say that you should not secure the scene until the proper professionals can get on scene to evaluate what they are seeing, but once

Essentials of Medicolegal Death Investigation. http://dx.doi.org/10.1016/B978-0-12-803641-9.00010-0

the scene can be cleared of signs of foul play or a significant medical history is discovered that could have led to the child's death the families should be able to hold their child. This is no different than when a medicolegal professional examines an adult decedent on scene and rules out trauma and/or foul play then allows the family to sit with, talk to, and touch their loved one before they are removed from the scene. Treating parents and caregivers like they may have committed a crime can irreparably destroy a relationship that you as the medicolegal investigator need to ascertain, and it can even create a negative public perception of the office in which you work.

As with any death investigation, the first step medicolegal death investigators should make when arriving on scene is to introduce themselves to the family and covictims on scene. This is not the time to get their version of the events but is instead used to notify them that you have arrived on scene, that you will be taking a look at their loved one, and that you will be back to speak with them. This brief conversation will aid in setting the stage for a trusting relationship that is essential to get all of the information you will need including the Centers for Disease Control (CDC) Child Death Investigation form and the doll reenactment.

Documenting the Scene

When documenting a child's death, investigation photographs are essential. The text will discuss shortly the need to properly photograph the doll reenactment portion of the investigation, but general photographs are also extremely important. As with any scene, the medicolegal professional should document the scene in such a way that the forensic pathologist handling the case gets a thorough understanding of the scene conditions. The best place to start is from the outside of the dwelling.

With a homicide investigation you might expect to take pictures of the house in a 360-degree fashion showing all points of ingress and egress. This may not be necessary with a child's death where there are no initial suspicions of foul play, but there should at least be a photograph documenting the outside form of the structure. After this is completed, a complete picture of pertinent rooms is necessary for a complete investigation.

Photographs showing the common areas of the home are important. The medicolegal professional should take care to document certain conditions in the residence to outline the cleanliness and order of the home. The same would be true if the child died at a care center. Any food, beverages, and medications that are out should be fully documented. The medications are important as they may explain why a certain drug shows up in a toxicology screen, which could have come from the mother passing on the drug during breastfeeding, as an example. Additionally, when in the kitchen, a photograph of the inside of the refrigerator should be secured to show the availability of nutritional foods to those who live in the house. If it is not immediately apparent, the medicolegal death investigator should also photograph the child's formula, if applicable, and other age-appropriate foods. If a bottle is found, it should be secured as evidence for possible testing if necessary. Sleeping environments are also essential to document.

The documentation of the sleeping environment is something that will be discussed in the doll reenactment discussion, but showing the areas where the child slept can be very important to an investigation. It is important to know whether the sleeping environment was age appropriate. Did the child sleep in a crib or on a soft surface such as a regular bed or couch? If the child slept in a crib, were there other items in the sleeping area such as excess blankets, pillows, railing cushions, or toys? Was the padding in the crib firm or soft? Additionally, was the room hot, warm, cool, or cold? Was there working air-conditioning for warmer seasons or a working furnace if it was cold outside? Other photographs a medicolegal professional should take revolve around the routine care given to the child.

The presence of appropriate supplies such as baby wipes, new diapers to replace soiled ones, clean clothes, and age-appropriate toys should not cloud medicolegal death investigators' perception of an environment if the quantity or quality of items does not meet what they would perceive as someone "being a good parent." The idea of looking for these items speaks more to the parent(s') preparation and care given to the child. Any diapers that are soiled in the house, particularly if the deceased child appears to have a clean diaper on should be collected as evidence. Prior to packaging it would be appropriate to examine and photograph the diapers.

The child's diaper(s) should be photographed to show how it appeared when medicolegal death investigators located it. Additionally, it should be documented in the case notes how the diaper(s) appeared. Was it wet or dry? Was there fecal matter present? How about signs of trauma present in the diaper like bright red blood? This one piece of documentation could hint to the medicolegal death investigator a number of key issues associated with the care of the child. In addition to scene photographs, pictures showing how the child presented at the time of the investigation are also important.

When photographing a child, the basic recommendations that one follows during the investigation of an adult death should be followed. Initial photographs should be taken to show the child within the environment with which it was found. Additionally, any items touching or near the decedent that could potentially be important to the investigation should be photographed at a medium range to show its relation to the body and then at a close range to document details of the particular item. These items could be a bottle, blankets, toys, or any other object the medicolegal death investigator feels is important. Once that is completed, an identifying photograph should be taken showing the decedent's face. Then overall photographs that overlap should be obtained showing both anterior and posterior aspects of the decedent. With adults this usually requires three overlapping photographs to document the whole body, but with a small child two are usually sufficient. If the child was fully clothed at the time he/she was found and clothing items can be lifted up to expose further areas of the body; without having to completely remove the item, this should be done. However, if the clothing items do not easily lift up or down it is in the best interest to leave the clothing as is and wait until the forensic autopsy to photograph the covered aspects of the child's body. Some close-up photographs may also be useful.

The close-up photographs that one might consider taking are of the child's genitalia, anus, hands, and side profile pictures of the child's head. While there may not be any evidence of trauma with these photographs, documenting negative findings is just as important as showing injuries. Often times with deaths, regardless of the age of the decedent, family members, friends, or even the media in high-profile cases will hear rumor or believe that there was evidence of foul play. Being able to properly document that there were no signs of foul play on examination of scene is very important.

Postmortem Changes of Children

The postmortem changes of a small child progress at different rates than those of an adult. However, just like with adult decedents there is no hard-and-fast rule regarding how to give an exact time of death. Instead, and just like with adults, a range could be provided based on the postmortem changes that are noted. Additionally, just like with adults, the longer the postmortem interval the less accurate an estimation would be. An example of this would be the accuracy of a postmortem interval where changes that appear consistent with only a few hours, versus a child who is severely decomposed.

As with adults, the three postmortem changes the medicolegal death investigator is looking for are livor, algor, and rigor mortis. There are, however, differences in the general time frame for when these changes will occur in small children. Children tend to cool more rapidly than an adult decedent, and their rigor mortis will be more difficult to appreciate. Because of these issues, it is more difficult to provide an accurate postmortem interval range.

CDC Form and Doll Reenactments

In the summer of 1996, the CDC (2016) published its first Sudden Unexplained Infant Death Investigation Reporting Form, as well as guidelines and recommendations for how to handle these deaths. However, the agency's involvement started well before this date by recognizing the need for standardizing this important subset of death investigations. By recognizing the wide manners in which these deaths were investigated, or not investigated, across the country there was an obvious opportunity to properly review these deaths to decrease infant mortality. Additionally, by having a common form that all agencies would theoretically use, there is a greater amount of researchable data available to epidemiologists. The epidemiologists can then evaluate what trends are present in the data.

Examples of situations that are unsafe for the child would be a soft sleeping surface, the presence of soft, padded objects in the sleeping environment, and cosleeping are among many risk factors for sudden death in infants (Task Force on Sudden Infant Death Syndrome, 2005). The CDC form helps identify these issues in a standard format. The form is separated into the following sections:

- Investigation data that include the decedent's information as well as the witness' information.
- Witness interview that covers 34 different questions that range from recent traumatic history, how the child was placed in a sleeping environment, multiple environmental factors, to whether or not resuscitative efforts were performed and how.
- Infant's medical history that covers everything from birth to recent signs or symptoms of illness.
- Infant's dietary history that covers information related to last feeding and types of food the child had.
- Pregnancy history that asks questions about the mother's prenatal care and any medications she may take, as examples.
- Incident scene investigation that focuses on the conditions and features of the house such as heating and cooling sources.
- Investigation summary that allows for certain investigative times to be recorded, and an area to identify additional information or inconsistencies between witnesses.
- Investigation diagrams that allow for the scene to be sketched along with an infant body diagram to indicate findings just as the medicolegal death investigator would with any scene examination.
- Summary for pathologist that provides a brief overview of all the information collected.

At times, not all of the information will be readily available for the medicolegal death investigator. However, every effort should be made to collect all of the information possible to help paint a complete picture for the forensic pathologist ahead of the autopsy. With these deaths in particular, scene findings could be the only aspect of the investigation into a child's death that could identify the cause and manner of death instead of having to sign the case out as an undetermined death. The CDC form is one of the first steps in this process, and the doll reenactment further solidifies the events that may have led up to the infant's death.

The doll reenactment is an essential tool for the medicolegal death investigator, and though it is emotionally draining for all involved to perform, it provides a wealth of information related to the death. This does take some practice on the part of the medicolegal death investigator to have a proper flow to the reenactment, but the CDC has a document and resources on how to properly perform this important aspect of an investigation. Part of having a successful doll reenactment is the preparation that goes into this before one of these deaths occur.

The most important piece required for the doll reenactment is a proper doll to perform this function. This might seem like an obvious statement, but there are a few features the doll should have to get the most information possible out of the reenactment. First, the doll must be an appropriate size for the child whose death you are investigating. Since these reenactments are done when a child less than one year of age dies, the doll should be comparable to a child of that age. Second, the doll should have simple, asexual clothing that allows for the anterior and posterior aspects of the doll's body to be easily identifiable when someone is reviewing the photographs or video at a later time. Some offices will write a large "F" for front on one side and a large "B" for back on the other. Third, the doll should have a head and neck that rotate similarly to an actual child's. This is important because regardless of a child's position, the medicolegal death investigator will want to be able to show how the child's head was turned. This is important as the direction of a child's head, and particularly where his/her mouth and nose was located, is an essential component to understanding if the child could have potentially died an asphyxial death. When the time comes that there is a child death to investigate, documenting the process is essential.

Photography is an essential component of the doll reenactment so that it can be reviewed later by the forensic pathologist, law enforcement officials, and even the district attorney's office and jury members if the case is criminal in nature. Videography could also be considered, but it is not essential. The photographs should fully document the entire process from when the child was last placed to where he/she was located, and through resuscitative efforts prior to the arrival of first responders. It is the easiest to think of the reenactment in these three segments: how the child was placed, how the child was found, and what resuscitative efforts whre performed and how they were performed.

How the child was last placed is very important as it can provide the investigator with clues as to what may have happened. Have the parent or care provider placed the child down to show how he/she accomplished this. Encourage him/her to place the child exactly as he/she did, including covering the child with any blankets or placing any objects like a stuffed animal next to the child. Photographs of this stage illustrate the child's relationship to potential hazards. Were there too many blankets? Were there soft objects near the child or was the child on a soft surface that could create a suffocation scenario? Was the child near an edge of the surface it was placed on to from where it could fall into a gap and become wedged? Was it in a sleeping environment with a parent where it could potentially be smothered? All are important to consider.

How the child was found is the next step in the doll reenactment process. This includes the need to examine the sleeping environment where the child was found and if that contributed to his/her death. A retrospective study of child death cases in New York City illustrates the need to do a thorough investigation into the death of a child. The study by Senter, Sackoff, Landi, & Boyd, (2011) was examining sudden unexplained infant deaths and trying to look at how unsafe sleep environments contribute to these deaths. The autopsies in these cases did not reveal any gross or microscopic findings. So, without a thorough scene investigation, including a doll reenactment, a cause or mechanism of death may never be known in a large number of child deaths.

The medicolegal death investigator should pay particular attention at this point to illustrate what changed between the environment in which the child was placed and the environment in which it was found. Developmental milestones will be discussed shortly, but in brief, if the child was not found where it was last placed or if it fell and was wedged in a particular area does it make sense based on its age that this could have occurred. An example would be a caretaker telling the medicolegal death investigator that the child must have rolled off the surface it was placed on down to a hard floor causing trauma. If the child was at least four months old, this could be a possibility. If the child is younger than this age, it is highly improbable that the child was able to do that on its own.

What resuscitative efforts were performed and how they were performed is the last segment of the doll reenactment. When a parent or caretaker finds a child not breathing and unresponsive and emergency services are called, the dispatcher will give instructions on how to perform CPR. This is important to note and have the caretaker or parent demonstrate so that if there is evidence of trauma to the thoracic cavity the knowledge of how CPR was performed could explain the injuries. If a child was placed on a hard surface or on the forearm of the caretaker and two fingers were used to perform compression on the midline chest there might be contusions of fractures noted on the anterior aspect of the chest wall. The second method, by which CPR can be provided to an infant, though usually only done by someone with medical training, is to hold the child's chest wall in the provider's hands and use the thumbs to perform the chest compressions. In this scenario, you could still see the previously mentioned signs of trauma, but you might also note some posterior trauma. If the rescuer or caretaker used his/her fingertip to press on the chest wall incorrectly, since only the thumbs are supposed to be used for compressions, there could be the possibility of trauma. However, it is important to note here that the breaking of a child's ribs is very difficult since they are still composed of a significant amount of cartilage. Meaning, the ribs of a small child should not break as easily as an adult who has CPR performed on them.

The pictures included here illustrate important moments of the doll reenactment that should be documented on every case. Fig. 10.1 shows the

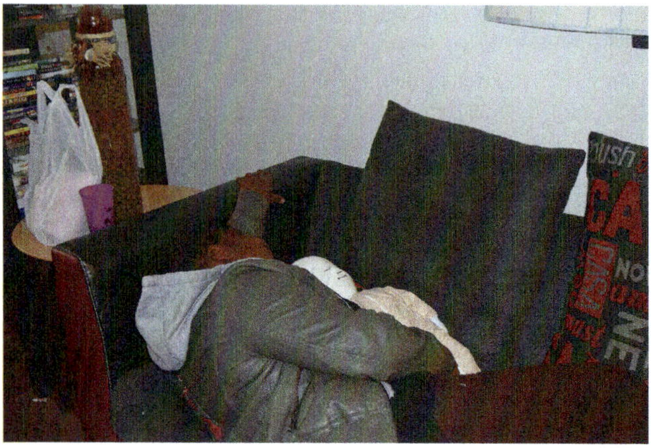

FIGURE 10.1 A mother described laying down with the child prior to falling asleep.

mother described laying down the child prior to falling asleep that evening and Fig. 10.2 is how she reported finding the child after waking up in the middle of the night. It is incumbent on the medicolegal death investigator to know if that is something that is a possibility. Milestones in development will be discussed next, but the investigator should consider if a child could have moved himself/herself into the position in which he/she was found. It is also important to remember that just because a story does not completely add up, does not mean that something criminal has occurred. Discrepancies should, however, always be noted. Fig. 10.3 illustrates another keep moment to document and that is the caretaker showing how CPR was performed. Lastly, a picture of the environment free of individuals should always be

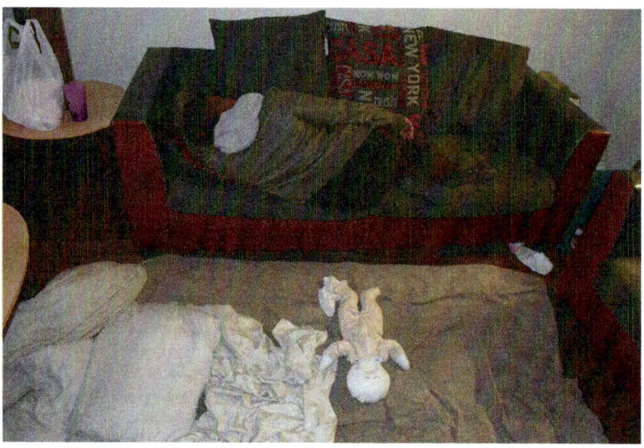

FIGURE 10.2 A picture of how the mother claimed she found the child in the middle of the night.

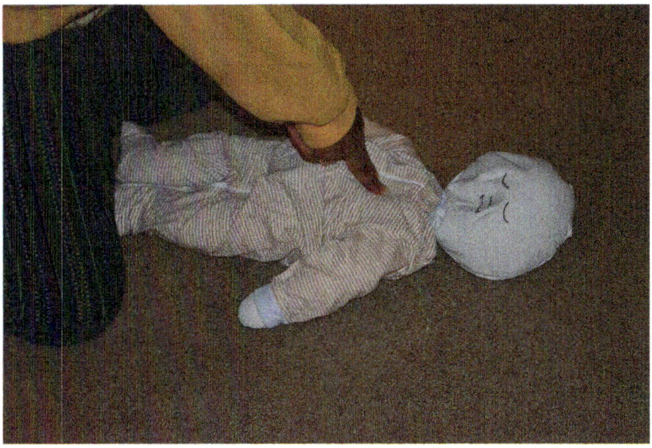

FIGURE 10.3 A picture of the caretaker showing how CPR was performed on the child.

documented. Fig. 10.4 shows the environment in which the child was put to sleep and later found unresponsive. A stain can be noted on one of the couch cushions that could be consistent with purge. It is possible in this scenario that the medicolegal death investigator could be looking at an overlay situation with the mother in advertently laying over the child on this soft surface, making normal respiration impossible.

Knowing certain milestones is also important as it could indicate the plausibility of a particular event happening. The following are general guidelines, though they may vary slightly from child to child. Additionally, a child that is born premature will reach milestones based more on his/her due date as opposed to the day in which he/she were actually born. By 1 year,

FIGURE 10.4 A picture showing the environment in which the child was put to sleep and later found unresponsive.

however, the child should catch up. The basic milestones for investigative purposes are given as follows (Denver II, 2015):

- By 1 month:
  - lifts head and chin slightly while in a prone position,
  - keeps hand in a tightly closed fist, and
  - simple vocalizations.
- By 2 months:
  - lifts head approximately 45 degrees while in a prone position and
  - opens hands.
- By 3 months:
  - lifts head approximately 90 degrees while in a prone position,
  - can hold head upright and steady without support when held in a seated position, and
  - can grasp and hold onto a rattle that is placed in its hand.
- 4–5 months:
  - rolls over,
  - raises chest and supports self with its arms while in a prone position,
  - bears some weight when held in an upright position, and
  - starts to work toward and reach for objects in front of it.
- 6 months:
  - begins to feed self,
  - sits upright without the use of props on a firm surface, and
  - keeps head level with body.
- 7–8 months:
  - stands with the assistance of an object and
  - can pick up objects.
- 9 months:
  - crawling starts,
  - can hold a bottle and use hands to feed self, and
  - can stand with the assistance of an object from a seated position.
- 10–12 months:
  - beginnings of being able to stand and walk independently and
  - able to use thumb and fingers together to aid in holding objects.

The common accidental deaths that the medicolegal death investigator should be considering based on the scene findings and the child's developmental age are whether or not there was a possible smothering due to a soft surface or other objects in the sleeping environment, wedging as a result of falling into a tight area that does not allow the child's chest wall to breathe normally, and whether or not the child was cosleeping with another child or a parent as to whether or not the possibility is present that there was an overlay situation. All of these scenarios require a proper scene investigation to properly certify the death certificate because many of these events are unlikely to produce injuries that would be visible at the time of autopsy.

Additionally, the possibility should always be considered that the child was intentionally harmed. When a child is intentionally killed by another individual 24 h of being born, it is referred to as neonaticide, and if the child is killed after 24 h but is less than one year of age, it is referred to as infanticide. The generalized individual who kills his/her child within the first 24 h after giving birth generally does so to remove any evidence of an unwanted pregnancy. The children who are killed within the first 24 h are generally delivered outside of a hospital setting. Infanticide is similar in that a percentage of the deaths are because a parent wants to remove the presence of an unwanted child. Infanticide is different in that the majority of the other cases happen because an individual is retaliating for a perceived wrong committed by another individual, or the death happens as a result of abuse of neglect (Porter & Gavin, 2010).

Regardless of whether or not there is suspicion of foul play, fully investigating child deaths is essential, and this includes performing a complete medicolegal autopsy to look for hidden signs of trauma. The only exception for the need to perform a forensic autopsy might be if the child had a history of a disorder and he/she was not expected to live. In these cases, a scene investigation is important to simply rule out the presence of foul play and no autopsy would then likely need to be performed. However, it is important to note that an autopsy is may be the only way certain traumas are noted since not all traumas are readily visible or palpable. Even traumatic head injuries can occur where there may not be any accompanying skull fractures that an investigator could palpate during his/her examination (DiMaio & Dana, 2007). This is true too in abdominal injuries to children due to the lack of a boney prominence, which would create contusions more easily from blunt trauma (Trokel, DiScala, Terrin, & Sege, 2004). For these reasons, and many others, an autopsy should be performed for all forensic cases.

Following-up With Families

As mentioned earlier in this chapter, working with families and other covictims throughout these death investigations is imperative. The trust that is needed to fully investigate these deaths starts before you even get to a scene. This starts with the policies that the office and medicolegal system adopt for how to handle these cases.

Regardless of whether an office is a large medical examiner system or a small county coroner, there should always be a focus on following best practices for handling these and ever other death. Putting the decedent and his/her loved ones first will always result in the best possible outcome for any scenario. However, just having the right policies does not mean anything if the agencies that the office routinely interacts with is not on board. The law enforcement and fire/emergency medical services (EMS) systems need to understand the proper way to handle these cases in the initial stages prior to the medicolegal office even being notified. Working with the various first responder professionals to inform them of the policies as well as the reason behind them can help ensure that a family is not already unwilling to work with the medicolegal death investigator simply because of the way the family was treated prior to the arrival of law.

After the medicolegal death investigator has completed his/her scene investigation and has performed the doll reenactment there should be a sit down conversation with the legal next of kin(s), at a minimum. It is up to the medicolegal death investigator as well as the next of kin(s), whether other family members or friends on scene should be part of this conversation. A conversation should first take place with the law enforcement agency to discuss what the medicolegal death investigator found, and to discuss what information is appropriate to share with the family at this point. If there is a concern that something improper occurred, then there might not be a lot of findings discussed with the family. However, if nothing appears suspicious, there should be a conscious effort to share as much information as possible. With this in mind, it is important to simply state that something is not currently known, if that is in fact the case. Regardless, there needs to be a time where the medicolegal death investigator can discuss what findings if any are present, what the next steps of the investigation are, and be able to answer questions the family may have.

Once the medicolegal death investigator has answered the questions he/she can, there should be a reiteration of what the next steps are, and information should be left on how the family and covictims can contact the medical examiner/coroner's office. It is important to emphasize the timeline for the family. This will also reduce unnecessary calls to the office from families that are unaware of what is going on. Developing this relationship also helps if follow-up is needed on the case.

Families that believe the medicolegal professionals are doing everything possible to find out what happened to their loved one will be more willing to cooperate as the investigation continues. It would not be uncommon for follow-up questions to occur during the investigation of a child death. While you will discuss who the child's pediatrician was, you might need to follow-up to see if the child had been seen by any other providers. When interviewing parents and covictims, it would not be uncommon that the stress of the situation clouds the family's memory. Additional information may be apparent after the family has a chance to sit back and reflect on the previous history of the child. Without the proper trust, a child's family may be unwilling to assist in providing additional information, or they may not feel comfortable coming to the medicolegal death investigator with additional information that they have concerns about.

In conclusion, the investigation of a child's death is one of the most stressful cases a medicolegal death investigator can be a part of. What is important to keep in mind is to always follow best practices, be truthful and upfront with the family, and for the medicolegal death investigator to know when to ask for help if they are uncomfortable or unsure about something related to the investigator or examination. The proper scene investigation, doll reenactment, and follow-up work may be the difference between a family having answers for why their child died and a death that is signed out as cause or manner of death undetermined.

WATER DEATHS

A water-related death occurs at a rate of 10 deaths per day in the United States (CDC, 2016). This is even more significant when one considers that this prevalence does not include boating-related fatalities. Certainly, depending on where the medicolegal office resides will impact the regularity of the investigation of a drowning death. If an office is located in a costal environment or one with many lakes, it is likely that it will experience more possible drowning cases than those who work in an area without large bodies of water. However, individuals can certainly still drown in a residential setting such as in a tub or pool, but they could also die from drowning related to a natural disaster like a flood. These cases present unique challenges that the medicolegal death investigator must consider when faced with a possible drowning case.

The diagnosis of drowning tends to be a diagnosis based on scene findings and the exclusion of other causes of death. Some research showed that pre-autopsy CT revealed a very high prevalence of fluid in the sinuses as well as in the trachea and bronchus, the branched out airways after the trachea that enter the lungs, of individuals who were suspected of and signed out as drowning cases (Levy, Harcke, Getz, Mallak, Caruso, Pearse, et al., 2007). This is important as it provides a diagnostic finding to indicate a high suspicion for drowning versus other possible diagnosis. Additionally, drowning could be the diagnosis but it could be in the presence of another significant contributing factor.

If an individual exhibited signs and symptoms of a myocardial infarction, such as a bystander hearing the decedent complaining of chest pain and looking pale, prior to going unresponsive in the water this condition would be a contributing factor, but if the decedent is pulseless and apneic when he/she are eventually pulled from the water the case may very well be signed out as a drowning. Said another way, if this particular case was signed out as a drowning with heart disease as a contributing factor the forensic pathologist believes that without the decedent being in water he/she may have survived the cardiac event. Another common drowning death with a significant contributing factor is those who die with significant drugs of alcohol in his/her system.

Individuals have been known to drown in very low levels of water, particularly when substances of abuse are involved. If individuals are incapacitated due to a substance they ingested, they may not be able to lift their head and or body from a dangerous position the same as they would if they were not affected by drugs or alcohol. The substance, usually water, need only be deep enough to occlude the mouth and nose of the decedent. In an instance like this, if there is minimal water present to cause drowning the key moving forward is determining if the decedent was disabled in any way, had a medical condition that could leave him/her unresponsive, or presenting evidence that the decedent may have been abusing a substance. Of course, once the toxicology results come back after the autopsy this will show definitively what was in the decedent's system and at what levels. Obtaining a detailed medical history, as previously mentioned, is also very important as part of the investigation of a suspected drowning death as it may indicate a medical condition that too could have left the decedent unresponsive and unable to move his/her body from a dangerous position in a liquid.

If a decedent dies in a large body of water, such as a river or lake, particularly in fresh water, the body will sink, particularly if the individual has a lot of clothing on, which will act as further dense weight on the body after the articles become soaked. If a body becomes submerged, even in moving water like with a river, the body tends to not travel far from the location where it went under. The time it takes for a body to return to the surface, assuming it is not caught on any objects under the water, depends on how long it takes for the body to decompose. The gases formed from the decomposition process aid in the decedent coming to the surface. This being known, it stands to reason that the water temperature is an important component to how long it will take for a body to resurface.

Whether a body resurfaces due to decomposition or it is recovered by a dive team, there are a few scene findings that the medicolegal death investigator should look for. First, the presence of what is known as washerwoman hands will be present to some degree depending on time in the water. This rigid development of the top layers of skin of the hands generally starts with the fingertips and will eventually progress to the entire hand. This is not specific to drowning, of course, as anyone who has washed dishes for a prolonged period of time or swam in a pool has experienced this. Another nonspecific finding associated with drowning is a cone of foam coming from the decedent's mouth and/or nares. This is a result of fluid building up in the lungs. The other findings deal with postmortem artifacts. These could be injuries noted to the body due to the decedent coming into contact with low branches or rocks in the water in which he/she was submerged. Additionally, activity from fish or other sea life could create artifacts similar to what might be expected if small animals were biting or eating the decedent. In addition to medical conditions or substance abuse, large scale disasters can cause a situation where there may be multiple drowning fatalities at one time.

Natural disasters also account for a fair amount of drownings each year. The cases that most individuals think of when discussing drownings related to natural disasters are with excessive rainfall in a short period of time that causes flash flooding or a tsunami; however, drownings can be associated with natural disasters where flooding is a byproduct of a different natural disaster such as when a tornado occurs. Regardless of how the death occurred, the proper recovery of the body must occur to avoid losing any potential evidence.

Often times, when a body is found in water there is very little known about the circumstances at the time of the scene investigation. Thus the preservation and collection of evidence, especially the body, is extremely important. Recovering the body presents a unique challenge if the decedent is in a large body of water. If the same decedent were found on land, there would be a standard procedure for limiting the movement and removal of items prior to sealing the body in a body bag. However, when it comes to a water fatality very few have a plan for examining and securing the body in a bag while limiting the potential loss of evidence.

Part of this problem is access to the body. If a decedent is submerged or in a body of water with a current, it might be unsafe for the medicolegal death investigator to handle the removal. Preplanning and training with the dive teams a medicolegal office is likely to work with will assist in ensuring a body is recovered in the best way possible. Regardless of who recovers the decedent from a body of water, the investigator or a dive team member, the general process involves placing the body as gently, safely, and quickly as possible into a body bag specifically designed for water use. These bags are generally made of a synthetic material and are mesh to allow for easier usage under water. Without this, bodies are often pulled through water, lifted out of the water by a small team into a boat or onto land, all this time possible evidence is lost during the transportation process. These bags help minimize this loss. Fully documenting the scene in which a decedent is found in water is also important and sometimes difficult to document.

Taking photographs of the scene is very important as it is with any death investigation. Documenting the area as well as possible points of entry into the water can not only help paint the picture for law enforcement investigators and the forensic pathologist, but it can also be a valuable piece of documentation if someone wants to recreate the scene at a later time. If a body is recovered from underwater, a statement from the dive team should be obtained to provide a detailed scene description of the conditions below the surface. This could help identify where certain injury patterns came from, or if there was an eddy line that could have trapped the body underwater in a spiral pattern. Regardless of the type of outdoor body of water where a decedent is located, there are certain measurements that need to be collected on every scene.

These measurements include the air temperature, water temperature, water levels, and if applicable, the current speeds from the time the individual was last seen alive until the time he/she was located and removed from the water. This information can be used at the time of autopsy for explaining certain postmortem changes.

ELECTROCUTION

Often times when discussing electrocution deaths, the general public will have the image of a decedent receiving a shock from an electrical item. Instances of this type of low voltage electrocution could be directly touching a source of electricity like an outlet or coming in contact with an exposed wire associated with an electrical appliance. Deaths are not uncommon when someone without the proper training as an electrician attempts to do electrical work in his/her own home. While these are electrical deaths, many other situations or events could be categorized in this section.

Other instances where there could be an electrical death include lightning strikes and live power lines, particularly during or after a storm. These two examples would produce high voltage situations where a decedent would likely die from severe internal burns to various organ systems. The example of an electrocution as a result of a faulty small appliance would likely cause a cardiac arrhythmia that would lead to death. Regardless of the specific voltage, there will be burns present.

If an individual is the victim of an electrocution, there will be a burn associated with where the electrical current entered the body as well as one where the current left the body. This path within the body travels in the path of least resistance. In other words, the current will take the shortest distance to exit the body at a point where it is grounded. So, if a person is standing and touching a live wire the current will travel down to his/her feet to exit the body. However, if we take the same example but the individual was leaning against a countertop, the current would leave the body through the chest or abdomen, whichever was in contact with the countertop.

The first step to investigating this type of death is to ensure that the scene is safe. If there was a faulty appliance, outlet, or exposed wire, the power to that room and possibly even the entire house should be shut off. If the source is a downed wire or related to a commercial electrical source, the electrical company must be called to the scene to make the area safe. Lastly, if it is weather related does it make sense to perform the scene investigation at this time or is it advisable to wait until the storm passes. There could even be a situation where the individual was in water during a natural disaster and the electrocution occurred as a result of the current being conducted through the flood water. In the example where water played a role, it is even more important to ensure that all electrical sources in the area are powered off. Once the scene is made safe, the examination of the burns can begin.

The size of burns seen on scene by the medicolegal death investigator can also vary greatly depending on the voltage. If the death involved a low voltage source, there are likely to be a small or multiple small burns where the decedent's body comes in contact with the source. The same would be true for the exit burns. However, with a higher voltage source or if the death was the result of a lightning strike the external burns could be very severe and cover a large area. Regardless of the injury pattern, accurately documenting the scene and the possible source of the electrical current is essential, especially if the source is a low voltage one since there might not be internal injuries seen at the time of autopsy. One finding that is associated with lightning strikes is ferning or arborescent.

ENVIRONMENTAL DEATHS

For the purposes of this chapter, we will be considering the two most common types of environmental deaths. However, many situations could be classified as environmental deaths such as deaths occurring as a result of a forest fire, a strong storm such as a hurricane or tornado, or even communicable disease if the living environment of those affected were unsanitary. The two environmental deaths we will discuss are hyper and hypothermia. Depending on the environment where the medicolegal office is located, one or both could be a likely possibility at certain times of the year.

Hyperthermia is caused when the environment is too hot for an individual's body to process through normal means such as sweating. Often times when a medicolegal death investigator is examining someone for a possible heat-related death, it is due to a prolonged event without the proper protective factors. This is regularly seen by offices in the southwest United States as individuals attempt to travel by foot across the United States and Mexico border. These travels take many days and are generally done in extreme heat. The prolonged heat and physical exertion is too strenuous on individuals' bodies and he/she eventually succumb to the conditions. This can also happen if there is a prolonged heat wave in a specific area.

When there is the potential for a prolonged heat wave that could have devastating effects on the general population, particularly individuals who are elderly or have chronic health conditions, the local and state health departments will generally issue a warning. Some of the preventive measures that these health warnings will discuss are things that the medicolegal death investigator should be looking for to see what contributing factors may have been present. These include but are not limited to: whether the residence where the decedent was found had working electricity, whether there was a functional cooling element in the structure such as a fan, swamp cooler, or air conditioning, and what type of structure he/she was found in and at what level. If there is not a proper cooling element and an individual lives on a higher floor of a tall building he/she are more likely to suffer the effects of a heat wave than someone on a lower floor, as an example.

Death from heat in vehicles has also become a regular topic in the summer months as of late, particularly when it involves a child being left in a car. The make, model, year, and even the color of the vehicle are important to describe when investigating a possible hyperthermia death. Additionally, as with any potential heat-related death, the medicolegal death investigator should collect zip code—specific information from the National Weather Service to show the weather.

Lastly, making sure to document drug and alcohol use as well as the medications someone takes can be an important factor to consider when investigating this type of death.

Hypothermia is caused when the environment is too cold and an individual's body is losing heat quicker than it can generate heat. This could be a more severe problem for individuals who are on certain medications, particularly psychiatric, or are chronic alcoholics. Any condition that causes a difficulty in regulating body temperature will put individuals at greater risk for hypothermia when they have prolonged exposures. If an individual is found in an environment that might indicate the individual may have died from hypothermia, such as being found outdoors, in a vehicle, a makeshift home, or in a structure with insufficient heating or insulation, there are a few pieces of information the scene investigator must collect.

On the scene, the medicolegal death investigator needs to document the lack of appropriate shelter as well as layers of clothing. This could include an outdoor shelter and multiple layers of clothing if the individual is found in an outdoor environment. If the decedent is found inside of a structure, the medicolegal death investigator should note whether there was a heating element present in the structure. This could be a furnace to keep the entire structure warm or it could be a space heater meant to heat one particular area. Part of this is whether or not there was electricity to the structure. The power could be out due to lack of payment, or it could be related to a weather event.

Once back at the office, there needs to be a documentation of the weather conditions whenever medicolegal death investigators believe they may be dealing with an environmental death. There are multiple sources for this information but the important thing to remember is that for the case file there needs to be the most accurate information possible. Finding detailed hour-by-hour data from the nearest tower is essential. Providing only the high and low temperatures for a metropolitan region will not suffice as there can be great variations within a single region.

Lastly, it is not uncommon for the medicolegal death investigator to come across individuals who died from hypothermia and they are found to have removed layers of clothing prior to death. This is a condition known as paradoxical undressing. This is a phenomenon associated with the end-stages of hypothermia, and it is not uncommon to have the items spread out over a large area. The important thing for the scene investigator to keep in mind if an individual is found to be nude or nearly nude in an outdoor environment there must be a detailed examination to ensure there are no signs of trauma present. The concern, particularly if the decedent is a female, is whether an individual was a victim of a sexual assault.

Regardless of what the environmental condition that leads to an individual's death, if a decedent is transported to a local hospital, it is important to find the exact location where the individual came from. The location of death can certainly be different than the location of injury.

MASS FATALITIES

When discussing mass fatalities, it is important to first define what a mass fatality is. The most basic definition is that a mass fatality is an event which is too large for a jurisdiction to handle with its normal staffing and capabilities. Fig. 10.5 is from the terrorist attacks on 9/11 in New York City, which would be a mass fatality no matter how large of an office is, whereas Fig. 10.6 is from the Aurora Theater Shooting in Aurora, Colorado. This incident was a mass fatality for the office that handled it, therefore extra staff had to be called in to handle day-to-day operations in addition to processing the scene. Regardless of the size of the medicolegal office, preplanning is an essential function of any office so that it is as best prepared in the event that something does happen.

Preplanning is more than an office developing its internal plans as well as policies for how to respond to a mass fatality event, though these functions are very important, it is also working collaboratively with other agencies in the area. Tabletop exercises and discussions on multiagency policies are important but more important are the communication and familiarity that come from these meetings. When a large-scale event happens, showing up and knowing what you are going to get out of the people around you is invaluable. When this author responded to the Aurora Theater Shooting in the early hours of July 20, 2012 everyone in the command center was comfortable with each other as we had worked together many times in the past. Knowing what you are going to get out of someone allows those in charge to focus on what they need to focus on instead of worrying over whether someone else is going to get his/her job done. There are functions that are unique to each agency that responds to a mass fatality incident.

FIGURE 10.5 Terrorist attacks on September 11, 2001.

FIGURE 10.6 Aurora theater shooting in Aurora, Colorado.

When the initial 911 call comes into a dispatch center, the local law enforcement agency will likely be the first responders on the scene of a mass fatality incident. Their role is to secure the scene, make the scene safe or as safe as possible, and lay the groundwork for the potential criminal investigation that may follow. Frequently, there is an uncertainty surrounding whether an act was criminal or it is the result of some other issue. Did a structure collapse because there was a structural defect, or did someone intentionally bring down the structure? There will be times, like mass shootings, where it is unmistakably a criminal act. Some instances might not be as obvious. An example of this could be a large natural disaster like a flood or tornado. Did the individuals who were found after the incident die as a result of the incident, or did they die prior to? If they died prior to or unrelated to the natural disaster, finding out if foul play was involved becomes paramount even in the face of rising body counts as a result of the disaster.

The fire department and EMS are likely the next professionals who arrive on scene. With the help of the law enforcement agency, they are tasked with treating and saving the lives of as many victims as possible. At large scale events it is not uncommon to see the fire department and EMS setting up a triage area to best allocate resources to those patients who need it, as well as setting up a staging area for other responding units. The staging area is important so that there is a uniform manner in which resources are being dispatched, and so those on scene have an understanding of what resources they have available immediately if needed and what resources they are likely to have to wait on.

The crime lab and medicolegal office are generally dispatched as soon as practicably possible to help determine how to proceed with the investigation and how to best process the scene. As previously discussed, the criminalist, medicolegal death investigator, and the detectives should work as a cohesive unit to accomplish the goal of processing the scene. On the scene, the responsibility for certain kinds of evidence differs depending on the agency. As previously discussed, the medicolegal office generally has the responsibility for the body, anything touching the body, and anything that could be related to the cause and manner of death. The criminalist generally handles the overall crime scene documentation and collects items of evidentiary value. Often times the evidence will overlap. In these instances, while the medicolegal death investigator has a duty to fully document the evidence, a firearm is a great example, the crime lab will likely have professionals who have advanced knowledge in a certain specialty, so it is ultimately better for them to document the information related to that piece of evidence as well and then collect it for storage at the investigating law enforcement agency's facility. Processing large scenes can also feel overwhelming, but it can be managed with proper planning and execution.

To process a large scale event, it is often advisable to break up the large event into smaller scene investigations. In past events, offices have developed teams to handle multiple fatalities. These teams generally include a medicolegal death investigator, a criminalist, and a detective. This way, a team would only have to investigate a few deaths after an event versus trying to process and investigate all of the fatalities. Treating each death like its own scene within the context of the larger event can help focus the professionals and limit the possibility for mistakes to be made, which might be the case if the investigators are constantly thinking about all of the bodies they have to process. One last point of emphasis when examining decedents prior to transport to a medicolegal facility is that there needs to be an agreed upon numbering system for the bodies and other remnants that are recovered. This will decrease the confusion as the bodies are processed and examined further down the line. Even if medicolegal death investigators believe they can presumptively identify a decedent, it is best to make a note of that but allow the identification procedures for the office to go about making the positive identification and still give the decedent one of the agreed upon mass fatality case numbers.

Lastly, having a unified command with multiple stakeholders is essential in these instances. Inevitably, one individual will be in charge of the event but he/she will require the input and expertize of those around the individual to make the most informed decisions possible based on what is known at that moment. Additionally, the individual in charge can change over time depending on the phase the event is in. An example of this could be a large scale hazardous materials situation. Initially, someone from the fire department might be in charge of the event because he/she is the agency that would best know how to respond and mitigate this particular situation. It then might transition to a police department lead event to pursue whether or not a crime has occurred. Once bodies are located within the scene, the direction of the event might transition to the medicolegal office to best process the bodies and prepare them for examination. Each situation is unique and requires a flexible approach that is built on plans that were developed prior to the event. The response from the medicolegal office, what types of evidence is collected and when it is collected, and whether or not everyone needs to be autopsied are decisions that will need to be made.

As part of the preplanning process, knowing what an office can handle is essential to determining what the threshold is for having to call in additional resources to handle a response. Resources could be human capital as well as structures or tools. To understand what an office can handle, one must first look at the office's capacity to investigate deaths without interruption with the regular staffing that is on at one time. If a mass fatality event takes two investigators away from the office to focus on that one scene and they will likely be out there for multiple hours, can the other medicolegal death investigators maintain the other caseload that is constantly being reported to the office? If not, can you call people in without creating a situation where the office will not have well-rested staff to handled regular shifts two or three days after the event? If you do not have the staff for this, it might be time to activate a local response team or request additional staff with surrounding offices that you have agreements with. Additionally, if it is a truly large scale event that will be drawn out over many days, weeks, or even months, the medicolegal office then needs to be willing to call in DMORT (Disaster Mortuary Operational Response Team) if the event has been declared a national emergency. The medicolegal facility is also a common concern when preplanning for a mass fatality event.

The vast majority of medicolegal offices in this country are not equipped to handle the sudden, dramatic increase in caseload that occurs when a mass fatality occurs. Knowing what an office can handle is essential. The number of spaces in the refrigerated cooling area is important to know, but does not paint a complete picture. If an office has room for 50 bodies but its normal body count is around 40 bodies at any given time in the cooler, anything more than 6–8 additional bodies from a single event will start to put the office in a bind. Many offices have memorandums of understanding with providers to allow them access to refrigerated trailers that could be utilized, if needed, to store bodies for a defined period of time. Additionally, if an event is a federally declared emergency and DMORT comes in, the medicolegal office will also likely need to set up one or many field sites where bodies can be safely stored and examinations can be performed. Being part of the discussion with the various stakeholders on the front end to plan for these events will greatly improve the ability for a medicolegal office to provide quality service with an appropriate turnaround time for all of the families impacted.

ANTHROPOLOGY

Deaths involving skeletal remains often require the assistance of an anthropologist. However, there are things that the medicolegal death investigator can do to ensure the successful recovery and processing of skeletal remains. There are also instances that occur more frequently that will not require a scene response from an anthropologist but may require a consultation later on. It is not uncommon for someone to find a bone, or what he/she believes to be a bone, and report it to a local law enforcement agency or the medical examiner/coroner office.

When a single item believed to be a human bone is found by a member of the general public, it is not uncommon for them to remove the item from where it was found prior to reporting it. The good news is often times these "human" bones turn out to be animal remains that the seasoned medicolegal death investigator can easily spot based on the remains' size or shape. However, for the ones that are likely from human remains, it is essential that there is a coordinated effort to have the individual who found the bone(s) take you back to the exact location so that a search of the area can be performed.

The first step, whether remains were located and left in place or located and removed, is to secure the scene for processing. If human remains decomposed fully are exposed to the environment, meaning they were not buried, bones and tissue may be spread out over a very large area due to animal activity. As with any scene, it is better to secure more area and be able to move into a more defined area than it is to start with a smaller scene and try to expand it.

The next step, as with any scene, is to document how the scene presents, including any landmarks that might be in the area. If the medicolegal death investigator is presented with a large outdoor scene, a proper search of the area should be preformed. If items are located that might be human remains, searchers should mark the item with a flag and the search should continue until the entire area has been examined. At this point, medicolegal death investigators can go back and take a look at the various items to see if they are in fact human remains. When in doubt, collect. If a near complete skeleton is found to be partially or fully buried in the ground, a grid over the area should be configured prior to excavating the remains.

Utilizing a forensic anthropologist can greatly improve the efficiency of a dig for possible or suspected human remains. While a medicolegal death investigator could be trained to create a proper grid over the ground to be searched as well as perform the actual excavation, having a trained professional has its obvious advantages. In addition to being able to provide on-the-spot information about the possible sex, age, and stature. Forensic anthropologists can also advise if the remains are from one individual or from multiple, and can help preserve the evidence and reduce the chance of creating artifacts during the excavation process. Since most makeshift graves that a medicolegal death investigator would come in contact with are shallow, it is important not to dig too aggressively. While some digs require large shovels or even a backhoe loader, the majority of cases require hand shovels and spades as well as paint brushes, to delicately remove small pieces of soil to expose the remains. Additionally, any soil that is removed should be sifted through using wooden boxes with wire mesh bottoms to ensure that small items are not discarded. Some of the potential small objects that might be located at such a dig could help piece together the story of who the decedent was. Items of clothing could help with identification or even tell the story of potential trauma, for example, a stab or gunshot wound passing through the item. Small personal items like jewelry or other unique property can greatly assist with telling who this person was. A good example of this can be found when searching through cases of unidentified bodies in the National Missing and Unidentified Persons (NamUs) database. This publicly available system will often show personal items of unidentified remains in America's morgues, because families can search the system, with limited capabilities, a unique necklace or watch might be all they need to know to determine if the John or Jane Doe could potentially be their loved one. Lastly, before and after removing the excavated remains from a dig, one must look for and document any signs of trauma or identifying features. If the medicolegal death investigator is dealing with a complete skeleton, there might be very few causes of death that can be opined and the evidence of trauma or changes due to natural disease might be all the medicolegal office has available when certifying the death. In addition to dental work, any chronic deformities to a skeleton could potentially help with identification. These could include previously healed fractures or unusual structural anomalies that differentiate the decedent from others. However, this is assuming that there is a potential identification for the John or Jane Doe and the medicolegal professionals have access to antemortem x-rays.

IN CUSTODY

Very few cases will garner as much attention as those that happen when an individual was in the custody of a law enforcement agency. The public, rightfully so, demands that those who are sworn to protect the community do so in a professional and safe manner. That being said, some instances occur where officers must use deadly force in a situation if their life or the life of another is reasonably at risk. When an individual dies as a result of a police action, the death will be ruled a homicide. This however does not mean, as we have previously discussed, that the officer did anything illegal. It just means that the individual died as a result of another person's actions; in this case a police action is the cause.

Reason for Fully Investigating These Deaths

In a time where law enforcement actions are a focal point of public interest, it is essential that the death of any individual who dies in police custody is fully investigated. In custody deaths could come in a number of settings. It could occur on the streets while the police are trying to effect an arrest, it could happen while the decedent was in a holding cell, or it may even happen postconviction inside of a state or federal penitentiary.

REFERENCES

Centers for Disease Control and Prevention. (2016). *Web-Based Injury Statistics Query and Reporting Systems*. Retrieved from: http://www.cdc.gov/injury/wisqars.

Denver II. (2015). *Denver Developmental Activities*. Retrieved from: http://denverii.com.

DiMaio, V., & Dana, S. (2007). *Handbook of Forensic Pathology* (second ed.). Boca Raton, FL: CRC Press.

Levy, A. D., Harcke, H. T., Getz, J. M., Mallak, C. T., Caruso, J. L., Pearse, L., Frazier, A. A., & Galvin, J. R. (2007). Virtual autopsy: two-and three-dimensional multidetector CT findings in drowning with autopsy comparison 1. *Radiology, 243*(3), 862−868.

Porter, T., & Gavin, H. (2010). Infanticide and neonaticide: a review of 40 years of research literature on incidence and causes. *Trauma, Violence, & Abuse, 11*(3), 99−112.

Senter, J., Sackoff, J., Landi, K., & Boyd, L. (2011). Studying sudden and unexpected infant deaths in a time of changing death certification and investigation practices: evaluating sleep-related risk factors for infant death in New York city. *Maternal & Child Health Journal, 15*(2), 242−248.

Task Force on Sudden Infant Death Syndrome. (2005). The changing concept of sudden infant death syndrome: diagnostic coding shifts, controversies regarding the sleeping environment, and new variables to consider in reducing risk. *Pediatrics, 116*(5), 1245−1255.

Trokel, M., DiScala, C., Terrin, N., & Sege, R. (2004). Blunt abdominal injury in the young pediatric patient: child abuse and patient outcomes. *Child Maltreatment, 9*(1), 111−117.

Chapter 11

Ethic/Legal Issues

Chapter Outline

When working as a medicolegal professional it is important to have a strong working knowledge of the applicable local, state, and national laws. Additionally, as a public agency that is tasked with a very important public health and safety function it is imperative to be as transparent in nature as possible. If a medical examiner or coroner's office does not have the trust of the stakeholders in their community, it makes it impossible to do the necessary work. As discussed in previous chapters, medicolegal death investigators depend on a strong relationship with family members and covictims of the decedent just as they do with the law enforcement community. That being said, this chapter will provide a basic overview of how to handle the remains of decedents, property of the decedent, and any evidence collected so that there is a proper chain of custody and to avoid any improprieties.

REMAINS

From the time the medicolegal death investigator arrives on scene, they are responsible for the decedent's remains. This responsibility does not end until care has been passed on to a funeral director who will handle final arrangements, which will likely include a traditional burial or a cremation. When most individuals think about having the responsibility to care for an individual's remains, they generally think about properly identifying the decedent and making sure the right body is released. However, there are a number of ethical and legal decisions that must be considered. These include how the body is handled through transportation, respecting family's wishes and religious beliefs, and handling every case the same regardless of who the decedent was.

Starting with performing a scene examination, to removing the decedent from the home, through transfers to and from the autopsy table the decedent

Essentials of Medicolegal Death Investigation. http://dx.doi.org/10.1016/B978-0-12-803641-9.00011-2

should be handled with the upmost care. The general rule of thumb for medicolegal death investigators is, if the family saw how you handle their loved one would they be upset? It would not be an unusual request for a family member to want to stay with the medicolegal death investigator while they perform their external exam. In some instances, such as a homicide investigation, this would not be appropriate. However, if there are no signs of foul play, unusual trauma, and the decedent had significant history that could account for their death it would not be improper to allow the next of kin or another close family member in the room during the examination. The viewing of the examination could be a necessary part of the surviving individual's healing process and the request should be strongly considered when at all possible. Conversely, there will be times that it would not be appropriate for a family member to be in the area while the medicolegal death investigator is performing their investigation.

One such instance is likely when the body is being moved, particularly upstairs or downstairs, or in a confined area. While every care could be taken in these scenarios, the reality is that this could not be a pleasant visual for families to absorb. When situations like this arise, or a family member does not feel comfortable seeing their loved one removed from a scene, it is best for the medicolegal death investigator to take the family into another area of the house they are in, or if the scene is outdoors, take them around to an area where they are less likely to see their loved one leave. In addition to handling the decedent's body with care, the medicolegal death investigator should do everything within their ability to adhere to the family's wishes and religious beliefs.

Families that have strongly held wishes and religious beliefs will generally inform the responding personnel about those requests. It is the medicolegal death investigator's job to determine what can legally occur and what is reasonable given the circumstances he/she is facing. In a separate chapter there is a more in-depth discussions of religions that are the most prevalent one will encounter during the commission of their job, but below are a couple of examples of cases where there was a request and it must be considered as to whether the request is legal and it is reasonable.

The first hypothetical scenario involves an American Indian man who has died from a possible illicit drug overdose. The tribe's beliefs involve placing ash inside of the decedent's palms and closing the hands. Additionally, there is a requirement for a member of the tribe to be with the decedent at all times until he is buried. Both of these could potentially create conflicts as such a death would require an autopsy to confirm the cause and manner of death.

In this scenario the medicolegal office would not be losing any evidentiary value, if there were no signs of foul play, to allow family to place the ashes inside of the decedent's hands and close them. The forensic pathologist should be made aware of this so during the autopsy they can protect the hands, possibly even bagging the hands during the autopsy so as not to get the hands wet or to minimize the loss of the ashes. The second practice of staying with the body could present a unique challenge.

It would be a best practice for medicolegal offices that have a large American Indian population in their jurisdiction to build relationships with the tribe early. This way, when issues come up or deaths occur there is an understanding from the medicolegal office as to the customs and traditions they should expect. Additionally, the tribe could be made aware of what legal acts the medicolegal office must perform. Going back to the practice of having someone with the decedent at all times, it would be impractical and unhealthy for the member staying with the body to stay in the body cooler for a prolonged period of time just as it would be unwarranted to have them in the autopsy suite during the performance of the autopsy. In these situations every possible measure should be taken to allow the individual accompanying the body to stay in the facility as long as the safety of the staff is not negatively affected. If there is a secure waiting room or lobby where they could stay until the completion of the autopsy then this request should be honored. Another example would be the family's request to see a homicide victim before the decedent is removed from the scene.

The request from a family member or covictim to see and touch a decedent before they leave the scene is a very common one, and one that should be honored whenever practically possible. There are times, however, when this would not be considered a best practice. The problem with allowing a family member to see and touch a homicide victim is that they could inadvertently add or remove evidence to the scene. Locard's exchange principle tells us that every individual who enters a crime scene will take something with them, as well as leave something behind. This is as true for the investigators as it is for bystanders. However, the investigators need to be in the scene to process it and take every precaution to limit their disruption of the scene. Distraught family members or covictims do not have the same training, universal precautions, or due to the stress of the situation an emotional stability like that of the investigators. In these instances, the medicolegal death investigator should explain to the family that to preserve evidence for a potential trial it is necessary to not allow them in at this time. However, the family and covictims should be assured that once the autopsy is complete they will be able to touch, hold, and see their loved one. In some instances, once the body is sealed in a body bag, placed on a gurney, and covered with a quilt or other covering the family may be allowed to place their hand on top of the quilt to have a brief moment outside of the primary scene before loading the body into the transport vehicle. While not the same as actually being able to see and feel their loved one, this may be an acceptable alternative for the time being. This would be conditional on the medicolegal death investigator and the law enforcement professionals feeling that there would not be any incidents associated with this act and that the family members were small in number and that they were as cooperative as could be expected under the current circumstances.

Regardless of the specifics of a case, every attempt should be made to handle every case in the same general way. Certain cases will undoubtedly be higher profile than others, or will present unique challenges, but the basic care and investigation into someone's death should be the same regardless of their social, political, or ethnic background. Each death marks the end of an individual's life, and they deserve to be handled in a respectful and professional manner. Too often, medicolegal offices will make adjustments or take special action if the decedent was a well-known figure in the community or has a relationship to an elected official. By doing this, an office may be winning favor with a certain group of individuals, but if the general public finds out that special treatment has been provided it can greatly reduce the trust that they hold in the entire system. The one caveat is when there is a high profile case.

High profile cases can be a complete drain on office's resources. Medicolegal offices tend to be scarce of additional employees above the bare necessities. So, when a high profile case occurs, particularly cases with multiple fatalities, they greatly tax the available resources. In these instances, due to the stress on the system, which includes demands from local, national, and even international media, it is often in the best interest of the medicolegal office to expedite the autopsies and laboratory testing to clear these cases from their workload. In these rare events, the general public is accepting and supportive of the increased effort in these cases.

PROPERTY

After the proper handling of the decedent's remains, the handling of the decedent's property is of the upmost importance. Medicolegal offices can get into trouble at times if they do not have a proper system in place to collect, document, track, and release personal effects for the deaths that they investigate. The first step is to develop the appropriate policies associated with this process. While policy alone will not provide all of the necessary safeguards to avoid an unfortunate event, it can delineate what is expected of the staff so that there is an expected guideline in place.

Anytime an office is developing a policy for their practice there are two sources, at a minimum, which should be considered. The first source should be the laws and statutes that affect the jurisdiction. Knowing what is legal to collect, under what circumstances it can be collected, and to whom the property can be released to are extremely important. The second source should be the appropriate accreditation body for the field. For medicolegal offices there are currently two organizations that handle accreditation: the National Association of Medical Examiners (NAME) and the International Association of Coroners and Medical Examiners (IAC&ME). At the present time, there is no national requirement that a medicolegal office be nationally accredited, though this may change in the future. Regardless, the accreditation standards that are outlined by NAME and IAC&ME provide a known industry standard that any office can access and utilize as a guide for developing their own best practice. One essential aspect of any policy related to a decedent's property is the appropriate documentation.

Whether a department uses a paper system or a completely computer-based property management system there needs to be a well-developed system in place to track a decedent's property. This starts at the scene and continues all the way until after the items have been released to the appropriate party. Once an item is collected by the medicolegal death investigator it must be fully documented prior to being placed in a sealable container, often a paper or plastic bag depending on the contents. It is easy to simply log that a wallet was collected, but there should be a more complete record that details the style of wallet and the exact contents. If a detailed record is not kept, the medicolegal death investigator can expect to field calls and complaints asking where a specific item or amount of money is located. If your records only state that you had a wallet and there was no mention of money the office could be in a precarious position having to explain where the money may or may not be. However, if a complete record shows that the wallet only had $20 in it, and the family is asking about where the $2000 the decedent had with him/her is, there will at least be a record showing that it was never in the possession of the medicolegal office and thus they bear no responsibility. Some additional helpful reminders when documenting personal effects include the following:

- Do not state a specific brand or material. Speak more generally about the item and if there is writing on a wallet, as an example, simply put the words in quotation marks.
- Do not describe a stone as a diamond, ruby, or emerald, as examples. Instead, state that there is a clear, red, or green stone.
- Do not describe the type of metal of an object such as gold or silver. Instead, state that the item is a yellow or white metal.

Once the items have been collected, they must be secured. This could range from the items being stored in a locked closet to a digital system with a bar code feature. Regardless of the resources of the office, there needs to be a way in which the access to the personal items are limited to only staff members with a genuine need. Some bare-bones systems, such as the locked closet, severely limit the ability to track who entered and removed items. So, what security measures can be taken should be taken. The same is true for medications that are recovered on scene, which will be discussed a little later in the chapter. Additionally, the medicolegal death investigator needs to be aware of what they can legally collect.

The legal requirements around who can collect items should be an important point of emphasis for any medicolegal death investigator's initial training with an office. The legal standards are different in each state. In general, the medicolegal death investigator will collect items that are on the decedent and anything that will help them determine the cause and manner of death or find next of kin. However, not everything needs to be collected.

Personal effects should not be collected just for the sake of collecting them. The fewer items the medicolegal office takes possession of, the less likely the chance for something to be damaged or misplaced. Examples of this could be the decedent dying in their own home where items could be left behind and the residence secured. Another example would be when the decedent's next of kin is on scene. The caveat here is that if there is any chance that there could be a disagreement about who is the legal next of kin, the personal items should be collected by the medicolegal death investigator. If items were collected, once the appropriate individual is identified to release the effects to, it is important to ensure that there is appropriate documentation showing why this individual was the legal next-of-kin and when the items were released.

Properly documenting of the release of personal effects generally involves the person whose items are being released to signing a standard form of some kind. It may also be appropriate to document the government-issued identification that the individual presents when picking up the items. In some jurisdictions, the items are released to the mortuary that is handling final arrangements. The only point of emphasis here is that the legal next of kin who signs the mortuary release should also indicate on the same form that they give permission to pick up the personal effects too. While great care should be taken with the documentation, collection, storage, and release of personal effects, even greater care should be taken when collecting evidence.

EVIDENCE

The first and most important concept of evidence collection is the idea of maintaining the chain of custody. The chain of custody is the documentation showing who has collected, sealed, examined, and eventually released an item. This is done by ensuring each individual who comes into contact with an item signs and records the date and time on both the package the item is sealed in and a standard tracking form. The form used for tracking could be as simple as a handwritten document with multiple lines that the staff handling or testing the items could record the appropriate information on, or the items could be tracked electronically through an electronic records system.

Regardless of the system utilized to track the evidence collected by the medicolegal office, it is imperative that there is a complete record of everyone who touched that piece of evidence. Without this, there is no way for an agency to ensure that the piece of evidence has not been tampered with prior to being introduced at trial. If an item is not admissible due to the mishandling of evidence, it could be the difference between a conviction and a case not even making it to trial.

Preparing evidence for packaging is the first step in the process to properly storing, maintaining, and tracking the item. Each item retained by the medicolegal office will need to be packaged separately. So, if two socks are recovered on a scene, they must be placed into separate paper bags and labeled as two where they came from. If an item is wet, it is not uncommon to collect the item as is on scene, and once the medicolegal death investigator returns to the office the item can be removed from the sealed paper bag and placed on a drying rack. If wet items are not properly dried, mold will develop over time and degrade the possible evidence on the item.

In most instances, prescription medications that are collected on scene can all be placed in one large bag to be processed later. The reason being is that the medicolegal death investigator and the forensic pathologist are generally only concerned with which medications were found on scene, does it appear that the decedent was taking them as prescribed, and then when the toxicology results come back the substances found in the decedent's system can be compared to the medication log. Oftentimes the medications can provide a window into what was going on with the individual.

If medications are present that reveal the decedent had a number of chronic health conditions, it may not be necessary to perform an autopsy. Conversely, if certain medications such as sleeping aids or narcotic pain medications are present, an autopsy may be required to determine if those medications played a role once the decedent's medical history and other scene findings are weighed. Also, medication bottles that have fewer pills remaining than that would be expected based on the day in which they were filled, the total number filled, and the prescribed frequency may indicate one of two scenarios. In one scenario, the decedent took too much of their medication. This is generally associated with prescription medications that have a high rate of abuse such as the narcotic pain medications and the sleeping aids. In the other scenario, the decedent did not take enough of their medications. This too is important to know because it speaks to the overall health of the decedent. Take diabetics for example. If they were not staying on schedule with their medication regiment it is unlikely that their diabetes was well controlled. The same would be true of an individual with medications for cardiac issues. Without the medications, it is not difficult for the medicolegal death investigator to hypothesis that the decedent's conditions were only deteriorating over time due to a lack of care and maintenance. In most offices, if a death requires a scene investigation the medications are almost always inventoried and sometimes retained by the medicolegal office.

Information contained on the prescription bottles is extremely valuable for the medicolegal death investigator. The basic information on most prescription medications are the individual to whom the medication was prescribed; who was the prescribing physician; which pharmacy filled the prescription; and medication-specific information such as the prescription, generic or trade, the quantity prescribed and the quantity filled this particular time, the dosage as many medications can be prescribed at various dosages, and at what frequency the individual is supposed to take the medication. Documenting this information as well as the exact number of pills remaining is crucial to having a complete investigative report to provide the forensic pathologist prior to a medicolegal autopsy. This information can also help the medicolegal death investigator track down a more complete picture of the decedent's life and health.

A common occurrence is when a decedent is found in his/her home by someone who is not a member of his/her family. Once law enforcement and the medical examiner/coroner arrive on scene, one of the items investigators are looking for is information regarding who the decedent's next of kin is. This can even be more challenging as technologies continue to advance and people do not write names, addresses, and phone numbers in address books anymore. Today, most individuals keep their contact information on a cell phone, so tracking down families requires new techniques. An easy way to check, based on the medications, is to reach out to the prescribing physician's office to see if the decedent had filled out an emergency contact form. This is not always a fruitful effort, but it is just one way in which medications can provide more than just information on the decedent's health. It may also reveal a pattern of care.

If a decedent's most recently filled medications are from a provider who only sees patients in a hospital setting, like an emergency room physician or a hospitalist, it might indicate to the medicolegal death investigator that the individual's health was starting to deteriorate. The medical records from the hospital can oftentimes indicate that an individual was deteriorating in health or that a serious illness had just been diagnosed. This information would oftentimes not be readily known to a decedent's primary care provider as they may only see them occasionally. So if records from the primary care provider where the only ones requested, a forensic pathologist would not have all of the information necessary to them at the time a decision is made regarding whether to perform an autopsy or not. It is also worth noting that just because the medications may not seem of particular value while they are being collected on scene, but later on in the investigation and follow-up stages they could end up being an excellent resource for where to turn for additional information whether it is from a provider, a pharmacy, or a treating facility.

Regardless of the usefulness of a decedent's collected prescription medications, if the medicolegal death investigator takes them into their care, the medications' information must be fully documented and the bottles counted. Once this count is performed, the medications should be stored in a secure location so that only individuals with a legitimate interest are having access, do. Once the time comes to destroy the medications, a medicolegal office must have proper protocols for safely removing the medications. These include having them destroyed according to industry standards so that the disposal does not negatively affect the environment. Additionally, safety measures must be in place to ensure that the individual who counted the medications prior to placing them into a secure area is not the individual who disposes of them. A person separate from the case should count the medications again and log this number so that it can be compared against the original value. While no system is perfect, every measure possible should be taken to ensure collected medications are accounted for and destroyed properly. The same is true for illicit drugs that the medicolegal office collects on scene.

Illicit drugs, particularly heroin, are significantly on the rise in the United States. As previously discussed in this text, individuals dying from drug overdoses make up a noteworthy amount of cases each year. When encountered on a death scene, each office handles the collection of the related evidence a little differently, and state statute sometimes plays a role in who is ultimately responsible for collection on scene of illicit drugs and paraphernalia. If the medicolegal office has the authority to collect these items, as they often do, the proper procedures must be in place for ensuring the safe collection, storage, and destruction of illicit drugs.

The first step to ensuring an ethical collection of illicit drugs involves the documentation and properly packaging of items. At some point in their history, every office will go through some kind of scandal, and sadly, these sometimes are related to staff members stealing drugs for personal use. To avoid this type of a scandal, the thorough documentation of illicit drugs on a scene can be the first step in a series to provide an effective institutional guardian against this unethical and criminal abuse.

Documenting where the potential drug and/or paraphernalia was located on a scene with photographs and in writing on a scene report creates the start of a paper trail that an item was found and collected. This paper trail, or chain of custody, makes the theft of this type or any item substantially more difficult. This is because someone, at some point, will notice that the item(s) has been taken. Once the item has been documented where it was found, property collecting and sealing the item is the next guard against someone improperly accessing the item. Lastly, securing the item in a safe place, as discussed with the other items, personal property, and prescription drugs, limits the number of individuals who have access to the item and could possibly remove the drugs or paraphernalia.

HAVING THE RIGHT CULTURE

In some professions, law enforcement being one of them, there is often a culture that supports looking out for each other. Part of this is very admirable and helpful, particularly in high-stress fields such as law enforcement and forensics. However, the problem comes into play when the same culture precludes someone from reporting unethical behavior simply because they are afraid of hurting the individual or worse, be retaliated against. The theory of a "rotten apple" can lead to some believing an unethical behavior by a public safety professional is isolated (Delattre, 1989); however, this view may cause an organization or public to miss the actual systematic corruption that is occurring (White & Terry, 2008). Some research studies suggest that there is an importance for frontline supervisors to document and enforce unethical behavior to maintain an ethical culture (Lee, Lim, Moore, & Kim, 2013). This illustrates that the direction from the chief medical examiner or coroner, particularly in large organizations, is not always enough to set the tone for an office to support an ethical environment. In addition to the workplace, professionals in death investigation have ethical codes they must live up to in to maintain their certification.

CERTIFYING BOARDS AND MEMBERSHIP ORGANIZATIONS

Lastly, professional certifying boards as well as membership organizations provide a certain level of ethical guidelines that one of their certificants or members, depending on what setting you are discussing, must uphold. Forensic pathologists are physicians who have their own ethical guidelines consistent with their medical practice as well as their licensure. This section will not focus on them specifically but instead will focus on medicolegal death investigators.

Multiple states, particularly ones with strong medical examiner or coroner associations, have their own certification process that the medicolegal death investigators in that particular state must complete but the national organization that certifies these professionals is the American Board of Medicolegal Death Investigators (ABMDI). Part of ABMDI's (2014) code of ethics and conduct states the following:

- As a means to promote the highest quality of professional and personal conduct of its certificants, the following constitutes the Code of Ethics and Conduct, which shall be endorsed and adhered to by all certificants of the ABMDI.
  a) Every member of the ABMDI shall refrain from exercising professional or personal conduct adverse to the best interests and purposes of the ABMDI.
  b) Every member of the ABMDI shall refrain from providing any material misrepresentation of education, training, experience, or fact. Misrepresentation of one or more criteria shall constitute a violation of this section of the code.
  c) Every member of the ABMDI shall refrain from making statements that appear to represent the position of the ABMDI without specific authority first obtained in writing from the Board.
- Any member of the ABMDI who has violated any of the provisions of the Code of Ethics and Conduct shall be liable to censure or suspension/revocation of their Certificate by action of the Board.

This is just a portion of the ethics statement put out by the nonprofit organization that is considered the gold standard in certifying medicolegal death investigators not only in the United States but also those in other countries as well as in the armed forces. It may seem vague in nature, but this is not uncommon. Many of the cases are determined based on precedence, or what the ethics committee and eventually the board of directors determine is unacceptable based on previous decisions. However, this does not allow for much guidance to the peers of the certificants in question when determining what punishment is warranted, if any (Downs & Swienton, 2012). The difficulty with creating a more specific code of ethics is that there may be unintended consequences associated with limiting the scope of a certifying body's ability to control "bad actors" in the profession.

In a similar fashion, professional membership organizations attempt to accomplish the same goal but have less of an ability to negatively impact an individual continuing to work in the field. If an ethical violation was severe enough, a certifying body could suspend or revoke a medicolegal death investigator's credentials. This, in a number of instances, would make the individual no longer able to work as certification is often a requirement to maintain employment. With professional organizations such as the NAME, IAC&ME, and the American Academy of Forensic Science, having one of their members be found guilty of an ethical violation simply means they are removed from the organization. This would not, however, preclude them from working in the field the same as losing their certification would. This is not to say, however, that an issue brought before an ethics committee would not likely be handled too in a human resources setting.

Regardless of the ability of a certifying board or professional organization to fully investigate and safeguard the community from individuals who do something unethical or illegal at this point in time, the continual pursuit of greater accountability and protections from unethical behavior should be sought. As time progresses, particularly with certification possibly being mandated at a federal level, there could be greater professional accountability if all medicolegal death investigators in the United States are required to be certified to be employed in the field. Until that occurs, the ownness will continue to be placed on the individual offices and systems to have strong policies and procedures, require certification for all of their medicolegal death investigators, and have an office culture that adheres to a strong ethical code.

REFERENCES

American Board of Medicolegal Death Investigators. (April 2014). *Policies and Procedures.* Baltimore, MD.

Delattre, E. J. (1989). *Character and Cops: Ethics in Policing*. Washington, DC: American Enterprise Institute for Public Policy Research.

Downs, J. U., & Swienton, A. R. (Eds.). (2012). *Ethics in Forensic Science*. Oxford, UK: Elsevier Academic Press.

Lee, H., Lim, H., Moore, D. D., & Kim, J. (2013). How police organizational structure correlates with frontline officers' attitudes toward corruption: a multilevel model. *Police Practice and Research, 14*(5), 386–401.

White, M. D., & Terry, K. J. (2008). Child sexual abuse in the catholic church: revisiting the rotten apples explanation. *Criminal Justice and Behavior, 35*, 658–678.

Chapter 12

Working With Families

Chapter Outline

To be an effective medicolegal professional one must not only possess the necessary knowledge associated with his/her field, but equally, if not more important, is the professional's ability to work with the families and covictims of those who have died. This is an important component of a family member or friend being willing to communicate with the medicolegal death investigator throughout the investigative process. When dealing with the families, agencies should consider taking a team approach to ensuring proper communication.

During the investigation of a death, particularly if it is a homicide investigation, families may feel like they are not being kept in the loop about what is happening with their case. This can become a delicate balance between the medicolegal office and the law enforcement agency on how they communicate with these families. On the one hand, it is important for agencies to assure the survivors that everything is being done to find answers for why and how their loved one died. Conversely, there needs to be a certain level of secrecy, or keeping facts of the case close to the vest. If the medicolegal death investigator knows that a case is likely criminal in nature, and the office will be unable to let the family know everything up front then the family should be told as such up front. Letting them know the benefits of not divulging all the evidence to them in the initial stages will improve the law enforcement agency's ability to file a case with the district attorney to get a conviction. Compounding this, there is also evidence that families and covictims of homicide do not feel the same about their grief as those who have lost someone from other means.

Having and encouraging support groups is one of the many things a medicolegal death investigator can do for a family who is experiencing a sudden loss. However, there is evidence that families of homicide victims often do not find comfort in shared experiences of loss unless the loss experienced by another individual was from a homicide as well. Families can struggle to make a connection or understand that another's grief could possibly be the same as theirs. In the family member or covictim's mind, the other

Essentials of Medicolegal Death Investigation. http://dx.doi.org/10.1016/B978-0-12-803641-9.00012-4

person's loved one could not have possibly felt the fear or pain that their loved one did just prior to death (Wellman, 2014). This difference in the perception of loss suffered is important to understand and should be considered when finding resources for families. This all starts with the death notification.

MAKING A DEATH NOTIFICATION

An important and very difficult function that is almost always handled by the medicolegal death investigator is the notification of death to the next of kin. The proper handling of this responsibility is one of the ways in which the agency sets themselves up for as positive of an interaction with a family as possible. With this in mind, careful consideration should go into how a notification is made.

By taking a team approach to the next of kin notification, agencies can create a situation where there are multiple resources immediately present for when they hear the horrible news that their loved one has died. The team dispatched to handle the notification should include a law enforcement officer, a victim advocate, and a medicolegal death investigator.

The law enforcement officer serves two main functions as part of this team. First, their presence in uniform, or if in plain clothes the visibility of their badge, provides legitimacy that this is a real and official act. Many medicolegal death investigators do not wear a uniform similar to that of an officer. The general public is more likely to come in contact with a medicolegal death investigator who, while dressed professionally, is in plain clothes. This has to do with the jurisdiction in which the death occurs. Medicolegal offices that are part of a public health system are less likely to carry a badge or wear a uniform, whereas medicolegal death investigators who work in a public safety–based system might wear a badge and uniform. Some in a sheriff-coroner system might even be peace officers and carry a firearm. The second function of a police officer as part of the notification team is for knowledge.

When a death occurs there need not be a criminal investigation that is ongoing for a law enforcement agency to be involved. As examples, property could have been collected by the officers on the death scene and the officer could provide guidance to the next of kin on how those items could be collected. Additionally, there could be questions associated with who and when an individual could access the scene where a loved one died. The law enforcement officer would have the most knowledge to answer these questions and to provide direction on how to contact their agency. It is also important to address the emotional aspects of a death notification, and for this victim advocates are an integral part of the notification team.

The training and availability of victim advocates varies greatly depending on where someone lives. For departments that have victim advocacy programs, oftentimes there are only a few full-time employees who are supported by a large network of volunteers. Their backgrounds, regardless of employment status with the agency, tend to be in social work or counseling. Including these professionals as part of the notification team can provide the family member with someone who is specially trained in dealing with the emotional support needs of someone who is in the acute stages of trauma. Additionally, these professionals can provide a continuation of care for the family's mental well-being well after the initial notification. Most victim advocacy programs provide a list of resources and support groups similarly to what has been previously discussed in this text, some of which are specific to populations such as families of homicide victims or families who have lost a child. The victim advocate can also spend more time with the family on scene than the medicolegal death investigator can. This is often the case because even in large medicolegal offices there are usually very few investigators on to cover the jurisdiction in which they serve. The care provided by the victim advocate allows that medicolegal death investigator to get back into the field to handle the next case. In some instances there may not be the availability of resources to take a team approach to a death notification. Regardless of whether multiple professionals can respond to make a notification or not, every effort should be made to make the death notification in person.

The notification of death is often an unexpected event. As a medicolegal death investigator this may be handled by the first responders to an event. If the family finds their loved one unresponsive, notifies emergency services, and the decedent is pronounced dead on scene the family will be told by the pronouncing paramedics. However, it is often the case that the medicolegal death investigator will need to track down the decedent's family and notify them, unexpectedly of the death. Doing this in person is the preferred choice over making a telephone call.

Notifying the next of kin is difficult to perform over the telephone since you have no control over the environment they are in when the call is made, or the ability to provide proper assistance if they are alone and need support from someone close to them. However, this is the only option at times. This is particularly common when a decedent does not have a lot of resources or close family contact which would generate populated information into people-find software. A common example would be finding a decedent's phone with contacts that they routinely called or exchanged text messages with, but a search of the people-find software does not produce an active address for that number or individual. In these instances a phone call may be your only option to make notification within a reasonable time frame. Staffing issues could also be a limitation that drives a department to make notifications via a phone call versus in person.

Very large departments may justify making the notification of death by telephone simply because they do not have the staff to send to execute this in person. However, the consequences of how a death notification is made can have lasting consequences as described by Stewart (1999):

> *Although the content of a death notice...undeniably presents numerous challenges and adjustments that may have unhealthy and long-lasting effects, the process of a death notification...can significantly affect the extent to which the survivors cope with these challenges (pp. 302–303).*

As public servants, medicolegal death investigators should do everything within their control to serve the needs of their stakeholders, and this should extend to the covictims. If a decedent's next of kin lives outside of the medicolegal death investigator's jurisdiction, it is a common practice to notify an agency in the jurisdiction of the individual to be notified and ask for assistance making the notification. While the medicolegal death investigator will not have any control over how the outside agency handles the notification, it will at least be made in person and the family can then be given the investigator's office information to call to have their questions answered when they are able. Before ending the telephone conversation with a decedent's family member the medicolegal death investigator should be sure to articulate which office is handling their loved one's death, and contact information should be provided so someone can be reached to answer further questions or concerns that may arise. This is more easily handled when the death notification is made in person.

Medical examiner/coroner offices and/or the victim advocate unit, usually housed in a law enforcement agency, should create a brochure to hand out to families that they make notification to. This provides an easy to use source when dealing with bereaved families. Oftentimes the initial information provided to families during a death notification is not remembered due to the stress and shock associated with the event. By providing an easy to use reference, families will be able to review and look up information whenever they are able to better process the information.

The brochures for families can be very different depending on the jurisdiction, but there should be three standard sections to any good handout. First and most importantly, there should be contact information for the multitude of agencies the family may need assistance from or have a question for. This should include at a minimum the medical examiner/coroner office, the various law enforcement agencies that are served by the particular medicolegal office, and the victim assistance unit. Second, the brochure should discuss some of the emotions the family may experience after a sudden, unexpected loss. This will help the family members better understand what they are going through and will also provide the sense that they are not alone in feeling a particular way about a loved one's death. Third, multiple resources should be included so that families can reach out for assistance if needed. The resources could be various support groups, crime scene cleanup companies, government assistance for burial expenses, and the resources may even list the mortuaries in the area. Anything the medicolegal office and other agencies within the jurisdiction can do to assist in the process will empower families to take tasks on when they are emotionally ready and can decrease the number of unnecessary calls to investigators simply because they are unaware of the process.

CULTURAL/RELIGIOUS ISSUES

There are a number of religions that are practiced regardless of where an office is located. Obviously, large metropolitan communities tend to have a greater diversity of religions present, but regardless it is important to understand how a religious practice may influence the investigation into someone's death. This text will focus on three Abrahamic traditions which are some of the most common religions that one might encounter during the commission of his/her work. They are Christianity, Islam, and Judaism. The religion of a decedent is important because it could have an impact on the medicolegal death investigator's dealings with the family, and there could be legal implications since some states require the medical examiner or coroner to consider religious beliefs prior to determining if an autopsy is necessary (Bierig, 2001). This section will not focus so much on the overall beliefs of the religions, but on how those beliefs impact their interactions with medicolegal offices.

Christianity. The majority of Christians will not object to an autopsy, at least on a religious basis. The belief among Christians is that when individuals die, their soul is raised to God for judgment. Thus, as long as their body is treated with respect there is not likely to be an issue. However, there is scripture in the Bible regarding the resurrection of the dead. For this reason, some Christians believed that a body should not be cremated. However, this is no longer a common belief. Many of the concerns of Christians regarding an autopsy deal with how the procedure will affect their funeral options.

If a Christian family is concerned with an autopsy being performed, the medicolegal death investigator should focus the conversation on the fact that an autopsy is a medical procedure and it will not preclude them from having an open casket, describe the benefits to the family members to possibly identify health concerns they should discuss with their primary care providers, and describe the need for the procedure to determine what happened to their loved one. The key with Christians, as with all individuals, is to accurately and compassionately communicate your position for the need for the autopsy to be performed.

Islam. Families who practice Islam have a number of objections that affect how the medicolegal office can proceed with an autopsy. The first is that the Islamic faith teaches that an individual's body belongs to God and that no part of his/her body should be removed or even donated (Campbell, 1998; Green & Green, 1992). Thus, eviscerating organs for examination and keeping sections of tissue for histology, as examples, would be against this belief. The second issue that generally arises when dealing with the death of an individual of Islamic faith is the belief that their loved one must be buried within 24 h of his/her time of death.

When an instance such as a religious objection to an autopsy occurs, the medicolegal office should always weigh the religious beliefs of the decedent against the need to protect public safety and health. There is research that suggests certain cases based on probable manner of death, suicide, accident, and natural, are more likely to be signed out with less invasive procedures when a religious objection is made by the family (Carpenter, Tait, Adkins, Barns, Naylor, & Begum, 2011).

Judaism. Families who practice Judaism believe that an individual's body was created in the likeness of God and upon death the soul remains near the individual (Mittleman, Davis, Kasztl, & Graves, 1992). As such, any alterations or discarding of tissue could be seen as an undignified treatment of a holy body. For this reason, Jewish families will often strongly object to the performance of an autopsy. However, there are agreed-upon standards for Jewish decedents whose death would require an autopsy.

When an autopsy is performed on a Jewish decedent, the key is to avoid collecting more than what is needed or in general wasting any tissues of the body including blood. So, only the blood that is necessary for testing will be collected, and no organs will be retained for examination at a later time. Additionally, surgical towels are often used to soak up the loss of blood and the drain at the foot of the autopsy table is usually plugged so that no fluids are lost. The surgical towels that have blood on them are often placed in the body when the examination is complete. Rabbis can be extremely helpful when families state that their religion does not allow for an autopsy.

Rabbis, in general, are aware of the benefits of an autopsy as well as the procedures in place to conform the procedure to honor the Jewish religion. If a medicolegal office encounters a Jewish community or Rabbi who does not have an understanding of this need and adjustments to the procedure, it is incumbent on the office's leadership to start the conversation before it becomes an issue on scene. It is often a smart practice for the office to initiate the conversation about bringing the decedent's Rabbi to the scene at the beginning of the investigation to help with the conversation about the need for an autopsy, in addition to the general support they could provide to a family member of covictim. The medicolegal death investigator should also be aware of what to do on the Shabbat.

There are weekly Shabbats that generally start on sundown Friday and end on Saturday night, and there are also Sabbaths associated with certain religious holidays. Regardless of the specific Shabbat, the medicolegal death investigator may find it more difficult to have access to the decedent's Rabbi or to have a mortuary discuss the specifics of the service as business transactions are discouraged during this time. However, mortuaries that handle Jewish services will still respond to and take possession of the body regardless of the day as there is a focus on preparing the body for burial in the earth as soon as possible.

PROPER COMMUNICATION AND FOLLOW-UP

In this text, we have discussed the need for setting an appropriate tone with family members at the beginning of the investigation in order to foster a trusting relationship that will hopefully last throughout the investigation until the death is certified, and in some cases even after. In the investigation of someone's death, as is the case with any relationship, there must be effort put in at all stages to continue to have success. In the context of a medicolegal death investigation, this means communicating when their loved one can leave the care of the medicolegal office and be released to a mortuary, following up with family members if they have questions or concerns, and notifying them when the investigation is complete and the death certificate is ready to be signed out.

The last step to be completed prior to leaving a death scene is to talk with the family and other covictims present on scene. In this text, the information that is needed for the investigation has been discussed. This includes the timeline leading up to the death, the decedent's past medical, social, and work history, to name a few. However, to continue to have a strong working relationship with the family the medicolegal death investigator must address their needs too in addition to the medicolegal office's needs. This includes informing the family of the next steps in the process, providing resources which could include a list of mortuaries in the area, support services, and financial assistance for burial expenses, and it also includes where their loved one's body is going to be taken and when it can be released.

Family members and other covictims are likely to know where the decedent is at all times. This starts from the scene through to the funeral. By letting the family know where the medical examiner or coroner office physically is it provides them with an understanding about where the decedent will be located. At this point it is also important to stress to the family that their loved one will be safe or, said another way, will be in a secured facility until a final decision is made by the forensic pathologist about whether or not an autopsy will be performed. Additionally, some offices will contact the family at the same time they contact the mortuary to make sure everyone is on the same page as far as the decedent being ready to be released from the medicolegal office and into the care of the funeral director. Once the body has been released, this does not end the communication between families and the office.

Following up with family members who have questions or concerns in a timely manner is important to maintain a strong working relationship. A single medicolegal office could handle a significant number of cases in a day, but the workload is not important to a family who has a question that they feel is urgent and needs resolution. It is important for the medicolegal death investigators to maintain perspective about these concerns as they will expect a quick response if they themselves have a follow-up question as part of the investigation that they would like answered. Oftentimes the questions one gets from a family member or covictim are not one that the medicolegal death investigator should handle, but being the referee and finding the right resource to address, the issue is just as important for building trust. Knowing the local laws is also important as this could affect who can receive what information.

Some states, such as Colorado, are what are called open records states. This means that anyone, with or without a legitimate reason, can call up or write the medicolegal office and request information about a case. This could include the entire case file, assuming there is not an ongoing investigation or that the file has not been sealed by court order. There are other states, such as Iowa, that will only allow the release of the cause and manner of death, with the exception of the legal next of kin, who can request a copy of the autopsy report. There are obvious benefits as well as challenges that present depending on the particular state's laws. Regardless of the openness of the medicolegal office's records, the medicolegal death investigator must be aware of the particular laws governing his/her jurisdiction. If there is any doubt, legal counsel should be sought out from the appropriate state, county, or city office. The last key component of quality communication with a decedent's family is letting them know when the death has been officially certified.

Notifying the next of kin when the investigation is complete and the death certificate is ready to be signed out is the last step in the process of handling the investigation into a decedent's death. This is an important step that too many offices overlook. Having the ability to contact the next of kin directly to inform them of the cause and manner of death that will be on the death certificate allows the office to adequately explain why the death is being certified in that fashion, and what it means more specifically based on the findings of the investigation and autopsy. Additionally, this provides the opportunity for the family to ask follow-up questions in a timely manner to improve their understanding.

WORKING WITH FAMILIES AFTER THE CERTIFICATION

Just because a case has been signed out does not mean that the medicolegal office no longer has contact with the decedent's family. While some families will find out how their loved one's death certificate was filled out, and the office will never hear from them again. Others will call from time-to-time, or they will ask for an autopsy report months or even years after their family member's death. Sometimes covictims are not ready to know the details about how someone they loved died. For some, the passage of time and/or the nagging questions in their head will bring them to a point where they are ready for more information. If this time comes, the medicolegal office should provide an avenue for them to seek answers, even if it is years since the death was investigated.

Whether the death just occurred a few months earlier or it occurred a few years ago, talking with families over the telephone or in the office provides a level of professionalism that all offices should afford their constituents. While it can be difficult to carve out time in a busy day to meet with families, being able to go over the case in great detail with an individual or family might be the best way to fully inform them and reduce the likelihood that they will need to call back multiple times to get the answers they are seeking. This is often seen when the death is one that is not easily accepted by the family, like when an individual commits suicide.

When someone commits suicide, there is often a social stigma attached to that certification. As such, many families will have difficulty accepting this ruling. One way in which a medicolegal office can improve the family's understanding is by showing them all of the facts that lead the office to make that certification. This is not always effective, but oftentimes the totality of the evidence that supports a ruling, in this case suicide, is helpful for families to understand why the medicolegal office made the decision that they did. There are also less direct ways that a medicolegal office can communicate their priorities and commitment to the community in which they serve, including taking part in public events to honor those who have died.

Holding memorial services for crime victims, individuals who committed suicide, or those who are unidentified is a way in which a medicolegal office can build lasting relationships with the community in which they serve, as well as highlight their commitment to important social issues. These events can be put on with other community stakeholders as a way of showing that someone's death went unnoticed. It is also a way to bring awareness to a particular issue. In addition to simply bringing awareness to an issue, medicolegal offices can improve the outcomes in cases by working with multidisciplinary working groups.

One issue that many multidisciplinary teams have tried to address in recent years is the number of homicide cases that do not have a legal resolution. Assisting with cold case teams as a way to continue to serve the community by providing expertize in reviewing findings from case files to help generate new ideas for tackling the unresolved cases. Additionally, there are also multiple federal initiatives to help guide public policy on a number of issues from improving public health research by standardizing certain information on all cases, to developing standards of practice.

The profession of a specially trained, educated, and nationally certified medicolegal death investigator is a relatively new development in the field of forensics. As with any profession, there should be a concerted effort by all who practice to improve the way in which the field operates and provides services to the population in which they serve. As with any young profession, there are endless opportunities to effect change, but it takes commitment and the dedication of resources to ensure that the field of medicolegal death investigation is an evidence-based practice. This textbook ends with a challenge, whether you are a student hoping to enter the field or a seasoned investigator, have a goal to advance the profession. It does not have to be through federal legislation or working with a national certifying body to improve standards of practice. It can be on an individual level by striving to provide exemplary service to those in the community who have been thrown into a system after an unexpected death. John F. Kennedy once said, “efforts and courage are not enough without purpose and direction.” The purpose of the medicolegal death investigator is always to provide answers for the people who are left behind after a death, and to respect those who have died by working tirelessly on their case regardless of how their life was lived.

REFERENCES

Bierig, J. (2001). Informed consent in the practice of pathology. *Archives of Pathology and Laboratory Medicine, 125*, 1425–1429.

Campbell, C. (1998). Religion and the body in medical research. *Kennedy Institute of Ethics Journal, 8*, 275–305.

Carpenter, B., Tait, G., Adkins, G., Barns, M., Naylor, C., & Begum, N. (2011). Communicating with the coroner: how religion, culture, and family concerns may influence autopsy decision making. *Death Studies, 35*(4), 316–337.

Green, J., & Green, M. (1992). *Dealing With Death: Practices and Procedures*. London, UK: Chapman and Hall.

Mittleman, R., Davis, J., Kasztl, W., & Graves, W. (1992). Practical approach to investigating ethics and religious objections to the autopsy. *Journal of Forensic Sciences, 73*, 824–829.

Stewart, A. E. (1999). Complicated bereavement and posttraumatic stress disorder following fatal car crashes: recommendations for death notification practice. *Death Studies, 23*(4), 289–321.

Wellman, A. P. (2014). Grief in comparison: use of social comparison among cold case homicide survivors. *Journal of Loss and Trauma, 19*(5), 462–473.

Index

'*Note:* Page numbers followed by "f" indicate figures'.

T

W

CPI Antony Rowe
Eastbourne, UK
September 20, 2019